DATE DUE

Goddesses
&
Wise Women

The Literature of
Feminist Spirituality
1980-1992
An Annotated Bibliography

Anne Carson

 The Crossing Press • Freedom, CA 95019

Printed in the U.S.A.

Library of Congress Cataloguing-in-Publication Data

Carson, Anne, 1950 Dec. 16-
    Goddesses and wise women : the literature of feminist
spirituality, an annotated bibliography / Anne Carson
        p. cm.
    Sequel to her Feminist spirituality and the feminine divine.
    ISBN 0-89594-536-3 (cloth)
    1. Women and religion—Bibliography. 2. Feminism—
Religious aspects—Bibliography. I. Title.
    Z7963.R45C37 1992
    [BL458]   91-47603
                                                        CIP

Table of Contents

Introduction

This compilation of books, articles, periodicals, and audio-visual materials is a companion volume to my *Feminist Spirituality and the Feminine Divine: an annotated bibliography*, published by The Crossing Press in 1986. With the exception of entries for a few journals and some books which are in new editions, it does not duplicate the earlier work but is an entirely new text. The first bibliography described works published from 1833 to 1985; the new volume contains primarily entries for works published from 1980 to early 1992, with a few items dating from the late seventies that were not included in the earlier book. Of the most important books of the women's spirituality movement, almost all have gone into new editions, which are listed herein. Annotations for those that have not, such as Merlin Stone's *When God Was a Woman*, can be found in the earlier volume.

In the six years since the publication of *Feminist Spirituality and the Feminine Divine*, a river of books, articles, magazines, newsletters, and audiotapes touching upon women's spiritual experience and the renaissance of interest in the Goddess has flowed quietly but steadily. The movement has attained enough academic respectability that doctoral dissertations are being written about it, while media interest in such New Age phenomena as channelling has come and gone and the price of crystals has probably peaked. Marija Gimbutas, Vicki Noble, and Riane Eisler have become widely read, and Lynn Andrews, Diane Stein, and Barbara Walker have gone on to become prolific authors.

Among the more recent trends in women's spirituality, there is a strong interest in healing of all kinds; indeed, it may be said that the essence of feminist spirituality consists of healing the female self. Since the mind and body are not judged to be separate entities, feminist theories of healing have always had a psychological dimension. Women's knowledge of folk medicine and feminist emphasis on self-care have developed into the Wise Woman tradition, under the leadership of herbalist Susun Weed. Recovery from addictions and abuse has become an important part of mainstream psychotherapy, and as women participate in the proliferation of Twelve-Step programs, attendant issues have arisen for feminists over the male-oriented, Christian-based language common in the literature of Alcoholics Anonymous and similar groups. In response to what some critics perceive as an attitude of perpetual victimhood, there have been attempts to formulate a feminist philosophy of recovery.

Feminist literature also reflects a growing interest in the sacred aspects of menstruation. For some women, menstruation is being transformed from curse to blessing, monthly bleeding being one feature of our bodies that all women can share and celebrate, whether we are heterosexual or lesbian, mothers or childless. My own regular ritual practice has shifted from the full and new moons to my personal cycles. In *Feminist Spirituality and the Feminine Divine* there were only two titles that dealt with this subject; this book lists nearly two dozen.

Three other currents in contemporary feminist spirituality are much more far-reaching. First, we see a new appreciation for archaeological research and a reconstruction of the Goddess-worshipping cultures of Neolithic Europe and the Near East, comparisons being made with our own society. In the early women's movement, theorists seized upon the Marxist concept of a primitive matriarchal and communal stage of social organization, the "we invented it first" school of history. The following decade witnessed some criticism of this paradisaical model. Scholars now postulate from the material evidence that ancient Goddess-centered peoples were egalitarian and essentially peaceful, if not politically matriarchal, and that it is this ancient model we should be striving for in our rejection of patriarchal patterns of domination. Some of the leaders in this work are archaeologist Marija Gimbutas, who has been contributing to scholarship in this area for decades, historian Ruby Rohrlich, and social scientist Riane Eisler. The work of these and other scholars serves to legitimate the intuitions of feminist spirituality and the values of feminist politics, for they provide evidence that a society in which men do not oppress women might be one in which men do not oppress each other.

In the seventies, creators of woman-centered religion tended to draw upon witchcraft and the pre-Biblical religions of the ancient Near East. Although the Craft and the ancient goddesses are certainly still with us, today the trend is towards the practice of shamanism by both men and women. It may be said that, after motherhood, shamanism is the real "world's oldest profession," and some feminist authors such as Vicki Noble consider the origin of shamanic power to be intimately linked with the inner power of woman. In their quest to serve twentieth-century civilization as bridges or conduits of deep wisdom and vision, so-called urban shamans employ the many surviving traditions of shamanism and tribal religion, most often those of Native Americans.

Within the feminist community, women continue to be attracted to various Third World spiritualities, and not all newcomers to Vodun and Santería are Black or Hispanic. Moving beyond the reconstructing or re-visioning of Paleolithic religion, Native Americans like Dhyani Ywhaoo, Brooke Medicine Eagle, and Twyla Nitsch are bringing authentic tribal wisdom to a multiracial audience, yet some Native Americans are not happy with the boom in workshops offering glimpses into Native spirituality, as if the teachings were meant to be everyone's property. Look to your own heritage, whites are often advised, and not just by Native Americans. Both Z Budapest and Starhawk remind seekers that Europe also has a shamanic tradition, and some white people are trying to lend authenticity to the Pagan traditions by researching the pre-Christian and folk traditions of Europe, placing them on a par with other indigenous "technologies of the sacred." For most Americans, however, any connection with the European pagan tradition does not extend beyond Christmas customs and folktales, while even in Europe, indigenous (not revived) pagan religion survives only among the Lapps and possibly the Gypsies, peoples with very little presence in North America. The issue has been raised whether someone who has not trained with an indigenous shaman and been initiated by him or her has the right to assume the title of shaman, or, even more seriously, whether a field of study can be declared off-limits to someone because of her or his race. Can the question of appropriateness—and appropriation—of shamanism be settled as it has been in the Neo-Pagan community, where a witch is someone who says she's one, or is Native-American style shamanism merely a game that people from the dominant culture can safely play once a week?

The most important theme to come out of feminist spirituality in the past decade has been eco-feminism, which has become a political philosophy in its own right. Eco-feminist politics have contributed significantly to Green Party platforms, uniting feminist principles and women's concerns with activism on behalf of environmental protection, sustainable development, anti-nuclear protest, the promotion of vegetarianism, and animal rights. If the nineties are to be the decade of genuine concern for ecological well-being, feminism will play an important part in the setting of agendas and the choice of political rhetoric. On the biological front, witness the current fascination with the Gaia Hypothesis, formulated by James Lovelock and promoted by Lynn Margulies, who postulate that the Earth as a whole is a living organism, metaphorically personified as Gaia, the pre-patriarchal Greek Earth Mother. Ethical treatment of the environment and its creatures is also a topic of discussion in Christian circles, where a number of theologians are referring to the Earth as "the body of God," contemplating the meaning of stewardship, and developing "creation spirituality."

More concretely, eco-feminists point out, in most of the world women and the environment are already intimately involved well beyond the level of metaphor, since the majority of the world's agricultural workers are women and in most societies the acquisition and preparation, if not the production, of food is almost wholly the work of women. Similarly, in the United States, it is often women who have initiated investigations into the safety of commercial food and the presence of toxins in the ground and water. Women are the ones who first recognize the long-term social consequences of economic and political decisions our leaders make, since we bear most of the responsibility for our children's well-being. Couching women's concern for nature in Goddess language is therefore only employing a spiritual metaphor to describe a real-world relationship.

Not everyone is comfortable with the rhetorical alliance of woman and nature, however. A number of feminist thinkers have been disturbed by what they perceive as an Orwellian tendency among some radicals towards "XX good/XY bad" (which has its roots in the early seventies), as well as a headlong willingness to embrace all values, behaviors, and qualities which have been

4

traditionally associated with women (nurturing, negotiating, mysticism, etc.), thus making a virtue out of what was once a curse. Despite the many studies which indicate that human males really do seem to be more aggressive, whether men or women are inherently more *anything* may be a judgement on which the jury is still out.

The original challenge to the women's spirituality movement remains: is (re)constructing a religious tradition a suitable endeavor for women, when our economic status, medical rights, and personal safety appear to be dwindling before our eyes? Never mind the loss of the Equal Rights Amendment, critics warn; when laws are being passed restricting the availability of abortion, when a quarter of our children are in poverty, when college students are routinely raped on campus, who cares whether a matriarchy existed ten thousand years ago?

Those women who do celebrate the values of the Feminine counter that we can clearly see where the values and interests of men have gotten us; surely, responding to the concerns of women will provide a balance. Despite cogent criticism of some writers' fuzzy-mindedness, skeptics are mistaken if they believe that spiritual feminists are ignorant of the socio-political forces that make us what we are at this point in history. Rather, we strive to acknowledge our heritage while we work to re-define "woman" and "man," "creation" and "God."

In this bibliography entries are separated into several broad categories: "Feminism and Women's Spirituality" (the largest single section), "The Goddess Through Time and Space," "Witchcraft: Traditional Europe and Feminist Wicca," "Christianity and Judaism: Woman-Centered Re-visioning," "Fiction and Fantasy Literature," "Children's Literature," "Audio-Visual Materials," "Periodicals," and "Bibliographies and Additional Resources." Each item is listed under the author or creator of the work, or under title for periodicals and most edited works. Interviews with well-known figures are generally listed under the name of the interviewee, not the interviewer; some authors will be found in more than one section. A subject index is at the back of the book. I have added English translations for foreign titles, and apologise for any linguistic infelicities.

Many of the titles listed here might not be found in bookstores, but they usually can be borrowed from libraries around the country through your own library, often for free. Photocopies of articles can be obtained through the same channels, or a copy of the periodical issue itself ordered from the publisher. Academic dissertations and theses may be available on interlibrary loan; if not, copies of doctoral dissertations can be purchased from University Microfilms, 300 N. Zeeb Road, Ann Arbor, MI 48106 (this service is quick but not cheap). Master's theses are available from the university issuing the degree.

In order to illustrate the reception the movement has received from the mainstream, scholarly, and religious media, I have also included entries for books and articles which are critical of or openly hostile towards feminist theology and the Goddess movement. The Christian churches are finally taking feminism seriously, discourse no longer being limited to arguments over ordination and liturgical language. While there are many thoughtful discussions within conventional theological circles over the place of women and the role of the Feminine, there is also a great fear of change—in fact, according to David Neff, managing editor of the popular magazine *Christianity Today,* fear (of mainstream education, women's changing roles, AIDS, cult religions and general loss of control) is generally what drives much popular conservative Christian writing (quoted in *Publisher's Weekly*, Aug. 16, 1991, p. 19).

Perhaps we should be flattered at being taken seriously: sensing the real threat we present, some members of the Protestant and Catholic Right have organized a number of rhetorical and political attacks on feminist theology, witchcraft, Neo-Paganism, and the New Age movement, pandering to the ignorance of the general population by conflating all occult and esoteric work with Satanism and by characterizing eclectic women's worship services as witchcraft. See, for example, Johanna Michaelsen's *Like Lambs to the Slaughter* (Eugene, OR: Harvest House, 1989), an "exposé" of New Age and occult influences in education and children's entertainment, which, like many such evangelical books, is well-researched but appallingly obtuse. She confines her examination of Goddess religion to a description of the cult of the Carthaginian goddess Tanit, who was worshipped with child sacrifice two thousand years ago. In another case, the curator of the Human Sexuality Collection at Cornell University mounted an exhibit of various materials on sexuality from the libraries' collections. I helped prepare a display case on witchcraft, selecting illustrations from the Rare Books Department, several Tarot cards from the Daughters of the Moon deck, the "Women of Color" issue of *Woman of Power,* and a reproduction of the Venus of Willendorf. After the exhibit opened, two male students, who identified themselves as Christians, promptly complained that we were "promoting" witchcraft, nor were they pleased that the exhibit portrayed Christianity only in the decidedly negative context of the witch-hunts. (In response the curator pointed out a nearby display of Indian erotic sculpture as an example of a sex-positive religion.) Some people's complacency is easily disturbed.

Although some of the authors represented here have completely rejected the Biblical tradition, even a brief perusal of the Christian/Jewish section will expose the reader to the beautiful and exciting work some women are doing in churches and temples. An explicitly feminist theology may be seen in both Christianity and Judaism, and women-centered liturgies have quickly grown in both faith traditions.

My own female-centered spiritual practice is now ten years old and eclectic. By now I have read hundreds of books and thousands of articles on women's spirituality, and while I don't spend as much time at my altar as I would like, I do have the pleasure of passing on the beauty and mystery of the ways of the Goddess to my small daughter.

Shortly before *Feminist Spirituality and the Feminine Divine* was published in 1986, I became selector for philosophy and religion for Cornell University's graduate research library. Since that time new references to materials on women's spirituality, the Goddess, and alternative metaphysics have flowed onto my desk almost every working day in the form of catalogues, flyers, and publication slips. Having the resources of a large university library has greatly facilitated my bibliographic work, but both books have had to be produced without research grants, student assistants, or sabbaticals. Therefore, heartfelt thanks go to Julie Copenhagen, Bill Ford, Janet Millman, and David White, my colleagues in Interlibrary Borrowing, for processing my countless requests; to Cynthia Lange and other friends who have brought new titles to my attention; to the booksellers whose cash registers I have gladdened; to my husband David Price who spent many hours slaving over a hot computer, working magic any Merlin would be proud of; and to my daughter Catherine, for bringing me to children's literature and for keeping my feet on the ground while my head was in the clouds. Finally, my gratitude to all those authors, artists, and healers whose burning certainty of the importance of the Feminine has produced so many fascinating works on the Goddess Reborn.

8

Feminism and
Women's Spirituality

1. Achterberg, Jeanne. *Woman as Healer.* Boston: Shambhala Publications, 1990. 241 p.

   A history of women healers in ancient civilizations, their victimization during the European witch-hunts (the "Burning Times"), women's heritage as midwives and nurses, and women's role in medicine and healing today.

2. Adair, Margot. *Working Inside Out: tools for change: applied meditation for intuitive problem solving.* Berkeley: Wingbow Press, 1984. 414 p.

   A much-loved book of meditations and visualizations for political work, self-healing, empowerment, envisioning a new society, and problem-solving in relationships. Not Goddess-oriented or even religious, for that matter, yet spiritual in the most profound sense, providing energy re-sourcement for activists of all kinds and for people of any religion or none.

3. *After Patriarchy: feminist transformations of the world religions.* Ed. Paula M. Cooey, et al. Maryknoll, NY: Orbis Books, 1991. 169 p.

   An anthology of insightful essays on women and religion: Rita Gross on Buddhism, Judith Plaskow on Judaism, Emily Culpepper on her own post-christian spiritual revolution, with other contributions on Christianity, Black women's spirituality, the goddess Kali, and women in Islam.

4. Albert, Mimi. "Women of Wisdom," *Yoga Journal,* May/June 1986, no. 68, pp. 26-29, 52-54.

   An interview with Tsultrim Allione, author of *Women of Wisdom* (Routledge and Kegan Paul, 1984), spiritual teacher, and former Buddhist nun, who speaks of the importance of motherhood to her spiritual life. (See also the entry for *Yoga*

Journal in the Periodicals section).

5. Aldridge, Felicity. *Goddess Changes: the ninefold cycle—faith and experience.* London: Unwin Paperbacks, 1991.

6. Allen, Paula Gunn. *Grandmothers of the Light: a medicine woman's sourcebook.* Boston: Beacon Press, 1991. 246 p.

   Myths from many different Native American peoples (Cherokee, Navajo, Iroquois, Aztec, Pueblo, and others), stories of ancient cosmogyny, tales of women's power and magic. Allen, who is herself part Native American, adds a postscript placing the various Indian peoples in historical and cultural context.

7. Anderson, Sherry Ruth, and Patricia Hopkins. *The Feminine Face of God: the unfolding of the sacred in women.* Foreword by Jean Shinoda Bolen. New York: Bantam, 1991. 253 p.

   The authors interviewed women from a variety of backgrounds about their experience of spirituality: author Maya Angelou, a Seneca elder, a rabbi, a former nun, women in a feminist spiritual community in Maine.

8. Andrews, Lynn V. *Crystal Woman: the sisters of the dreamtime.* New York: Warner Books, 1987. 269 p.

   Many people in the alternative spiritual community have become skeptical of Lynn Andrews' ever-changing spiritual adventures and the speed with which she writes books about them—some New Age bookstores actually shelve her works under "Fiction." Nevertheless, an Andrews book is a good read, and likely to be the year's bestselling metaphysical title. In *Crystal Woman* she recounts her experiences in Australia under the tutelage of her Canadian Cree teacher Agnes Whistling Elk and an Aboriginal woman shaman.

9. Andrews, Lynn V. *Jaguar Woman and the Wisdom of the Butterfly Tree.* San Francisco: Harper and Row, 1985. 194 p.

   The third book in Andrews's series of spiritual adventures. In this installment Andrews travels to the Yucatan with Agnes Whistling Elk to meet a Guatemalan Mayan woman shaman and is inducted into the Sisterhood of the Shields, a worldwide women's secret society.

10. Andrews, Lynn V. *The Power Deck: the cards of wisdom.* Cards illus. by Rob Schouten. San Francisco: HarperSanFrancisco, 1991. 128 p.

In *The Woman of Wyrrd* (see below), Andrews refers to a "power deck" used by her wise-woman teacher. This deck of 45 cards (for the 44 members of the Sisterhood of the Shields plus the reader) is quite different from the one her mediaeval teacher might have used. Most of Schouten's images are of surreal landscapes, often juxtaposing ancient and modern civilizations. The deck is packaged with a cardboard stand for meditation on an individual image and a book with interpretations of the images and glossary of terms.

11. Andrews, Lynn V. *Star Woman: we are made from stars and to the stars we must return.* New York: Warner Books, 1986. 246 p.

Further adventures with Native American teachers Agnes Whistling Elk and Ruby Plenty Chiefs, who are joined by spirit guides Twin Dreamers, a Native American medicine woman from ages past, and a mysterious white stallion, all of whom push Andrews to her spiritual limits and beyond.

12. Andrews, Lynn V. *Teachings Around the Sacred Wheel: finding the soul of the dreamtime.* San Francisco: Harper and Row, 1990. 145 p.

A workbook of contemporary shamanism, with meditations and exercises and a generous amount of space for notes.

13. Andrews, Lynn V. *Windhorse Woman: a marriage of spirit.* New York: Warner Books, 1989. 210 p.

Andrews's spiritual journeys in Tibet and Nepal.

14. Andrews, Lynn V. *The Woman of Wyrrd: the arousal of the inner fire.* San Francisco: Harper and Row, 1990. 214 p.

In a trance state under Agnes Whistling Elk's direction, Andrews goes back to the Middle Ages, discovering a past life as an Englishwoman who is initiated into the ways of the Goddess by an old wise woman.

15. Aurora. *Lesbian Love Signs: an astrological guide for women loving women.* Freedom, CA: The Crossing Press, 1991. 128 p.

A personality guide to women of the fire, earth, water, and air signs, followed by chapters for each sign, giving prognoses for relationships between women of the various signs.

16. Baker, Jeannine Parvati, Frederick Baker, and Tamara Slayton. *Conscious Conception: elemental journey through the labyrinth of sexuality.* Freestone Publishing (Box 398, Monroe, Utah 84754), 1987. 411 p.

Rituals structured around the four elements, each relating to a different aspect of conception. The authors bring a spiritual and feminist vision of conception as a sacred endeavor, teaching the reader to work with both male and female reproductive powers.

17. Barr, Judith. *A Menstrual Journey: through the old and the dark to the new, the light, and the possibility;* and *The Goddess Has Many Faces.* Mysteries, Box 552, Pound Ridge, NY 10576.

Two works in one book by a poet, therapist, and performance artist.

18. Barrington, Judith. "A Midlife Ritual," *Common Lives/Lesbian Lives,* Winter 1988, no. 25, p. 97-103.

19. Bartkowski, Frances. *Feminist Utopias.* Lincoln, NB: University of Nebraska Press, 1989. 198 p.

An analysis of speculative fiction by Charlotte Perkins Gilman, Joanna Russ, Marge Piercy, Suzy McKee Charnas, Monique Wittig, E. M. Broner, Margaret Atwood, Christiane Rochefort, and Louky Bersianik, demonstrating how the authors create ideal women's worlds, handle issues such as women working together, redefine the meaning of "woman," and criticize contemporary oppression of women in the context of futuristic dystopias.

20. Beck, Renee, and Sydney Barbara Metrick. *The Art of Ritual: a guide to creating and performing personalized rituals for growth and change.* Berkeley, CA: Celestial Arts, 1990. 192 p.

A workbook for developing your own earth-centered rituals for the seasons and life passages: learning the elements of ritual, constructing an altar or sacred space, personalizing ceremonies such as births, marriages, separations.

21. Beechsquirrel, Nicola. *Sacred Women, Sacred Blood: a celebration of menarche.* The author, Blaenberem, Mynyddcerig, Nr. Llanelli, Dyfed, Wales SA15 5BL.

    The sacred aspects of menarche, with herbal remedies for menstruation's discomforts.

22. Bennett, Jennifer. *Lilies of the Hearth: the historical relationship between women and plants.* Camden East, Ont.: Camden House, 1991. 191 p.

    From Earth Mother to private gardens to ecofeminism, for thousands of years women have had an intimate knowledge of plants for food, medicine, and beauty. A interesting history of an often disparaged part of our heritage.

23. Bennett, Robin. "Herbal Wisdom," *New Directions for Women,* July/Aug. 1991, 20(4):5.

    A healer in the Wise Woman tradition writes that women are reviving the traditional healing knowledge which was lost for many generations.

24. Bergner, Paul. "The Wisdom of Susun Weed: reclaiming the Wise Woman healing tradition," *East-West,* June 1989, p. 22-27.

    On Susun's work as Green Witch and spiritual teacher, and on the Wise Woman tradition of healing. Susun describes herself as a "backwards pioneer" whose philosophy of healing concentrates on working with the natural powers of the body, as opposed to the "heroic," often anti-woman, tradition of most schools of alternative medicine.

25. Bernard, Hélène. *Great Women Initiates, or, The Feminine Mystic.* San Jose: Supreme Grand Lodge of AMORC Printing and Publishing Dept., 1984. 151 p.

    A translation of a French Rosicrucian's study of women mystics from ancient and modern times.

26. *Betwixt & Between: patterns of masculine and feminine initiation.* Ed. Louise Carus Mahdi, et al. La Salle, Ill.: Open Court Press, 1987. 513 p.

Contributors such as Marie-Louise von Franz, Robert Bly, Helen Luke, Victor Turner, and Marion Woodman point out the paucity of initiation rituals in our culture compared with those of other peoples. See especially Part 4, "The Initiation of Women," with essays on menstruation, shamanism, African and Apache women, and a Vietnamese Buddhist nun, and Part 7, "Initiators: Ancient and Modern," with articles on therapy and dream incubation. Includes a list of films whose theme is initiation (e.g. *The Wizard of Oz, An Unmarried Woman, Girl Friends*).

27. *Beyond Domination: new perspectives on women and philosophy*. Ed. Carol C. Gould. Totowa, NY: Rowman and Allenheld, 1984. 321 p.

   Papers delivered at a conference, including "Sexism, Religion, and the Social and Spiritual Liberation of Women Today" by Rosemary Ruether, and "Liberating Philosophy: an end to the dichotomy of matter and spirit," by Hilde Hein.

28. Biehl, Janet. "Goddess Mythology in Ecological Politics," *New Politics* (Brooklyn, NY), new series, Winter 1989, 2(2):84-105.

   Biehl is a Green Party activist who is dismayed at the prevalence of Goddess-based rituals among the Greens. In a well-argued critique, she rejects the use of mythic history in achieving socio-political change, and challenges Marija Gimbutas's findings (and their incautious adoption by spiritual feminists) regarding matriarchal Old Europe and the assumption that worship of "the Goddess" always goes hand in hand with peace and democracy. In sum, she warns that paying homage to the Goddess infantilizes us.

29. Biehl, Janet. "The Politics of Myth," *Kick It Over* (Toronto), Nov. 1988, no. 22, p. 2-4.

   "Goddess worship is less a cause for hope than a symptom of malaise." Biehl worries that by allowing any kind of spirituality to be part of the Green Party's agenda, political activism will be diluted and a new religious orthodoxy will be perpetuated.

30. Biehl, Janet. *Rethinking Eco-Feminist Politics*. Boston: South End Press, 1990 (also published in a slightly more

expensive edition as: *Finding Our Way: rethinking eco-feminist politics* [Montreal and New York: Black Rose Press, 1990]). 200 p.

Biehl is not opposed to eco-feminism per se, but she seeks to make eco-feminist thought more analytical, politically astute, and less dependent on what seems to be the fundamental irrationality (and anti-rationality) of Goddess thealogy and cultural feminism. To Biehl, woman does not equal nature and the statement "The Earth is alive" is neither profound nor true. She is particularly skeptical that any myth (e.g., of the Goddess or Gaia) can be a useful political image.

31. Biehl, João Guilherme. *De Igual Pra Igual: um diálogo crítico entre a teologia da libertação e as teologias negra, feminista e pacifista [Equal to Equal: a critical dialogue between liberation theology and black, feminist, and pacifist theologies].* Petrópolis, Brazil: Editoria Sinodal, 1987. 155 p.

A young Lutheran pastor brings North American liberation theologies to Latin America. Chapter 2 describes American feminist theology and the work of Judith Plaskow, Carol Christ, Phyllis Trible, Beverly Harrison, and especially the writings of Mary Daly and Rosemary Ruether.

32. Bleakley, Alan. *The Fruits of the Moon Tree: the medicine wheel and transpersonal psychology.* Bath, England: Gateway Books, 1984; New York: Interbook, 1985. 311 p.

John Rowan aptly described this as "a Christmas pudding of a book, indigestible in large quantities, delicious in small spoonfuls, and with the odd threepenny bit here and there." A poet-psychologist, Bleakley uses a combination of alchemy and the Native American medicine wheel (a symbolic system comparable to the Wiccan Pentacle) to explore the feminine and masculine forces within each of us, ranging in subject from the Black Goddess of menstruation, the Grail, and the shadow self, to the Celtic tree calendar.

33. *Blood Magic: the anthropology of menstruation.* Ed. with an introduction by Thomas Buckley and Alma Gottlieb. Berkeley: University of California Press, 1988. 326 p.

This book challenges the standard anthropological interpretation of menstrual customs as "taboos" indicating female subordination. The essays, which cover Africa, Turkey,

Borneo, Europe, Native America, and aboriginal Australia, stress that attitudes towards menstruation vary between cultures, and that ritual seclusion may be intended to protect the menstruating woman, not just the outside world.

34. Bogus, S. Diane. "Fighting Racism: an approach through ritual," *Lesbian Contradiction,* Fall 1984, no. 8, p. 10.

35. Bohn, Carole R., and Lorine Getz, comps. *A Registry of Women in Religious Studies.* 1981-82 ed. New York: E. Mellen Press, 1981. 46 p.
    A directory of women theologians and religion professors, with each woman's address, institutional affiliation, religious denomination if any, subject interests, degrees and thesis topic. Separate subject index.

36. *The Book of Rhianne.* Lux Madriana, An Droichead Beo, Burtonport, Co. Donegel, Ireland.
    Lux Madriana is a society of women who follow an ancient matriarchal heritage, living a strict, conventlike lifestyle.

37. Boulet, Susan Seddon. *Shaman: the paintings of Susan Seddon Boulet.* San Francisco: Pomegranate Artbooks, 1989. 112 p., 100 plates.
    A collection of visionary paintings of the embodied spirit in human/animal form, with quotations from Native American elders on the Path of Beauty. Most of the subjects are women from Native American or Arctic cultures. Boulet's stunning artwork graces the covers of a number of the books of the feminist spirituality movement.

38. Bowman, Meg, comp. *Memorial Services for Women.* San Jose, CA: Hot Flash Press, 1984. 155 p.
    A collection of feminist funeral and memorial services, sponsored by the Women and Religion Task Force of the Unitarian-Universalist Association.

39. Bowman, Meg. *Readings for Women's Programs.* San Jose: Hot Flash Press, 1984. 98 p.
    Quotations, poetry, chants, invocations, and reflections by women and men on feminism, sexism, and political action.

40. Bozarth, Alla Renée (Alla Bozarth-Campbell), Julia Barkley, Terri Berthiaume Hawthorne. *Stars in Your Bones: emerging signposts on our spiritual journeys.* St. Cloud, MN: North Star Press of St. Cloud, 1990. 100 p.

In poetry, prose, and visual art, three women—a poet and Episcopal priest, an artist, and a historian—recount their spiritual journeys during the period of the rise of the feminist spirituality movement.

41. Bridges, Carol. *Exploring the Great Mystery.* Box 158, Bloomington, IN 47402; 1987.

Bridges grew up a mystical Catholic who became attuned to Native American spirituality. This work is a coloring book and journal to be used with the Major Arcana of her Medicine Woman Tarot deck.

42. Bridges, Carol. *The Four Powers Coloring Book.* Box 158, Bloomington, IN 47402; 1987.

A workbook for the Minor Arcana of the Medicine Woman deck, which has suits of Stones, Pipes, Arrows, and Bowls.

43. Bridges, Carol. *The Medicine Woman Inner Guidebook: a woman's guide to her unique powers.* Rev. and expanded ed. Nashville: Earth Nation Publishing, 1987. 270 p.

Bridges created a women's Tarot deck based on Native American religion. Most figures in the cards are women from Native American or Polynesian-type cultures, painted in colorful, gentle images; the term "medicine" is used in the sense of "healing." This book is a comprehensive workbook to accompany the Medicine Woman Tarot deck, available separately or with the deck.

44. Brown, Michael H. *The Search for Eve.* New York: Harper and Row, 1990. 357 p.

Some biologists believe they have traced the roots of all of humanity back to one woman, or possibly a group of women, living in Africa some 200,000 years ago, lending some scientific support to the spiritual feminist mythos of a Mother Creatrix and the primacy of the female. Brown tells the story of the scientists' genetic quest in a breezy, *Newsweek* style, but his information is fascinating.

45. Budapest, Z. "In the Feminist Spirit," *Women's Review of Books,* Feb. 1986, 3(5):15-16.

A review of *Women's Spirit Bonding*, ed. by Janet Kalven and Mary I. Buckley (New York: Pilgrim Books, 1984), which constitute the proceedings of a multicultural women's spirituality conference held at Grailville, Ohio and attended by Christians, Jews, Moslems, and feminist witches such as Starhawk. (See *Feminist Spirituality and the Feminine Divine* for a summary of this book.)

46. Bunker, Dusty. *Quintiles and Tredeciles: the geometry of the Goddess.* West Chester, PA: Whitford Press, 1989. 177 p.

On the 72- and 108-degree aspects, relationships between signs in the astrological chart that are seldom taken into consideration. Although the author traces astrology back to the time of the Goddess, this book actually has very little to do with feminist spirituality. The second half consists of charts of celebrities and historical figures.

47. Buonaventura, Wendy. *Serpent of the Nile: women and dance in the Arab world.* Brooklyn, NY: Interlink Books, 1990. 207 p.

The author, a performer of traditional Arabic dance, reminds us of the incredible antiquity of using dance to stimulate sexuality and fertility, and the primordial identification of fertility with a Mother Goddess, who is known to have been worshipped with sexual dancing in India and the Near East. (Salome's "Dance of the Seven Veils" was actually a re-enactment of Ishtar's descent to the underworld). She traces the development of Arabic dance as a professional art-form up to its present-day popularization, and points out that, unlike most kinds of entertainment, in traditional belly-dancing and other forms of Arabic dance it is not necessary for the performer to be young and/or slender. The dance survived unchanged for hundreds of years until the 20th century when it became a Westernized entertainment.

48. Butler, Betty, ed. *Ceremonies of the Heart: celebrating lesbian unions.* Seattle: The Seal Press, 1990. 308 p.

A collection of interviews with and ceremonies by lesbian couples who have formally solemnized their relationships. The ceremonies range from Goddess religion to Jewish, Native American, Buddhist, and multicultural.

49. Carminhow, Joanne. *The Light of the Goddess (Lux Madriana)*. Robertsbridge, Eng.: The author, 1988. 123 p.
   A text of the Madrians, a matriarchal mystery school in England said to be thousands of years old. The author died in 1983; a copy of the book is in the British Library.

50. Carmody, Denise Lardner. *Women and World Religions.* 2nd ed. Englewood Cliffs, NJ: Prentice-Hall, 1989. 254 p.

51. *Celebrating Women's Spirituality: an engagement calendar.* Freedom CA: The Crossing Press, 1990—.
   A datebook illustrated with New Age goddess images, meditations, affirmations, and seasonal rites.

52. Chambers, Ellen, with Grace Walking Stick and seven other women in spirit. *Beyond the Eagle: an intervibrational perspective on woman's spiritual journey.* Wild Violet Publishing (Box 1311, Hamilton, MT 59840), 1990. 226 p.
   One of the few channelled writings in feminist spirituality. Chambers is a medium, and Grace and the others are disincarnate female entities who see themselves as simply variations in vibration. They speak individually and in turn on contemporary women's spiritual path, yin energy, the body and incarnation, crystals, the power of menstruating women, and spiritual merging during lovemaking between women, making for an unusual roundtable discussion.

53. Cheatham, Annie, and Mary Clare Powell. *This Way Daybreak Comes: women's values and the future.* Afterword by Gloria Anzaldúa. Philadelphia: New Society Publishers, 1986. 288 p.
   The authors travelled around America talking to the women who are building a new society, redefining the family, forming multicultural alliances, transforming spirituality and our relationship with nature. Spiritual women interviewed include Starhawk, Jean Mountaingrove, Hallie Iglehart, and members of the Pagoda community in Florida. The book is illustrated with examples of feminist art.

54. Chernin, Kim. *Reinventing Eve: modern woman in search of*

herself. New York: Times Books, 1987. 191 p.

Chernin writes beautifully on how we re-create and re-invent ourselves in ways that challenge patriarchal assumptions, keeping the Goddess alive in our hearts. She interweaves her own journey to self-understanding along with those of Eve, mystic and Holocaust victim Etty Hillesum, Queen Kaahumanu of Hawaii, and Chernin's own mother and daughter.

55. Christ, Carol P. "Dialogue, Accuracy, and Ambiguity," *Christianity and Crisis,* Feb. 16, 1987, p. 55-56.

A response to Rosemary Ruether's critique of feminist theology, "Female Symbols, Values, and Context" (see item 263), in which Christ points out some misinterpretations of her thealogical thought. Ruether responds briefly in turn.

56. Christ, Carol P. *Diving Deep and Surfacing: women writers on spiritual quest.* 2nd ed. Boston: Beacon Press, 1986. 157 p.

Christ's new preface reflects on the ways her book has helped women around the world to expand their vision of women's experience of the spiritual—which is something much broader and deeper than actual religious practice or feeling. She also describes how she uses this text and others to teach women's spirituality in a classroom setting.

57. Christ, Carol P. *Laughter of Aphrodite: reflections on a journey to the Goddess.* San Francisco: Harper and Row, 1987. 192 p.

Essays constituting a spiritual autobiography, reflecting her struggles as a feminist scholar of Biblical religion, her desire to reconcile her love for the Jewish and Christian traditions with a growing awareness of the value and necessity of a woman-centered spirituality, and her encounters with the Goddess in Greece and Turkey. Moving and powerful, essential for feminist thealogy courses.

58. Christ, Carol P. "Toward a Paradigm Shift in the Academy and Religious Studies," in: *The Impact of Feminist Research in the Academy,* ed. Christie Farnham (Bloomington: Indiana University Press, 1987), p. 53-76.

First of all, there is no such thing as "objectivity." What

is presented in male-defined academic research as rational and disinterested, in actuality derives from male experience. Christ criticizes assumptions about deity and text in conventional religious research (e.g. goddess images are often referred to as "fertility figures"), and summarizes feminist research in theology and ancient Goddess religions.

59.   Cole-Whittaker, Terry. *Love and Power in a World Without Limits: a woman's guide to the Goddess within.* San Francisco: Harper and Row, 1989. 239 p.
      A guide to success and happiness by a popular New Age teacher.

60.   Colegrave, Sukie. *Uniting Heaven and Earth.* Foreword by Robert Bly. Los Angeles: Jeremy Tarcher, 1989. 244 p.
      A reprint of *The Spirit of the Valley*, this is a profound study of feminine and masculine principles in the psyche and in history, based on the Chinese Tao and Jungian psychology.

61.   Collard, Andrée, with Joyce Contrucci. *Rape of the Wild: man's violence against animals and the earth.* Bloomington: Indiana University Press, 1989. 187 p.
      Collard challenges us to remember the Paleolithic matriarchal era, when descent was through the mother and all life was interconnected and infused with the spirit of the Goddess. Her book is an indictment of male domination of nature, with an emphasis on animal exploitation. Contrucci completed the book after Collard's sudden death.

62.   "Controversial Artwork Gift May Squeeze Books Out of the Library," *American Libraries*, Oct. 1990, pp. 835, 837.
      Judy Chicago tried to donate "The Dinner Party", her remarkable artistic celebration of women's history, to the University of the District of Columbia, which would have required extensive and expensive remodelling of the library at a time when the school could barely afford to stay open. It was the responsibility of Congress to approve funding for the university as part of the annual District of Columbia Appropriations Bill, and during the debate several Congressmen denounced "The Dinner Party" as "pornography" (*Congressional Record*, July 26, 1990, p. H5659-5670). Chicago withdrew her gift after students protested over this and other

financial issues.

63. *Cries of the Spirit: a celebration of women's spirituality.* Ed. by Marilyn Sewell. Boston: Beacon Press, 1991. 311 p.

A major collection of poetry and prose excerpts from a great number of women celebrating female spirituality in the broadest sense of the term. Most authors are 20th-century writers, with some contributions from earlier periods. The poems are grouped within the topics of the Self, intimacy, death, mothering, pain, hope, spirit, "Images of the Divine," and re-mything.

64. Crumbine, Nancy. *Religion and the Feminist Critique of Culture.* Wellesley, MA: Wellesley College, Center for Research on Women, 1983. (its *Working Paper*, no. 116). 16 p.

Reminds us that religion inspires our worldview, is often inseparable from politics, yet religion is frequently absent from feminist criticism of society.

65. Cunningham, Nancy Brady. *Feeding the Spirit.* San Jose, CA: Resource Publications, 1988. 118 p.

An attractive little guide to creating rituals, with examples of rituals for the moon, the Pagan Sabbats, the times of day, life-passages, blessings, and meditations. Based on Wiccan and Goddess religion, but eclectic enough to be useful to anyone.

66. Cushman, Anne. "Are All Women Healers?" *Yoga Journal,* Jan./Feb. 1991, pp. 37-42, 94-95.

Women have an ancient legacy as healers and make up 80% of our health care workforce, yet for centuries healing has been controlled by men. Feminists like Jeanne Achterberg, Diane Stein and Susun Weed are reviving the art of healing among women. Cushman concludes that both caring and knowledge are important for all healers.

67. Daly, Mary. *Gyn/Ecology: the metaethics of radical feminism; with a new intergalactic introduction by the author.* Boston: Beacon Press, 1990. 484 p.

First published in 1978, *Gyn/Ecology* goes far beyond Daly's previous theological work to effectively dissect and dismember the essences, forms, and manifestations of patriarchal thought in theology, politics, and medicine, using as examples women's horrific experiences with the witch-burnings, Western medicine, and bodily mutilation in China and Africa. Daly then leads us towards the future by constructing a truly liberated and female mode of thought and language. In her ironic and witty introduction to this edition, Daly describes her life in 1975 when she began work on the book, her difficulties with obtaining tenure at Boston College (where she still teaches), and how the book was written. An appendix by feminist philosopher Bonnie Mann describes the effect the book has had on many women who have read it: that of opening our eyes to the falsehoods of supposedly rational male thought.

68. Daly, Mary. "Spinning Wicked Webs: an interview with Mary Daly," *Iris: a journal about women* (Charlottesville, VA), Spring/Summer 1988, no. 19, p. 5-8.

Graduate student Kathleen Davies interviews Daly on the *Wickedary*, her ontology (approximating Modern Realism or Aristotelianism), and her critics in the feminist community. A review of the *Wickedary* follows.

69. Daly, Mary. *Websters' First New Intergalactic Wickedary of the English Language*. Compiled by Mary Daly "in cahoots with Jane Caputi"; original illustrations by Sudie Rakusin. Boston: Beacon Press, 1987. 310 p.

Anyone who believes that "militant" feminists have no sense of humor has never read Mary Daly. The *Wickedary* comprises a dictionary of her new language (*Gynophilia*, "women's space"), and her imagined free female society (*Webster*, "female weaver" of reality), and terms she has coined to describe patriarchal thought, religion, and society ("Bore-ocracy," "Papal Bully," "The/rapist"). As always, Daly is uncompromising in her standards for freeing the female mind.

70. Day, Phyllis J. "Earthmother/Witchmother: feminism and ecology renewal," *Extrapolation* (Wooster, Ohio), Spring 1982, 23(1): 12-21.

Describes two trends in science fiction: in contrast to the drearily male-oriented "advanced" societies of most science fiction, some writers are now showing women as capable and often independent of men. Sometimes the strong woman is called a witch, either positively or negatively. Secondly, many writers, not notably feminist, are writing "ecological" science fiction, which portrays nature more reverently, less mechanistically, and with less admiration for pure technology.

71. Deupree, Jenny. *The Feminine of History is Mystery.* Center for Archaic Studies (Box 445, Franconia, NH), 1985. 287 p.

   The right pages of this book contain mythic/magical history, with writings on goddesses, dreams, fantasies, and rituals on the left pages.

72. Dijk, Denise. "De Betekenis van de Goddess Movement [The Significance of the Goddess Movement]," *Tijdschrift voor Vrouwenstudies*, 1981, no. 8.

73. Dijk, Denise. "The Goddess Movement in the USA: a religion for women only," *Archiv für Religionspsychologie,* 1988, 18:258-266.

   An essay on the feminist spirituality movement as a woman-centered and -defined religion. She summarizes matriarchal herstory, feminist witchcraft, and describes Monica Sjöö as one example of a woman working to create a women's culture.

74. Dolfyn. *Shamanic Wisdom: nature spirituality, sacred power and earth ecstasy.* Earthspirit, Inc. (6114 La Salle Ave., Suite 362, Oakland, CA 94611), 1990. 182 p.

   A comprehensive and accessible guide to shamanic practice, emphasizing listening to the earth forces and seeking guidance from animal spirits. Contains meditations, visualization exercises, instructions on conducting a sacred circle, teachings on the medicine wheel, seasonal and moon rituals, guidelines for dreamwork, and methods of sending forth power.

75. Doty, William G. *Mythography: the study of myths and rituals.* University, AL: University of Alabama Press, 1986. 326 p.

   Of most interest is the section "A New Ritual Consciousness," pp. 101-104, which discusses contemporary women's rituals and the work of feminist anthropologist Kay Turner, publisher of *Lady-Unique-Inclination-of-the-Night* (see Periodicals section).

76. Downing, Christine. *Journey Through Menopause: a personal rite of passage.* New York: Crossroad, 1987. 164 p.

Unable to complete her book *Psyche's Sisters* because of intense feelings erupting during her menopause, Downing went on a round-the-world trip with a young male friend. They soon separated and she continued on alone. The journey made her fully appreciate home and Hestia, the goddess of home. During the journey she reflected on the Greek goddesses and our inevitable journey towards death.

77. Duerk, Judith. *Circle of Stones: woman's journey to herself.* San Diego: LuraMedia, 1989. 69 p.

A healing journey, a written retreat, in which we are called to listen to the voice of the ancient feminine, to nourish ourselves and rebalance our outer-driven lives; to envision a world where we can repair to women's space and be guided by elders. I felt as if the author were speaking to me personally.

78. Dunne, Carrin. *Behold Woman: a Jungian approach to feminist theology.* Wilmette, Ill. : Chiron Publications, 1988. 97 p.

79. Durdin-Robertson, Lawrence. *Priestesses.* Enniscorthy, Eire: Cesara Publications.

The author and his sister Olivia Robertson (see below) lead the Fellowship of Isis, a worldwide goddess-worshipping organization grounded in ritual magic. From their castle in Ireland they have published many books on goddess religion and the rites of the Fellowship of Isis. A profile appeared in the Manchester *Weekend Guardian*, March 9-10, 1991.

80. "Dyke Magic: a readers forum," *Lesbian Ethics,* Spring 1988, 3(1):72-84.

Short essays: "Healing with a Hex," by Sage Desertdyke (a ritual hex on rapists); "Dyke Magic," by Jeannette Silveira (the magic of lesbian separatism); "Sweet Mother, She's Alive!" by Reab Rose (the lesbian witch); "Playing Indian," by Iami and K. Moon (white women's appropriation of Native American spirituality); "A Lavender Tithe," by Jean Mountaingrove (on the 10% of humanity who are gay, serving as a tithe to the Goddess).

81. Edelson, Mary Beth. *Mary Beth Edelson: new work: an ancient thirst and a future vision.* Pittsburgh: Hewlett Gallery, College of Fine Arts, Carnegie-Mellon University, 1982. 35 p.

   Edelson was one of the first feminist artists of the seventies to incorporate themes of women's spirituality into her work. Her images are those of power and transcendence. This is an exhibit catalog, with two essays: "A Spiraling Journey," by Elaine A. King, and "Mary Beth Edelson: introduction," by Donald Kuspit.

82. Edelson, Mary Beth. *Shape Shifter: seven mediums.* The author (110 Mercer St., New York, NY 10012), 1990; available from Printed Matter Bookstore at Dia, 77 Wooster St., New York, NY 10012. 60 p.

   A survey of the forms her art has taken over the past decade: installations, paintings, sculpture, photography, ritual, "story-box," which is a kind of public questionnaire. Includes an interview and an appreciative essay by Adam Weinberg.

83. Edelson, Mary Beth. "Story Box: the spirituality question," *Heresies,* no. 24, 1989, p. 57-62.

   Edelson mailed out questions on several issues in feminist spirituality and received responses from Paula Gunn Allen, E. M. Broner, Carol Christ, Riane Eisler, Elinor Gadon, Chellis Glendinning, Susan Griffin, Sylvia Brinton Perera, Gloria Orenstein, Ntozake Shange, Starhawk, Charlene Spretnak, and Merlin Stone, among others.

84. Edelson, Mary Beth. *To Dance: paintings and drawings by Mary Beth Edelson with performance in mind.* Indianapolis: Patrick King Contemporary Arts, 1984. 28 p.

   An exhibition catalogue.

85. Eisler, Riane. *The Chalice and the Blade: our history, our future.* San Francisco: Harper and Row, 1987. 261 p.

   Building on the work of feminist scholars and archaeologists such as Marija Gimbutas, Eisler traces the degeneration of the peaceful, egalitarian societies of prehistory to today's global domination by warlike patriarchies. Her work has had a significant impact on spiritual feminist thought and the feminist philosophy of peace. Recognizing that historically, the opposite of patriarchy has not been matriarchy but equality, Eisler seeks to draw lessons from past Goddess-centered and essentially peaceful societies, such as Bronze Age Crete and Neolithic Europe. She warns that once again we have an opportunity to transform global political values and choose between the Chalice (the woman-inspired, life-affirming ethos) or the Blade (war and death). A study guide is available from the Center for Partnership Studies, Box 51936, Pacific Grove, CA 93950.

86.   Eisler, Riane. "The Long Journey Home: reconnecting with the Great Mother," in: *For the Love of God: new writings by spiritual and psychological leaders,* ed. Benjamin Shield and Richard Carlson (New York: New World Library, 1990), p. 13-19.

Born a Jew in Nazi Vienna, Eisler moved with her parents to pre-Castro, Catholic Cuba. As an adult studying the prehistoric Goddess, she realized that the dominator model of society and cosmology is not natural but is an aberration from our real heritage of partnership. She finds her spirituality in the Goddess and in honoring the Divine present in creation. Other contributors to this volume include Lynn Andrews, Brooke Medicine Eagle, Jean Shinoda Bolen, the Dalai Lama, Matthew Fox, Mother Teresa, and many other spiritual thinkers. These brief, beautiful essays on personal relationships with God do more to lead the reader to the spiritual path than any theology text.

87.   Eisler, Riane, and David Loye. *The Partnership Way: new tools for living: a practical guide for using the principles of* The Chalice and the Blade *in our lives, our communities, and our world.* San Francisco: Harper and Row, 1990. 242 p.

A guide to applying feminist, democratic, and Green principles to both personal relationships and public policy.

88.   Eller, Cynthia. *Feminist Spirituality and Social Transformation.* M.A thesis, University of Southern California, 1984. 122 p.

89. Engelsman, Joan Chamberlain. "Beyond the Anima: the female self in the image of God," in: *Jung's Challenge to Contemporary Religion,* ed. Murray Stein and Robert L. Moore (Wilmette, Ill.: Chiron Publications, 1987).

90. English, Jane Butterfield. *Different Doorway: adventures of a caesarean born.* Earth Heart (Box 1027, Point Reyes Station, CA 94956), 1985. 143 p.

    A physicist, artist, and translator recounts her ten-year journey to understand herself in terms of her birth experience via non-labor caesarean section. During this time she worked through her experience via dreams, meditations, artwork, and human potential exercises. Much is made in mythology and transpersonal psychology of our passage through the birth canal; English argues that a birth that occurs with no labor at all leaves its own distinctive psychic-spiritual imprint on the child. With planned caesarean births increasingly common, it is high time this birth experience was addressed in transpersonal terms.

91. Espin, Oliva M. "Spiritual Power in the Mundane World: Hispanic female healers in urban U.S. communities," *Women's Studies Quarterly,* Fall/Winter 1988, 16(3-4):33-47.

    A study of ten healers, mainly of Cuban descent, who practice Santería and charismatic Catholicism. Their calling as spiritual healers enables them to cope with living in a minority culture.

92. *Everywoman's Almanac 1992: appointment book and calendar.* Toronto: Women's Press, 1992—.

    Dedicated to "First Nations" (Native American) women of the United States and Canada; contains interviews with and quotations from Native American women, a bibliography, and a list of Native women's organizations.

93. Fairfield, Gail. "Inner Rhythms/Outer Signs: the astrological chart of Alix Dobkin," *Hot Wire*, May 1991, 7(2):20.

    Alix was one of the very first recording artists in the lesbian-feminist community and remains popular today.

94. Farias, Helen G. *The College of Hera: the first seven lessons.* Juno's Peacock Press, Box 8, Clear Lake, WA 98235.

The editor of *The Beltane Papers* presents guided visits to the temple of Hera, where women may come to know the power of their monthly bleeding.

95. Farrant, Sheila. *Symbols for Women: a matrilineal zodiac.* Winchester, MA: Mandala, 1989. 249 p.
Goddess-centered astrology.

96. Feldman, Christina. *Woman Awake: a celebration of women's wisdom.* New York: Arkana, 1989. 155 p.
A woman's guide to self-discovery through meditation.

97. Finson, Shelley. "Feminist Spirituality Within the Framework of Feminist Consciousness," *Studies in Religion/Sciences Religieuses*, June 1987, 16(1):65-78.
A fine defense of spirituality within feminism, which far from being an apolitical escape, arises from feminism itself: "Spirituality is being in the world; consciousness is being aware of oneself in the world."

98. Flowers, Felicity Artemis. *The P.M.S Conspiracy.* Circle of Aradia Publications (4111 Lincoln Blvd., #211, Marina Del Rey, CA 90292).
A feminist Wiccan view of the power of menstruation.

99. Ford, Lydia Ross. *Bleeding: a celebration.* Aguila Press (Box 252, Albion, CA 95410), 1983.
A reclamation of the sacredness of menstruation.

100. Francia, Luisa. *Der Africanische Traum [The African Dream].* Zürich: Stechapfel-Verlag, 1985. 81 p.
Luisa recounts her work with a West African priestess.

101. Francia, Luisa. *Berühre Wega, Kehr' zur Erde züruck: Trancen, Meditationen, und Rituale mit Sternen [Touch Vega, Return to Earth: trances, meditations, and rituals with stars].* Munich: Frauenoffensive, 1982. 112 p.
A handbook of rituals and meditations.

102. Francia, Luisa. *Dragontime: magic and mystery of menstruation.* Translation of *Drachenzeit* (Munich: Frauenoffensive, 1988) by Sasha Daucus; edited by Susun

Weed; introduction by Brooke Medicine Eagle. Woodstock, NY: Ash Tree Publishing, 1991. 137 p.

The dragon of folklore is the menstruating woman, the symbol of the fiery, serpentine power raised by the women who bleed. *Dragontime* is a high-spirited treasury of rituals, folklore, re-interpretations of fairy tales, meditations, physical exercises, and healing herbs for women reclaiming sacred menstruation.

103. Francia, Luisa. *Hexentarot: Trakt gegen Macht und Ohnmacht [Witches' Tarot: tract against power and powerlessness].* Zurich, 1981.

A handbook to accompany the feminist Tarot deck, beautifully drawn by Margrete Petersen. Cards available from Elisabeth Petersen, Lindenstrasse 4, D-8019 Netterndorf, Post Glomm, Germany.

104. Francia, Luisa. *Mond, Tanz, Magie [Moon, Dance, Magic].* Munich: Frauenoffensive, 1986. 138 p.

Thirteen moon rituals, each honoring a different aspect of womanpower.

105. Francia, Luisa. *Zaubergarn [Magic Yarn].* Munich: Frauenoffensive, 1989. 100 p.

"Magical stories of ordinary things."

106. Francis, Daphne. "Survivor of the 'New Age'," *Spare Rib*, Aug. 1985, no. 157, p. 52-55.

The author lived in the Findhorn Community for two years and is now very critical of the community's hostility to women-identified spirituality, its patriarchal, nuclear-family bias, and the tendency to foster a victim mentality among women.

107. Freer, Jean. *The New Feminist Tarot.* Revised, expanded, and reset edition of *Toward a Reclaimed Tarot* (London: Lamia Publications, 1982). Wellingborough, Eng.: Aquarian Press, 1987; San Bernardino, CA: Borgo Press, 1988. 128 p.

A lesbian-feminist guide to the Tarot, illustrated with examples from many decks and utilizing a number of spreads. Freer emphasizes numerology, and renames and renumbers some of the Major Arcana—the Emperor is called the Elder, and the Devil becomes the more positive Earth Dragon.

108. French, Marilyn. *Beyond Power: on women, men, and morals*. New York: Summit Books, 1985. 640 p.

A vast and profound criticism of the origins and effects of patriarchy. Like Eisler, French sees patriarchy as both unnatural and avoidable. She traces the human history of power from hominids, through ancient societies, the rise of capitalism, and the revolutions of the 20th century, and points out how men, too, are crippled by patriarchal forms of power. "Unless we embrace... values that historically have been considered feminine we are heading toward a totalitarian state."

109. Gardner, Kay. "Are White Spiritual Feminists Exploiting Native American Spirituality?" *Hot Wire: the journal of women's music and culture,* Jan. 1991, 7(1):52-53.

110. Gardner, Kay. *Sounding the Inner Landscape: music as medicine*. Stonington, ME: Caduceus Publications, 1990. 268 p.

Gardner has been composing woman-centered instrumental music for two decades, and has also been working with music's very real healing powers. Her book describes the unseen but scientifically documented energy forces that work on our bodies, and the physical effects of chanting, harmonics, rhythm, and melody. Fascinating, even for the non-musician. Also available from Ladyslipper on cassette with guided meditations backed by her music, as are her other albums and cassettes, some of which contain music for working on the chakras and meditations for people with AIDS.

111. Gardner, Kay. "Visiting Women's Sacred Mystery Sites," *Hot Wire,* May 1989, 5(2):54-56.

An account of a trip taken by Kay, feminist songwriter Chris Carol, and other women to sacred sites in England and Ireland, including Avebury, Silbury Hill, Glastonbury, and New Grange.

112. Garfield, Patricia. *Women's Bodies, Women's Dreams*. New York: Ballantine Books, 1988. 444 p.

Based on a study the author conducted with fifty women, and essential for any woman doing serious dreamwork. The chapters follow the dreams women have at each stage of adult life: menarche, sexuality, wedding dreams, dreams of pregnancy and birth, mothering, work, divorce, menopause, and old age. The author has recorded her own dreams for forty years.

113. Gaube, Karin, and Alexander von Pechmann. *Magie, Matriarchat und Marienkult: Frauen und Religion: Versuch einer Bestandsaufnahme [Magic, Matriarchy, and the Cult of Mary: women and religion: experiment with an inventory]*. Reinbek bei Hamburg: Rowohlt, 1986. 215 p.

A good overview of contemporary women's spirituality, with chapters on feminist theology, contemporary re-reading of Biblical texts, women in the history of Christianity, feminist criticism and the work of Mary Daly, research into ancient Near Eastern goddess cultures and the rise of patriarchal religions, matriarchal survivals in folklore and fairy tales, feminist witchcraft and magic (with an interview with Luisa Francia), and the new feminist spirituality.

114. *Gender and Religion: on the complexity of symbols.* Ed. Caroline Walker Bynum, Stevan Harrel, and Paula Richman. Boston: Beacon Press, 1986. 326 p.

Essays on how gender-related theological symbols reflect and affect cultural assumptions, with examples from Gnostic Christianity, Buddhism, Mormonism, and psychoanalysis.

115. Gidlow, Elsa. "The Spiritual Significance of the Self-Identified Woman," *Maenad* (Gloucester, MA), Spring 1981, 1(3):73-79.

116. Gilden, Nanda. *Feminisme en de New Age Movement: perspektieven op de natuurwissenschap [Feminism and the New Age Movement: perspectives on science]*. Groningen, Netherlands: Interfacultaire Vakgroep Energie en Milieu, 1986. 55 p. (its *Studentenverslag*, no. 25)

117. Gilligan, Carol. *In a Different Voice: psychological theory and women's development.* Cambridge, MA: Harvard University Press, 1982. 184 p.

Not a spiritual work, but extremely influential in the

formation of feminist ethics and thealogy. In a number of studies Gilligan has found that women and girls tend to make ethical choices on the basis of responsibility, caring, and awareness of consequences, rather than purely on legalistic grounds. It is connections, not abstract values, which are most important in female ethics.

118. Gladman, Sharon Mae. *Harbingers and Healers: a study of contemporary Goddess worshippers.* M.A. thesis, University of Calgary, 1988. 140 p.

119. *The Goddess Celebrates: an anthology of women's rituals.* Ed. Diane Stein. Freedom, CA: The Crossing Press, 1991. 272 p.

Observations and advice on creating rituals by Stein, Z Budapest, and Carol Christ, and a selection of rituals for celebrating bleeding, birth, handfasting, preparation for death, and healing from traumatic birthing or abuse, by Starhawk, Shekhinah Mountainwater, Antiga, Jeannine Parvati Baker, Marion Weinstein, and others.

120. *The Goddess Re-Awakening: the feminine principle today.* Comp. by Shirley Nicholson; introduction by Merlin Stone. Wheaton, Ill. : Theosophical Publishing House, 1989. 280 p.

An anthology of articles, most reprinted from other sources, on goddesses, the feminine principle in psychology, the sacred feminine in several religious traditions, and the need for a rediscovery of the Feminine in the world today. Contributors include Riane Eisler, June Singer, and Rabbi Leah Novick.

121. Goldenberg, Naomi R. "The Return of the Goddess: psycho-analytic reflections on the shift from theology to thealogy," *Studies in Religion/Sciences Religieuses,* June 1987, 16(1):37-52.

Comparing thealogy (study of Goddess rather than God) and psychoanalysis, she finds that both systems are concerned with re-evaluating the past, place us within a community, and utilize fantasy to create new futures.

122. Goodavage, Marion. "Return of the Goddess," *San Francisco Chronicle, This World Magazine,* Sept. 16, 1990; cover, pp.

10-11, 13.

On the feminist spirituality movement in the Bay Area and current interest in Goddess-centered archaeology, with interviews with Linda Lywandosky (proprietor of the Gifts of the Goddess shop), Starhawk, Gimbutas, Z Budapest, Jean Bolen, and others.

123. Goodison, Lucy. *Moving Heaven and Earth: sexuality, spirituality, and social change.* London: Women's Press, 1990. 498 p.

A blueprint for the transformation of consciousness and society, in which a woman-centered spirituality can lead the way. Goodison shows how we can exchange patriarchy's dualistic and alienated worldview for the being-in-nature consciousness of a society like ancient matriarchal Crete.

124. Goodman, Shuli. "The Soul of Liberation: the emergence of a gay & lesbian spirituality," *Lambda Rising Book Report,* 1988, 1(6):1, 9.

Goodman reports on the rising interest in spirituality of all kinds within the gay community, wonders whether there is such a thing as a gay spirituality, and describes how liberation struggles force us to re-examine our worldview. Much of this issue of *LRBR* is on the literature of spirituality and gayness: shamanism and Native Americans, Christianity and Judaism, gay priests and monks.

125. *Der Gott der Männer und die Frauen [The God of Men and Women].* Ed. Marie-Theres Wacker. Düsseldorf: Patmos, 1987. 172 p.

An interesting collection of essays on the return of the Goddess, the femininity of God, mediaeval God-as-Mother imagery, feminist theology in East Germany, and other topics.

126. Göttner-Abendroth, Heide. *The Dancing Goddess; principles of a matriarchal aesthetic.* Boston: Beacon Press, 1991. 254 p.

A translation of *Die Tanzende Göttin: Prinzipien einer matriarchale Ästhetik* (Munich: Frauenoffensive, 1984), a philosophical work on the intersection of feminist art and spirituality. The author, perhaps the most important figure in the German women's spirituality movement, discusses the role of art in patriarchal society, the matriarchal philosophy of art, contemporary feminist art, matriarchal spirituality, and seasonal ritual as art. An important contribution to aesthetic theory.

127. Göttner-Abendroth, Heide. "Hagia—Academy and Coven for Matriarchal Research and Experience," *Trivia*, Spring 1987, no. 10, p. 90-98.

An excerpt from the academy's catalogue describing a combination farm, coven, and women's academy located in Winzer, Germany, where research into matriarchal history and spirituality is conducted. See also an article on the author by Angela Lorent-Hofbauer in *Woman of Power,* issue 7, 1987.

128. Göttner-Abendroth, Heide. *Matriarchal Mythology in Former Times and Today.* Trans. from the German by the author with Lise Weil. Freedom, CA: The Crossing Press, 1987. 17 p.

An outline of the history, development, and overthrow of matriarchal society and religion in the ancient Near East, India, and Europe, with tables of correspondences in matriarchal and patriarchal religions. The author describes her personal discovery of feminist spirituality and its role today. Also published in *Trivia*, no. 7, summer 1985, as "Thou Gaia Art I."

129. Göttner-Abendroth, Heide. *Das Matriarchat [Matriarchy].* Stuttgart: Kohlhammer, 1988- . 4 vols.: Vol. 1: *Geschichte seiner Erforschung [History of its Development]*; vol. 2: *Das Matriarchat bei den Stammesgesellschaften [Matriarchy in Tribal Societies]*; vol. 3: *Das Matriarchat in Hochkulturen [Matriarchy in High Cultures]*; vol. 4: *Matriarchale Strömungen in patriarchalen Kulturen [Matriarchal Currents in Patriarchal Cultures].*

As of this writing, only the first volume has appeared. Volume 1 gives a history of matriarchal theory, from Bachofen and Engels to Briffault, Frazer, Graves, Mellaart, Gimbutas, and feminist scholars such as Elizabeth Gould Davis and Gerda Weiler.

130. Göttner-Abendroth, Heide. "Nine Principles of a Matriarchal

Aesthetic," in: *Feminist Aesthetics*, ed. Gisela Ecker (London: the Women's Press, 1985; Boston: Beacon Press, 1986), p. 81-94.

Matriarchal art is a form of magic because it seeks to change reality; it is process, not finished product, involves the audience and rejects power; it is ecstatic and erotic in the deepest sense.

131. Göttner-Abendroth, Heide. "Urania: time and space of the stars: the matriarchal cosmos through the eyes of modern physics," *Trivia,* Spring 1987, no. 10, p. 77-90 (also in *Goddess Rising*, Autumn 1988, no. 22, pp. 6-8, 11).

On the matriarchal concept of time (linked to cosmic transformations and movements of heavenly bodies), patriarchal timekeeping, and the divorce of science from the sacred.

132. Grahn, Judy. *Another Mother Tongue: gay words, gay worlds.* Updated and expanded ed. Boston: Beacon Press, 1990. 341 p.

Grahn's landmark study of the history of gay and lesbian culture and the origins of gay terminology (much of which she found to derive from pre-patriarchal Goddess religion). The book has been expanded to include terminology from Hispanic gay culture.

133. Gray, Elizabeth Dodson. *Patriarchy as a Conceptual Trap.* Wellesley, MA: Roundtable Press, 1982. 142 p.

A basic source for feminist and eco-feminist philosophy, skillfully delineating the Judeo-Christian origins of patriarchal thought, the concept of the Other, human chauvinism, nature as woman, and offering hope for a movement towards a more holistic mode of thought.

134. Gray, Francine du Plessix. "Women's Rites," *Vogue,* Sept. 1980 (reprinted in *Utne Reader*, Nov. 1987, no. 24, p. 61-66).

On the importance of ritual in our lives, particularly for women, which has been "civilized" out of us during the rise of 19th- and 20th-century technocratic culture.

135. Gray, Leslie. "Altered States: an interview on shamanism with Leslie Gray," *The Sun: a magazine of ideas* (Chapel Hill, NC), Mar. 1988, no. 148, p. 4-9.

An interview by D. Patrick Miller. Gray, a Native American psychologist and shamanic counselor, criticizes the rise of so-called shamanism among urban whites. She describes her methods of shamanic counseling, to be distinguished from traditional shamanism, and the nature of altered states of consciousness.

136. Griffin, Susan. "Celebrating All of Life: an interview with Susan Griffin," *New Catalyst* (Lillooet, BC), Spring 1988.

In this interview Griffin is highly critical of the New Age movement.

137. *Die Grünen und die Religion [The Greens and Religion]* . Ed. Gunter Hesse and Hans-Hermann Wiebe. Frankfurt: Athenäum, 1988. 302 p.

Contributions by Petra Kelly and others (chiefly women). Personal histories, "political prayers," and poetic prose on the spiritual relationship of members of the German Green Party to the world: a blend of Christian mysticism, Eastern spirituality, and anthroposophy (the philosophy of Rudolf Steiner and the Waldorf Education movement).

138. Hadditt, Marylou. *Rights of Passage: a celebration of mid life and menopause: a play.* PMZ Press (Box 475, Penngrove, CA 94951), 1983. 36 p.

A dramatic presentation and ritual, full of fun and high spirits, which celebrates menopause and the power and wisdom of the mature woman.

139. Haddon, Genia Pauli. *Body-Metaphors: releasing God-Feminine in us all.* New York: Crossroad, 1988. 256 p.

A rich, exuberant book that deserves to be better known, written and illustrated by an ordained minister and psychotherapist. Haddon prefers the term "God-Feminine" to Goddess or God, because it includes God and Goddess in one deity while still retaining ties to traditional religion. Her subjects range from the "testicular" or nurturing (as opposed to phallic and aggressive) aspects of God and opening to the feminine and masculine within each of us (pointing out that we are all initially female as embryos), to new liturgies, the Triple Goddess, the film *Aliens*, and the sacredness of our hormonal rhythms. She offers suggestions for encountering the Feminine Divine through meditation, therapy, and worship.

140. Hagan, Kay Leigh. *Prayers to the Moon: exercises in self-reflection*. San Francisco: HarperSanFrancisco, 1991. 224 p.

Fifty-two writing exercises to awaken self-awareness, with meditations and other activities. By a leader of feminist workshops.

141. Hajosy, Maria Dolores. "Celebrating the Wise Woman Way," *New Directions for Women*, July/Aug. 1989, 18(4):8-9.

An interview with Susun Weed, who explains that the Wise Woman tradition focuses on improving the Self while still allowing us our faults. Compassion and honor are the key, in contrast to patriarchy, which dismisses women as incompetent and sinful.

142. Hancock, Nancy K. "One Woman's Personal Quest," *New Directions for Women,* July/Aug. 1989, 18(4):10.

A massage therapist describes her odyssey from professor to spiritual therapist, the spirit guides she has met, and her awareness and balancing of masculine and feminine elements in herself.

143. Haney, Eleanor H. *Vision & Struggle: meditations on feminist spirituality and politics*. Portland, ME: Astarte Shell Press, 1989. 135 p.

The politics of feminist spirituality as experienced by the members of the Feminist Spiritual Community of Portland, grounded in Christianity but open to all forms of the Feminine Divine. An explanation of feminist politics and theology is followed by chapters on feminist spiritual understanding of oppression, alcoholism, and re-visioning of new forms of politics, spirituality, and sexuality.

144. Hanon, Gertrude Hatch. *Sacred Space: a feminist vision of astrology*. Ithaca, NY: Firebrand Books, 1990. 205 p.

A lucid, non-technical introduction to astrology from a feminist perspective: the association of Goddess religion with the observation of the heavens; astrology in ancient and mediaeval times; the astrological influence of the planets and how they have affected women's history; predictions for the 1990's.

145. Harris, Maria. *Dance of the Spirit: the seven steps of women's spirituality.* New York: Bantam Books, 1989. 223 p.

A low-key guide to the spiritual life which can be used by women of many religious paths, presented in seven steps: Awakening, Dis-Covering, Creating, Dwelling, Nourishing, Traditioning, Transforming. Each section contains text, meditations, and exercises.

146. Hart, Nett, and Lee Lanning, eds. *Awakening: an almanac of lesbian lore and vision.* Minneapolis: Word Weavers, 1987. 181 p.

Sequel to *Ripening* (1981) and *Dreaming* (1983), this is a collection of statements of lesbian philosophy, visions, poetry, artwork, self-care, ritual, and mythic memories, all arranged by the eight Wiccan seasons. Contributors include Shekhinah Mountainwater, Diane Stein, Sunlight, zana, and many other women.

147. Hart, Nett. "Radical Lesbian Spirituality," *Lesbian Ethics,* Spring 1988, 3(1):64-71.

Writing in the first person plural, as in *the Lesbian almanacs,* Hart describes lesbian spirituality as "not a set of beliefs or practices but an attitude" that encompasses reliance on immediate knowledge, inner trust, and a commitment to re-create the world.

148. Haught, Linda. "First Conference on Gay Spirituality," *off our backs,* Aug. 1986, 17(8):22-24.

A favorable report on the first annual Conference on Gay Spirituality, held January 1986 in Berkeley. The conference, which included men and women, offered presentations by Z Budapest, Paula Gunn Allen, Judy Grahn, and Sandy Boucher, and workshops on Yoga and Sufism.

149. *Healing the Wounds: the promise of eco-feminism.* Ed. Judith Plant. Philadelphia: New Society Publishers, 1989. 262 p.

Articles, poems, interviews, about half of them original, on the connection between the oppression of women and exploitation of the environment. Subjects include: feminist environmental activism worldwide; the spiritual base of eco-feminism and the presence of the Goddess in nature; and creating/working with an eco-feminist community. Original contributions by Anne Cameron, Vandana Shiva, Deena Metzger, Ursula LeGuin, Joanna Macy, Margo Adair, and Starhawk.

150. Healy, Eloise Klein. "Looking for the Amazons," *Lesbian Ethics,* Spring 1986, 2(1):50-64.

On the Amazons in mythic history and the meaning they hold for women, with references to Joan of Arc and the innovative and unconventional religious sisterhood of the Immaculate Heart of Mary, which the Vatican effectively suppressed in the 1970's.

151. Heine, Susanne. *Matriarchs, Goddesses, and Images of God: a critique of a feminist theology.* Minneapolis: Augsburg Press, 1989. 183 p.

"I write with a degree of scorn..." Heine, a German theologian, dismisses matriarchal theory, insists that ancient goddesses such as Anat are no model for women today, and promotes Jesus the man, who expressed humility in a way not possible for a woman of his time. Though she supports the goals of feminism, she takes a dim view of much of feminist theology and thealogy, and some of her criticisms may be well-taken.

152. Henes, Donna. *Dressing Our Wounds in Warm Clothes: Ward's Island energy trance mission.* Photos by Sarah Jenkins. Los Angeles: Astro Artz, 1983. 72 p.

With the enthusiastic support of the director of the Manhattan Psychiatric Center, Henes came to the facility to help the patients tie over 4,000 knots on trees and fences for luck and healing, culminating in a summer-solstice circle. Ritual knot-tying is an ancient and worldwide practice, especially among women.

153. Hester, Karen. "Why the Nonviolent Movement Needs Feminist Spirituality," *Women's Studies International Forum,* 1989, 12(1):87-89.

Part of a special issue on nonviolent resistance. States that ritual helps us to channel our anger, avoid burnout, empowers us, teaches us to revere the Earth, and enables us to work harder to protect her.

154. Heyward, Carter. *Touching Our Strength: the erotic as power and the love of God.* San Francisco: Harper and Row, 1989. 195 p.

Toward a renewed recognition of the sacredness of sexuality and personal relationships, a theology of lesbian/gay liberation, and a passionate call to use sexuality with honor, not domination.

155. Hinckley, Priscilla. *Women in a Patriarchal Culture: friendship, love, and spirituality.* Boston: Unitarian Universalist Association Women's Foundation, 1989. 60 p.

Material for a four-session workshop on lesbian-straight dialogue. Includes readings, discussion topics, music, handouts, and facilitator's guide.

156. Hoffman, Maryanne E. *The Goddess Guide.* Star Visions (Box 39683, Solon, Ohio 44139), 1990. 111 p.

A cheerful guide to becoming your own goddess, balancing relationships with men, working with astrology, colors, and gems. The book is unfortunately marred by having been printed in an elongated, computer-like typeface that is very hard to read unless you have astigmatism. Also available on audiocassette.

157. Holmberg-Schwartz, Debbie. "Giving Each Other Our Blessings," *Herizons* (Winnipeg), March 1986, 4(2):4.

Describes the new blessing ceremonies being performed by and for women, including a blessing for a friend which the author attended.

158. Hutchins, Charlie. *Hag Runes: poems.* Berkeley: Mistral Press, 1990. 83 p.

Finely crafted poems informed by Goddess religion, many of which deal with the poet's grief over the tragic death of her son.

159. *Images of the Untouched: virginity in psyche, myth, and community.* Ed. Joanne Stroud and Gail Thomas. Dallas: Spring Publications, 1982. 201 p.

Essays on virginity in myth, religion, and depth psychology, by Pamela Berry, D. L. Miller, James Hillman, and others.

160. *In Gods We Trust: new patterns of religious pluralism in America.* Ed. Thomas Robbins and Dick Anthony. 2nd ed., revised and expanded. New Brunswick: Transaction Publishers, 1990. 554 p.

This collection is divided into topics (e.g. Militant Traditionalism, Spiritual Innovation and the New Age), and contains a section on women's spirituality with articles on the Catholic Women-Church movement, an excellent history of the feminist spirituality movement by Mary Jo Neitz ("In Goddess We Trust"), an article on "Woman-Centered Healing Rites," and an essay on the growing number of Jewish women who are embracing Orthodoxy.

161. "Interview with a Lesbian Shaman," *Out!* (Madison, WI), July 1986, 4(9):12.

On Tasha Crystal Moonfeather, a shaman working in the Milwaukee area who follows Native American traditions in healing, using crystals, ritual, and the Japanese healing system of Reiki.

162. Iyengar, Geeta S. *Yoga: a gem for women.* Porthill, Idaho: Timeless Books, 1983. 404 p.

Hatha yoga for women.

163. Jackson, Lynne. *"Sorceress:* interview with Pamela Berger," *Cinéaste*, 1988, 16(4):45.

On the very popular French film about a mediaeval wise woman (see the Audio-Visual section). Berger describes her journey from art historian to film producer and screenwriter.

164. Jamal, Michele. *Shape Shifters: shaman women in contemporary society.* Foreword by Marija Gimbutas. New York: Arkana, 1987. 256 p.

Following an excellent introduction on the origins, development, and history of the contemporary feminist spirituality movement, Jamal interviews Starhawk, Tsultrim Allione, Lynn Andrews, Brooke Medicine Eagle, Vicki Noble, Joan Halifax, Luisah Teish, Rowena Pattee, and lesser-known women working in spirituality. Many of these women are redefining shamanism, bringing it into the context of a Western, industrialized society.

165. Jaskoski, Helen. "'My Heart Will Go Out': healing songs of Native American women," *International Journal of Women's Studies*, Mar.-Apr. 1981, 4(2):118-134.

A collection of songs of medicine women from several tribes.

166. Jeniva. "Witches as Warriors," *Open Road* (Vancouver), Fall 1986, no. 20, p. 6.

Both anarchism and feminist spirituality stress the responsibility of the individual. Spirituality can strengthen political action, while anarchists need to shed their pervasive mistrust of spirituality.

167. Joanne. "Spring Equinox," *Out and About*, April 1981, p. 9.

168. Jones, Christopher Burr. *Gaia Futures: the emerging mythology and politics of the earth.* Ph.D. thesis, University of Hawaii, 1989. 346 p.

An intriguing dissertation on the growing Gaia consciousness that is transforming society and global politics. Jones explores the various philosophies undergirding this movement: James Lovelock's biological hypothesis of the earth as a living system, named Gaia; eco-feminist and Neo-Pagan thealogy of the Goddess as immanent in the world; the mythology and symbolism of Gaia the earth goddess; and the deep ecology movement and environmental activism.

169. Judith, Anodea. *Wheels of Life: a user's guide to the chakra system.* St. Paul: Llewellyn Publications, 1987. 519 p.

A comprehensive guide to raising the Kundalini goddess, by a priestess of the Church of All Worlds. Each chapter contains a list of the occult correspondences to the chakra in question, the gods and goddesses associated with it, exercises and meditations, and ways to use the chakras in rituals, magic, and divination.

170. Judith, Suzanne. *Getting Acquainted with the Tarot.* The author, 461 Hanover Ave., Oakland, CA 94606.

The author has been teaching feminist Tarot for many years.

171. Kate. "Reclaiming the Righteous Rage of Women: a talk by

Mary Daly," *Hag Rag,* Jan.-Feb. 1988, 3(4):16-17.

A report on Daly's address at the Trafficking in Women Internationally Conference, in which she challenged women to name patriarchy's oppressions and oppressors, from reproductive technology to nuclear proliferation.

172. Kaye, Melanic. "Ritual: we fight back," in: *Fight Back!: feminist resistance to male violence*, ed. Frédérique Delacoste and Felice Newman (Minneapolis: Cleis Press, 1981), p. 334-338.

The text of a ritual performed at several women's gatherings, consisting of a litany of testimony by real women who killed their rapists or battering partners. Many of the women were jailed as a result of their actions.

173. Keller, Catherine. *From a Broken Web: separation, sexism, and self.* Boston: Beacon Press, 1986. 277 p.

An intense and deep work, drawing on psychology, theology, and feminist philosophy to identify the separation of self in Western patriarchal theology and philosophy, the matriarchal roots of Western religion, and the mythical defeat of the serpent (Tiamat) by the "hero" as the spiritual defeat of the female self.

174. King, Laurel. *Women of Power.* Berkeley: Celestial Arts, 1989. 289 p.

Interviews with women active in the New Age movement, including Lynn Andrews, Louise Hay, and Elisabeth Kübler-Ross.

175. King, Ursula. "Woman and Spirit," *Everywoman* (London), Mar. 1989, no. 48, p. 17-18.

On the feminist critique of religion in the U.S. and Great Britain. She reminds us that "women's spirituality" is not confined to the revival of the Goddess religion and feminist witchcraft, as there are great women to be found in many religions in the world.

176. King, Ursula. *Women and Spirituality: voices of protest and promise.* New York: New Amsterdam Books, 1988. 273 p.

Women worldwide are challenging the androcentric vision, promoting our experience as valid in formulating ethics and policy, reviving the Goddess, infusing feminism into theology and the peace and ecology movements. Includes a perceptive chapter on Goddess religion and matriarchal study groups. A very good overview of women's spirituality, suitable for classroom use.

177. Kitzinger, Celia. "Fundamentally Female," *The New Internationalist* (Oxford, Eng.), Aug. 1990, no. 210, p. 24-25.

A criticism of the female-chauvinist strain within feminist spirituality, which tends to suggest that women are innately more moral if not actually superior to men. She warns against biological determinism and draws an analogy to the rise in religious fundamentalism worldwide.

178. Knaster, Mirka. "Leslie Gray's Path to Power," *East West,* June 1989, 19(6):42-46, 78-81.

An interview with a Native American shamanic counselor who discusses white Americans' interest in Native American spirituality and shamanism, and what shamanism can offer as a form of psychotherapy.

179. Knaster, Mirka. "Raider of the Lost Goddess," *East West*, Dec. 1990, 19(12):36-43, 68-69 (cover story).

On the work of Marija Gimbutas, with criticism of her work by other archaeologists. Gimbutas in turn chides academics for looking only at objects instead of trying to get into the thealogy/theology that a material culture reflects.

180. Knaster, Mirka. "The Goddesses in Jean Shinoda Bolen," *East West*, Mar. 1989, 19(3):40-45, 71-73.

On Bolen's background and work as a psychiatrist, and her devotion to Greek goddesses as symbolic figures who can help us work through personal problems and life crises.

181. Koltuv, Barbara Black. *Weaving Woman: essays in feminine psychology from the notebooks of a Jungian analyst.* York Beach, ME: Nicholas-Hays; dist. by Samuel Weiser, 1990. 123 p.

Short essays on blood mysteries, mothers and daughters, sisters and the Shadow, the animus, women's creativity and wisdom, Hestia-Vesta, and the witch as wise woman.

182. Kovats, Alexandra. "Mysticism *Is* Feminism," *Creation* (Oakland, CA), Sept.-Oct., 1988, p. 34-35.

Mystics and feminists share a passion for life, a trust of one's own experience, and explore new vistas in language.

183. Kryder, Rowena Pattee. *The Faces of the Moon Mother: an archetypal cycle*. Preface by Vicki Noble. Golden Point Productions (Box 940, Mt. Shasta, CA 96067), 1991. 80 p.

Poetry, illustrations by the author, teachings and meditations on sixteen faces (phases) of the moon, each one representing the cosmic cycle, starting with the Primordial Mother and journeying through birth, growth, coming to wisdom, descent into the depths, and facing the Dark. Designed to bring the reader to a deeper appreciation for the power of the Moon in our lives.

184. Kryder, Rowena Pattee. *Moving With Change: a women's reintegration of the I Ching*. Foreword by José Argüelles. New York: Arkana, 1986. 300 p.

A new guide to reading and working with the I Ching; not specifically woman-centered, but aiming to re-integrate female elements into the androcentric traditional Chinese text. Each hexagram has a corresponding visual image which contains either a tiger or a dragon, a reading related to the moon, and interpretations for men and women. A set of the Tiger and Dragon cards is available from Golden Point Productions (see address above).

185. LaChance, Carol Wallas. *The Way of the Mother: the lost journey of the feminine*. Rackport, MA: Element, 1991.

On the spirituality of motherhood.

186. Lander, Louise. *Images of Bleeding: menstruation as ideology*. New York: Orlando Press, 1988. 227 p.

A feminist study of the ways images of menstruation have been used to oppress women up until the current feminist return to honoring our monthly blood; a good source for women who are reclaiming the sacrality of menstruation. Lander traces the shifts in attitude through history from menstruation as inescapable illness, to the better-living-through-chemistry philosophy of the past thirty years, up to contemporary metaphysical glorification.

187. LaPuma, Karen, with Walt Runkis. *Awakening Female Power: the way of the Goddess warrior*. SoulSource Publishing (Box 877, Fairfax, CA 94930), 1991. 225 p.

A guide to the spiritual life for women: chapters on awakening the Goddess within, building the will, exploring the Maiden, Mother, Venus, and Wise Woman, and cultivating the erotic.

188. Laura, Judith. *She Lives!: the return of our Great Mother: myths, rituals, meditations, and music*. Freedom, CA: The Crossing Press, 1989. 143 p.

Original myths and stories, seasonal and life passage rituals for women and men, and songs, including alternative Christmas carols.

189. *Leatherfolk: radical sex, people, politics, and practices*. Ed. Mark Thompson. Boston: Alyson Publications, 1991.

An anthology by practitioners of sadomasochism, including a shaman and Goddess worshippers.

190. Lee, Anna. "New Age Spirituality is the Invention of Heteropatriarchy," *Sinister Wisdom*, Spring 1989, p. 20-28.

191. Lee, Susan (Susanah Libana). *You Said What Is This For, This Interest in Goddesses*. Plain View Press (1509 Dexter St., Austin TX 78704), 1985. 12 p.

Poetry of the Goddess by a craftswoman who works with ancient goddess images. Published in a limited edition of 100 copies.

192. Lefkowitz, Mary. "Feminist Myths and Greek Mythology," *Times Literary Supplement,* July 22, 1988, pp. 804, 808.

A Classics scholar finds the conclusions of feminist herstory to be suspect, pointing out that feminist myth is a myth of power in the past, not power in the present, and that we are mistaken if we believe that Greek male mythographers and dramatists had a uniformly negative image of women.

193. Lerner, Gerda. *The Creation of Patriarchy*. New York: Oxford University Press, 1986. 318 p. (her *Women and History*, v. 1).

The origins of society, the role of women in the earliest

civilizations (Catal Hüyük and Sumer), and the development of patriarchal institutions of women's oppression, such as slavery, concubinage, and restrictive marriage customs; goddesses in ancient times; patriarchy in Biblical society and Classical mythology.

194. Libana (musical group). *A Circle Is Cast: rounds, chants and songs for celebration and ritual.* Libana (Box 530, Cambridge, MA 02140), 1986. 29 p.

Songbook to accompany their music cassette of the same name: contains chants from the women's spirituality movement and folk songs from Europe, the Middle East, and Native America.

195. Lindsey, Karen. "Starhawk's Spiritual/Political Vision," *Sojourner*, June 1988, p. 18-19.

An interview with Starhawk on the main themes in *Truth or Dare*: the nature of power, the importance of resisting oppression, how taking power functioned during the political actions against the construction of the Diablo Canyon nuclear reactor in California, and how Neo-Pagan spirituality supports concrete action in the world.

196. Lindsey, Karen. "Spiritual Explorers," *Ms.,* Dec. 1985, pp.38-39, 42, 89-90.

While Lindsey herself approaches spirituality tentatively, she recognizes that it has become a major subtext in the contemporary women's movement and feminist politics.

197. Lionne, Crystal. *Feminist Astrology.* Matriarchal Publishing Co. (Box 113, Encinitas, CA 92024).

198. Liston, Mary Kay. *Reclaiming the Body: essential element of revelation in feminist spirituality.* D.Min. thesis, Pacific School of Religion, 1985. 145 p.

199. Loehr, Mary. "Images for a Spiritual Journey," *Fellowship* (Nyack, NY), Dec. 1988, 54(12):8-10.

Her personal journey and that of three other women, including myself, from a spirituality of devout Catholicism to one grounded in feminist concerns.

200. MacAdams, Cynthia. *Rising Goddess.* Preface by Kate Millett; introduction by Margaretta K. Mitchell. Dobbs Ferry, NY: Morgan and Morgan, 1983. 116 p.

Striking photographs of nude women and girls by the sea, in the mountains, and in the Southwestern desert. With no human-made objects visible, the women are fully integrated into the landscape. These are images we want to look at again and again. In her introduction, Mitchell invokes the Goddess as Gaia and Artemis, the patron deities of woman-plus-nature.

201. Macy, Joanna. *Despair and Personal Power in the Nuclear Age.* Philadelphia: New Society Publishers, 1983. 178 p.

A powerful influence on feminist political activism, particularly in peace activism and anti-nuclear work.

202. Maia, Deborah. *Self-Ritual for Invoking Release of Spirit Life in the Womb: a personal treatise on ritual herbal abortion.* Illustrated by Sudie Rakusin. Mother Spirit Publishing (Box 893, Great Barrington, MA 01230), 1989. 25 p.

A journal account of a self-induced and spiritually conscious abortion accomplished over several weeks with the help of herbal preparations; cites the specific doses used.

203. Mankowitz, Ann. *Change of Life: a psychological study of dreams and the menopause.* Toronto: Inner City Books, 1984. 123 p.

A case study of the Jungian psychoanalysis of a menopausal Irish woman. The author views menopause as a rite of passage to a new definition of self that affects both marriage and sexuality. Women need the "facts of death" at menopause as much as we need the "facts of life" at menarche, since menopause forces us to confront our aging and ultimate death.

204. Marie, Jonna. *The Path Home: an exploration of women's search for identity and spirituality.* Ph.D. thesis, Union for Experimenting Colleges and Universities, 1988. 121 p.

205. Mariechild, Diane, with Shuli Goodman. *The Inner Dance: a guide to psychological and spiritual unfolding.* Freedom, CA: The Crossing Press, 1987. 198 p.

A handbook for women's transformation of self, using

meditations, trance journeys, and yoga exercises.

206. Mariechild, Diane. *Mother Wit: a guide to healing & psychic development*. New rev. ed. Freedom, CA: The Crossing Press, 1988. 180 p.

The text of this important handbook of feminist spiritual practice (first published 1981) remains largely the same. Over the years Diane has come to recognize that there are many political, economic, historical, and psychological forces shaping our lives, and that it is more accurate to say that we are *co*-creators of our reality, rather than to accept the New Age dictum that "we create our own reality."

207. Mattes, Kitty. "The Goddess Revived: the rise of ecofeminism," *The Amicus Journal* (National Resources Defense Council), Fall 1990, p. 32-35.

A good survey of eco-feminist philosophy and activity, illustrating its inherited connections to the matriarchal societies of Neolithic Europe as described by Marija Gimbutas. The author questions the "reromanticizing" of women within eco-feminist thought and the lack of political action on a national scale, but lauds eco-feminists for providing a forum for the ecological concerns of Third World women.

208. McCain, Marian Van Eyck. *Transformation Through Menopause: from fertility to wisdom*. Boston: Bergin & Garvey, 1991. 186 p.

The author, an Australian social worker, believes that a woman's post-menopausal years can be a source of great spiritual wisdom. Aging women should reject the West's linear emphasis on unending progress and adopt the Eastern concept of time as cyclical, wherein death is seen as a natural part of life instead of something to be shunned.

209. McClure, Vimala. *Some Still Want the Moon: a woman's introduction to Tantra Yoga*. Willow Springs, MO: Nucleus Publications, 1988. 122 p.

A handbook with exercises and meditations for women, with a guide to practicing yoga during pregnancy and preparing for birth, written by a mother and longtime practitioner of Tantric Yoga.

210. McClure, Vimala. *The Tao of Motherhood.* Willow Springs, MO: Nucleus Publications, 1991. 165 p.

Brief thoughts on parenting in accordance with the principles of Taoism: topics include discipline, flow, spirituality, forgiveness, admitting your own ignorance.

211. Medicine Eagle, Brooke. *Buffalo Woman Comes Singing: the spirit song of a rainbow medicine eagle.* New York: Ballantine Books, 1991, 495p.

The spiritual autobiography of a métis Native American spiritual teacher who has done much to encourage the finding of spirit within women and to promote the sacredness of menstruation.

212. Medicine Eagle, Brooke. "Women's Moontime: a call to power," *Shaman's Drum*, Spring 1986, p. 21.

In Native American tradition menstruating women gather together in small groups to ask for visions that will empower all people, not just themselves.

213. Meyerding, Jane. "Sympathetic Vibrations: shaking the spirit free," *Lesbian Contradiction*, Summer 1986, no. 16, p. 9.

Her odyssey from the Society of Friends, to atheism, to a recognition of the Spirit residing in all creation.

214. Mitchell, Julia Benton. "Feminist Theologians and Liberal Political Issues," in: *The Political Role of Religion in the United States,* ed. Stephen D. Johnson and Joseph B. Tamney (Boulder: Westview Press, 1986), p. 325-336.

A survey of the writings of reformist and revolutionary feminist theologians.

215. Modesto, Ruby, and Guy Mount. *Not for Innocent Ears: spiritual traditions of a desert Cahuilla medicine woman.* Sweetlight Books (Box 54, Angelus Oaks, CA 92305), 1980. 124 p.

Mount is an anthropologist who became interested in traditional midwifery after the home births of his children; Ruby Modesto was a shaman and healer of the Cahuilla Indians of southern California. In this book Ruby tells her life story, describes traditional Native American methods of healing, birthing, and relieving menstrual discomforts, and relates her people's myths and her experiences as a medicine woman.

216. Moore, Rickie. *A Goddess in My Shoes: seven steps to peace.* Atlanta: Humanics New Age, 1988. 139 p.

   A guide to enlightenment using the chakras. For each chakra there are yoga exercises, meditations, activities, and a story from the author's life.

217. Moore, Sylvia. "Contemporary Art/Ancient Sources," *Women Artists News,* June 1987, 12(2):8.

   A report on a panel discussion and slideshow on contemporary and ancient Goddess-inspired art, chaired by Nancy Azara and Gloria Orenstein, with Elinor Gadon, sculptor/architect Christina Biaggi, and Betty LaDuke.

218. Moorefield, Murf. "Spirituality," *I Know You Know* (Indianapolis), June 1985, pp. 9, 43.

   A good summary of the matriarchal/Goddess-centered theory of women's history: from the ancient peaceloving, earth-revering, Goddess-based civilizations, conquered by patriarchal hordes, to the present-day rebirth of feminist spirituality and Wicca.

219. Morgan, Ffiona. *Daughters of the Moon Tarot.* Original creation and design by Ffiona Morgan and Shekhinah Mountainwater; rebirthed and rewritten by Ffiona Morgan; illus. by Kate Taylor with Lily Hillwomyn. Daughters of the Moon (Box 888, Willits, CA 95480), 1984. 88 p. and card deck, each available separately.

   A round deck based on the traditional Major and Minor Arcana. The Major Arcana cards are generally given the names of the appropriate goddesses (the Devil is replaced by Pan, the only male figure in the deck, or Coyotewomon, for a completely female deck). There are five suits (Earth, Air, Fire, Water, and Aether [spirit]), which show gracefully-drawn women of many races, appearances, and abilities.

220. Murdock, Maureen. *The Heroine's Journey.* Boston: Shambhala, 1990. 213 p.

   The journey of the Heroine is the life journey of Everywoman towards a sense of self, from her psychological separation from her mother, her cleaving to the father and patriarchal values, to her rejection of "success" and descent to the Goddess within, where she reconnects with the Feminine, reconciles with the masculine forces, and ultimately finds wholeness. Murdock grounds all of this in Goddess imagery, from Ishtar to Spider Woman, Oshun, and Athena. A healing book.

221. *Das Mutterrecht von J. J. Bachofen in der Diskussion [A Discussion of J. J. Bachofen's* Mother-Right]. Ed. Hans-Jürgen Heinrichs. Frankfurt: Edition Qumran, 1987. 464 p.

A re-assessment of the work of the 19th-century theorist of anthropology, who, observing that women often had greater power in "primitive" societies than in civilization, concluded that matriarchy preceded patriarchy in the historical development of human society, with traces remaining among many tribal cultures. His work, while scientifically embryonic, has been important in the history of law, sociology, and women's studies.

222. Naish, Francesca. *The Lunar Cycle: astrological fertility control.* Australasia: Nature and Health Books; New York: dist. by the Avery Pub. Group, 1989. 157 p.

Physician Eugene Jonas found that a woman tends to be fertile when the moon is in the same phase it was at the time of her birth. Naish explains the influence of the moon on fertility, using the moon as a guide in conception, contraception, and sex selection, and how to re-align one's monthly cycle with the moon.

223. Navarro, Sonia L. "Is Goddess Worship Finally Going to Put Men in Their Place?", *Wall Street Journal*, June 7, 1990, pp. 1, 9.

An article on the feminist spirituality movement, with comments by musician Ruth Barrett and other Los Angeles women; also mentions the men's spirituality movement. The tone of the piece is strictly "Isn't this stuff weird?" It prompted several responses by women and men in defense of the Goddess movement (July 19, 1990, Letters section, p. 11).

224. Naylor, Gloria. "Hers: Spiritualism Has a Place in the Age of Disbelief," *New York Times,* Feb. 13, 1986, p. C2.

The noted Black novelist writes about urban psychics as

the inheritors of witches, explains why their clients are mostly women and why spiritualism arose in response to patriarchal oppression.

225. Nelson, Cheryl Michalko. "What Is the Heart of Ritual?" *WARM Journal*, 1987, 8(2):34.

A report on a panel discussion by women artists on the nature of ritual and its importance—and frequent absence—in women's lives.

226. Noble, Vicki. "Female Blood: roots of shamanism," *Shaman's Drum,* Spring 1986, p. 15-20.

Noble believes shamanism to have orginally been the province of bleeding/birthing women until it was usurped by males. The life-force is contained in our blood and our innate birthing power, both threatened by modern medicine.

227. Noble, Vicki, and Jonathan Tenney. *The Motherpeace Tarot Playbook: astrology and the Motherpeace cards.* Berkeley: Wingbow Press, 1986. 207 p.

The husband-and-wife authors met when Jonathan, a psychologist and astrologer, took a Tarot class from Vicki, who immediately recognised how well the Tarot and astrology mesh. The first half of the book is by Vicki, who expands upon the use of the round Motherpeace deck she created with Karen Vogel in greater detail than was possible in her original text (*Motherpeace: a way to the Goddess through myth, art and Tarot* [Harper and Row, 1983]). She discusses the People ("Court") cards, the interpretation of tilted cards, and how the cards relate to the chakras. Jonathan then connects the Tarot to astrological houses, elements, modes, aspects, and planets. The reader would be advised to have her chart drawn up before working with this section of the book; the experienced Tarot reader can use the book independently of the *Motherpeace* text.

228. Noble, Vicki. "Printer Refuses to Print *Snake Power*, Cancels Mid-Job," *Feminist Bookstore News*, Mar.-Apr. 1990, 12(6):15-17.

Vicki relates her difficulties in finding a printer for her new magazine of women's shamanism, due to homophobia and religious bigotry. The first issue's printers refused to continue because they considered the images pornographic and objectionable on religious (i.e. conservative Christian) grounds.

229. Noble, Vicki. *Shakti Woman: feeling our fire, healing our world: the new female shamanism.* San Francisco: Harper San Francisco, 1991. 255 p.

Vicki has no qualms about claiming the name shaman: since shamanism has its roots in the power of women's blood, it follows that women have a shamanic tradition extending back into prehistoric times. This wonderfully rich book helps us acknowledge and reclaim our heritage as intermediaries between the mundane and the divine, using such tools as astrology, dreams, art, trance, and sexuality. Vicki also relates her own experiences as a healer and as a mother in several different family situations, noting the mutual influence of her spirituality and motherhood.

230. Noel, Daniel C. "The Many Guises of the Goddess," *Arché: notes and papers on archaic studies* (Franconia, NH: Center for Archaic Studies), 1981, v. 6, p. 93-111.

A charming account of the author's experience as a professor of religious studies amid the growing feminist spirituality movement, and his discovery of a Cornish village named Wicca during a trip to England.

231. O'Brien, Paddy. *Birth and Our Bodies: exercises and meditations for the childbearing year and preparation for active birth.* London: Pandora Press, 1986. 123 p.

232. Orenstein, Gloria Feman. "Interview with the Shaman of Samiland: the methodology of the marvelous," *Trivia*, Spring 1988, no. 12, p. 93-102.

An interview with a Lapp (Sami) woman shaman, whose father is the Great Shaman of the Sami people.

233. Orenstein, Gloria Feman. *The Reflowering of the Goddess.* New York: Pergamon Press, 1990. 211 p.

A celebration of the powerful voice of the Goddess, who speaks through contemporary artists such as Leonora Carrington; the matristic renaissance of the 1970's; performance art as journey to the Earth Mother; and the emergence of feminist art that is not separate from spirituality or politics. Reading this rich work on the rebirth of the Goddess is itself a transforming experience.

234. Paige, Sarah C. "Matriarchy," *I Know You Know*, Apr. 1985, 1(5):20-21.

Herstory, from the prehistoric, Goddess-worshipping matriarchies to patriarchal overthrow and Church-driven persecution of women during the witch-hunts. Paige identifies witchcraft as "the love of women and nature" and regards lesbianism as an integral part of Goddess religion.

235. Parrish-Harra, Carol E. *The Book of Rituals: keys to personal and planetary transformation.* Santa Monica, CA: IBS Press, 1990. 304 p.

A minister and founder of the Light of Christ Community Church has compiled a useful guide to seasonal and moon rituals, prayer, dance, astrology, and the feminine principle in metaphysical and esoteric Christianity.

236. Phoenix, and Bärbel Messmer. *Venus ist noch fern: unsere Suche nach einer weiblichen Astrologie [Venus Is Still Far Away: our search for a feminine astrology].* 3rd ed. Munich: Come Out Lesbenverlag, 1981. 141 p.

Lesbian-feminist astrology.

237. Pilon, Debra. "Jean Brereton: the art of feminist astrology," *Herizons* (Winnipeg), July 1985, 3(5):32-33.

Brereton works in Ottawa and learned astrology from her mother. She hopes to reintroduce the feminine principle into male-dominated traditional astrology.

238. Pintar, Judith. *A Voice from the Earth: the cards of winds and change.* London: Unwin, 1990. 185 p. and card deck.

An accomplished Celtic harpist has created a set of 49 divinatory cards based on Native North American spirituality.

239. Pollack, Rachel. *The New Tarot.* Wellingborough, Eng.: Aquarian Press, 1989; Woodstock, NY: Overlook Press, 1990. 176 p.

A longtime teacher of Tarot reviews seventy Tarot decks

and similar card systems that have been created in the past two decades. Each deck is discussed for a few pages, illustrated with examples of the cards. One section treats feminist decks, with notes on the remaking of myth and history in women's spirituality. Woman-centered decks in other sections include the Medicine Woman Tarot and the Secret Dakini Oracle. Provides an essential and concise resource for evaluating new Tarot decks.

240. Porter-Chase, Mary. *Circle of Love: a women's unity ritual.* Samary Press (Box 892, Cotati, CA), 1987. 94 p.

A personal account of a bonding ritual between two older lesbians, both students of Buddhism, which is not simply a wedding ceremony but a ritual designed to produce unity among all those assembled. Included are reactions from people who attended the ritual.

241. Porterfield, Amanda. "Feminist Theology as a Revitalization Movement," *Sociological Analysis*, Fall 1987, no. 48, p. 234-244.

Revitalization movements, sometimes called "cargo cults," are new religions of hope which arise as a means of coping with cultural and social stress, chiefly among indigenous peoples. The author describes feminist spirituality in these terms, not unsympathetically, distinguishing between reformers of Biblical religion like Rosemary Ruether, and other women who practice Goddess religion or otherwise reject patriarchal religion (she calls Mary Daly "the prophet of Goddess religion").

242. Potts, Billie. *Witches Heal: lesbian herbal self-sufficiency.* 2nd ed. Ann Arbor: DuRêve Publications, 1988 (first edition 1982). 189 p.

An important handbook of herbal medicine from the Wise Woman tradition, substantially the same text as the first edition, with an index and some observations from the intervening six years. The author does not mention the comfrey controversy of 1986-87; when she refers to the "comfrey danger scare about two years ago" she is referring to the early 1980's, not the subsequent research.

243. Qualls-Corbett, Nancy. *The Sacred Prostitute: eternal as-*

pect of the feminine. Foreword by Marion Woodman. Toronto: Inner City Books, 1988. 171 p.

Using psychology, myth, ancient religious practices, and clients' dreams, a Jungian analyst redraws the ancient connection between spirituality and women's sexuality, long neglected in patriarchal culture. In the ancient Near East the priestess of sexual rites offered initiation and healing to both women and men, and we have much to learn from her. There are chapters on the Goddess's servant as Anima and the residual traces of the Sacred Prostitute who can be seen in Mary Magdalene and the Black Virgins.

244. Rabuzzi, Kathryn Allen. *Motherself: a mythic analysis of motherhood.* Bloomington: Indiana University Press, 1988. 248 p.

A more introspective *Of Woman Born,* the author asks, what does it mean for the female Self to become a mother? Rabuzzi looks at the mother goddesses and father gods, how motherhood defines or constricts women, the reclamation of women's power in feminist spirituality, and the mysteries of birthing, now threatened by technological medicine.

245. Rainbow (Sue Williams). "Croning at Pagoda," *Broomstick: by, for, and about women over forty,* Mar./April 1988, 10(2):13.

Pagoda is a women's spiritual teaching center and retreat in Florida, in operation for over a decade.

246. Ranck, Shirley A. *Cakes for the Queen of Heaven.* Boston: Unitarian Universalist Association, 1986.

The Unitarian Church has been the one established church that has welcomed the inclusion of Goddess and Pagan spirituality. This is a packet for a ten-session adult program on feminist spirituality. The boxed set includes Charlene Spretnak's *Lost Goddesses of Early Greece,* Naomi Goldenberg's *The Changing of the Gods,* Jean Baker Miller's *Towards a New Psychology of Women,* a leader's guide, a handbook of readings, and a filmstrip. The latter three items are also available separately from UUA as "Cakes in a Bag."

247. Randour, Mary Lou. *Women's Psyche, Women's Spirit: the reality of relationships.* New York: Columbia University Press, 1987. 239 p.

The author, sympathetic to feminist concerns vis à vis religion, interviewed a number of women about their views of Self, relationship, death, God. Most of the women are fairly conventional (one woman studies Sophia) and are not particularly feminist, tending to image God as male.

248. Reid, Lori. *The Female Hand: palmistry for today's woman.* Wellingborough, Eng.: Aquarian Press, 1986; San Bernardino, CA: Borgo Press, 1988. 208 p.

249. *Reweaving the Web of Life: feminism and nonviolence.* Ed. Pam McAllister. Philadelphia: New Society Publishers, 1982. 440 p.

An anthology of essays, poetry, and fiction by many women (and a few men) that tell stories of nonviolent political action, identify the connection between violence and patriarchy, and offer visions for the future. Altogether they constitute a powerful set of documents. Contributors include Barbara Deming, Mab Segrest, Karla Jay, Alice Walker, Sally Gearhart, Grace Paley, Karen Lindsey, Linda Hogan, Joan Baez.

250. *Reweaving the World: the emergence of ecofeminism.* Ed. and with essays by Irene Diamond and Gloria Orenstein. San Francisco: Sierra Club Books, 1990. 320 p.

Passionate, powerful essays by Charlene Spretnak, Riane Eisler, Paula Gunn Allen, Carol Christ, Starhawk, Susan Griffin, Carolyn Merchant, Ynestra King, and many others, on women's ancient roots of respect for nature, eco-feminist politics and ethics, women in the ecological present, healing the planet and ourselves, and the presence of the Goddess in creation.

251. Richardson, Alan. *Priestess: the life and magic of Dion Fortune.* Wellingborough, Eng.: Aquarian Press, 1987; also published in 1991 as *The Magical Life of Dion Fortune, Priestess of the 20th Century.* 256 p.

A biography of the celebrated British esotericist and author, one of the founders of the 20th-century occult revival.

252. River, Lindsay, and Sally Gillespie. *The Knot of Time: astrology and the female experience.* London: Women's

Press, 1987; New York: Harper and Row, 1988. 291 p.

Woman-centered astrology, its roots traced back to matrifocal times: an accessible and well-researched introduction to the basics of astrology, the planets, signs, and houses, their mythic elements, and the interrelationships among them.

253. Robb, Christina. "In Goddesses They Trust: feminists eschew tradition in pursuit of 'deeper' worship," *Boston Globe*, July 9, 1990, pp. 22, 36.

On the "Cakes for the Queen of Heaven" course in feminist spirituality offered by the Unitarian Church, and a Massachusetts bookstore and spiritual center called Native Spirit. Includes many thoughtful and moving observations by women participatants.

254. Robertson, Olivia. *Ordination of Priestesses and Priests*. 2nd ed. Enniscorthy, Eire: Cesara Publications, 1983. 16 p.

The rite of initiation of priestesses of the Fellowship of Isis.

255. Robertson, Olivia. *Panthea: initiations and festivals of the Goddess*. London: Cesara Publications, 1988. 67 p.

The rites of the Fellowship of Isis.

256. Robertson, Olivia. *Sybil: oracles of the Goddess*. London: Cesara Publications, 1989. 44 p.

257. Rochester, Sherry. "Spirituality," *I Know You Know*, Dec. 1985, 2(1):9.

On learning to hear the deep wisdom within.

258. Rohrlich, Ruby, and June Nash. "Patriarchal Puzzle: state formation in Mesopotamia and Mesoamerica," *Heresies*, 1981, 4(1):60-66.

Much attention has been paid to the transition from the peaceful, egalitarian societies of ancient Europe and the Near East to class-based, militaristic patriarchies. Here anthropologist Rohrlich contributes evidence from the civilizations of Central America. On both continents, emphasis on the Goddess shifted to gods, society became male-dominated, and new law codes indicated the oppression of women.

259. Romanic, Gloria. *Healing Circles Manual II: for women, men, and couples.* Soaring Hawk Enterprises (Box 22213, Barrie, Ont. L4M 543), 1990.

260. Romanic, Gloria. *Women's Healing Circles: manual I.* Soaring Hawk Enterprises (Box 22213, Barrie, Ont. L4M 543), 1988. 73 p.

261. Roszak, Betty. "The Spirit of the Goddess," *Resurgence*, Jan./Feb. 1991, no. 144, p. 28-29.
An excerpt from a speech delivered at the 1990 Swedish Green Party Summer Conference, in which she questions the eco-feminist identification of women and nature and the emphasis on woman as Mother. Does Goddess spirituality actually ghettoize women?

262. Rowan, John. *The Horned God: feminism and men as wounding and healing.* London; New York: Routledge and Kegan Paul, 1987. 155 p.
A British therapist active in the men's liberation movement uses the images of the Goddess and the pre-patriarchal Celtic god as paths towards a more authentic, non-dominating male identity. More inclusive of the Feminine than Robert Bly, the author is a committed and reverent feminist whose thought is influenced by Starhawk and Monica Sjöö.

263. Ruether, Rosemary Radford. "Female Symbols, Values, and Context: moving beyond 'Who killed the Goddess?'" *Christianity and Crisis*, Jan. 12, 1987, p. 460-464.
Calls for a dialogue among Christian, Jewish, and Goddess thealogians, criticizing Goddess feminists' statements regarding the existence of matriarchy in ancient times, the assumption that polytheism and goddesses indicate egalitarian societies, and that the institution of Christianity automatically wiped out goddess-worship.

264. Ruether, Rosemary Radford. "The Future of Feminist Theology in the Academy," in: *Trajectories in the Study of Religion: addresses at the seventy-fifth anniversary of the American Academy of Religion,* ed. Ray L. Hart (Atlanta: Scholars Press, 1988).

265. *Sacred Dimensions of Women's Experience.* Ed. Elizabeth Dodson Gray. Wellesley, MA: Roundtable Press, 1988. 244 p.

An important and sensitive collection of essays on the sacredness permeating women's lives, based on a lecture series at Harvard Divinity School, with sections on creativity, giving birth, housework, feeding, caregiving, creating sacred space, and the wisdom of the female body. Authors include Elizabeth Dodson Gray, Corita Kent, Elinor Gadon, Kathryn Allen Rabuzzi, Carol Christ, Emily Culpepper, and many lesser-known women.

266. Sams, Jamie, and Twylah Nitsch. *Other Council Fires Were Here Before Ours: a classic Native American creation story as retold by a Seneca elder, Twylah Nitsch, and her grand-daughter Jamie Sams* [creator of the *Medicine Cards*]: *the Medicine Stone speaks from the past to our future.* San Francisco: HarperSanFrancisco, 1991. 147 p.

267. Saussy, Carroll. "Discovering Goddess," *Pastoral Psychology,* Spring 1988, p. 169-171.

268. Saussy, Carroll. *God Images and Self-Esteem: empowering women in a patriarchal society.* Louisville: Westminster/John Knox Press, 1991. 192 p.

Saussy is a theologian whose recognition of Goddess helped her understand that religious patriarchy is as damaging to women's self-image as sexism is in the socio-political sphere. In her book she outlines the problems we face in sexist society and suggests ways in which we can build our own or others' self-esteem.

269. Schlehe, Judith. *Das Blut der fremden Frauen: Menstruation in der anderen und in der eigen Kultur [Strange Women's Blood: menstruation in our own and other cultures].* Frankfurt: Campus Verlag, 1987. 267 p.

Western, usually male, ethnographers report that tribal peoples equate menstruation with uncleanness, but in many cases are actually projecting Western values onto other cultures. The author reviews European attitudes towards menstruation from antiquity to the present, summarizes anthropological and psychoanalytic theories about menstrual taboos, and gives examples of menarche rites. Includes a lengthy bibliography with many English-language citations; this book would be welcome in an English translation.

270. Sells, Jennifer, and Helen Cordes. "New Goddess Worship Troubles Skeptics: is there a danger of a new eco-orthodoxy?" *Utne Reader,* May/June 1991, no. 45, p. 19-20.

A criticism of eco-feminism by some progressive and feminist thinkers.

271. *Sex and God: some varieties of women's religious experience.* Ed. Linda Hurcombe. New York: Routledge & Kegan Paul, 1987. 296 p.

An anthology of poetry, essays, and stories, many previously published, by British and American women from a wide range of spiritual traditions. Starhawk, Susan Griffin, Rosemary Ruether, Sara Maitland, Catholic theologian Mary E. Hunt, Episcopal priest Alla Bozarth-Campbell and others write about women in Christianity, motherhood, sexuality, lesbian identity, and justice. Indexed.

272. Shaffer, Carolyn R. "The Way of the Doll," *Yoga Journal,* Nov./Dec. 1989, no. 89, p. 56-61.

On Cassandra Light's workshops for women, in which the participants construct ritual dolls that symbolize the deep self. Illustrated with photographs of the artist's own amazing dolls.

273. *Shaping New Vision: gender and values in American culture.* Ed. Clarissa W. Atkinson, et al. Ann Arbor: UMI Research Press, 1987. 228 p.

An anthology on American women's religious experience and contemporary trends in theology. See especially Emily Erwin Culpepper's essay, "Contemporary Goddess Religion: a sympathetic critique." Culpeppper finds too much focus on the Western Mediterranean/Near Eastern cultures, to the neglect of women's experience in Asia, India, and Africa, and rejects the emphasis on the motherhood of the Goddess and the very concept of "the" Goddess.

274. Shinn, Thelma J. *Worlds Within Women: myth and mythmaking in fantastic literature by women.* Westport, CT: Greenwood Press, 1986. 214 p.

On women writers' reworkings of myth, especially Celtic myth, as in the writings of Evangeline Walton and Moyra Caldecott, and on the new myths being created by feminist authors. Other writers discussed are Marion Zimmer Bradley, Sally Gearhart, Andre Norton, Doris Lessing, Joanna Russ, and Suzy McKee Charnas.

275. Shuttle, Penelope, and Peter Redgrove. *The Wise Wound: myths, realities and meanings of menstruation.* Rev. ed.; foreword by Margaret Drabble. New York: Grove Press, 1988; Bantam, 1990. 416 p.

A landmark study of the deeper meaning of menstruation, as it is experienced by women. The authors stress that medical science still has very little understanding about this basic human bodily function and suggest that, rather than being a curse, the sensations and emotions of PMS can help us attain a heightened sense of reality, greater access to creativity, and a realization of the forces of the cosmos. With chapters on the real and metaphoric effect of the moon on menstruation, bleeding in shamanic practice, and cinematic portrayals of the mysteries of women's blood. Includes an afterword with notes on recent research findings.

276. Signell, Karen A. *Wisdom of the Heart: working with women's dreams.* Foreword by Riane Eisler. New York: Bantam, 1990. 325 p.

A guide to dreamwork, demonstrating the use of dreams to explore the self, make important decisions, confront the Shadow, work through relationships and sexuality, and accept the wisdom offered by the archetypal Wise Old Woman. The author, a Jungian analyst, illustrates the text with many dreams from the women she has worked with.

277. Silvermarie, Sue. *Imagine Her Satisfaction.* Midwife Press (Box 92482, Milwaukee, WI 53202), 1985. 141 p.

Powerful poems by a woman who loves women, the Goddess, and the earth's female beauty.

278. Singer, Victoria. *Songs of Earth-Worship: the music of feminist spirituality.* The author (Box 973, Santa Cruz, CA 95061), 1988. 211 p.

The folk roots of the songs and chants that have been

composed for women's rituals and the underlying spiritual and political philosophies contained in the lyrics. Includes the words for over fifty songs and a list of tapes and records they can be found on.

279. Singleton, Judith. *I Am a Spiritual Woman.* Mother Earth Speaks (1999 NE Division, #27, Gresham, OR 97030), 1982.
A workbook based on a 12-week women's spirituality program. Many of the activities involve journal-writing.

280. Sjöö, Monica. *New Age and Armageddon: the Goddess or the gurus?: towards a feminist vision of the future.* London: Women's Press, 1991.

281. Sjöö, Monica. "New Age, Same Old Story?" *Everywoman* (London), Dec. 1989, no. 57, p. 15-16.
When one of her teenage sons became mortally ill and the other died suddenly, Sjöö became involved with rebirthers and New Age healers. She soon found that the prevalance of sexist language and male gurus, the victim-blaming "create your own reality" ideology, and dualistic emphasis on the light over the dark all act to perpetuate male dominance rather than lead the way towards a truly new mode of being.

282. Sjöö, Monica. "Rebirth from the Mother Pot; My Sons in the Spiritworld; Indwelling Goddess of Glastonbury Tor; West Kennet Long Barrow: abode of the Dark Mother of death and rebirth," *Calyx,* Summer 1990, 12(3):22-25.
Black-and-white reproductions of four of Sjöö's paintings, inspired by Neolithic British motifs, with a brief commentary by the artist. She also did the cover for this issue of *Calyx.*

283. Solstice, Angela. "The Goddess Within," *Everywoman* (London), Oct. 1988, no. 43, p. 12-14.
An English healer and spiritual teacher gives an overview of women's spirituality, its philosophy and goals, and its forms of expression such as research, healing, therapy, and artistic creation.

284. Spencer, Jim. "Worshipping the Goddesses," *Chicago Tribune,* Oct. 25, 1987, Sec. 6, pp. 1, 7.

A respectful piece on the feminist movement within the Church, the revival of goddess religion, and Starhawk's work. Includes phone numbers for Limina, a Chicago women's spirituality group.

285. *The Spiral Path: essays and interviews on women's spirituality*. Ed. Theresa King O'Brien. St. Paul: YES International, 1987. 447 p.

Women, and a few men, from the major Eastern and Western religions discuss prayer, power, marriage and the family, and mysticism.

286. *Spiritual Parenting in the New Age*. Ed. Anne Carson. Freedom, CA: The Crossing Press, 1989. 290 p.

An anthology and guide for parents whose spirituality is eclectic or non-traditional, and who want to share their beliefs and ethics with their children. Arranged by age groups (infancy, young children, older children, and adolescence), with original essays by Diane Mariechild, Amber K, Margot Adler, and Gail Fairfield, among others. Contains rituals, meditations, and nature activities, from the Pagan, Goddess, Jewish, Buddhist, Krishna Consciousness, and Baha'i traditions. Includes a list of resources for parenting, New Age children's literature, tapes, and records.

287. *Spirituality and Society: postmodern visions*. Ed. David Ray Griffin. Albany: State University of New York Press, 1988. 162 p.

Includes two feminist essays: "Postmodern Directions," by Charlene Spretnak, and "Toward a Postpatriarchal Postmodernity," by Catherine Keller.

288. Spivack, Charlotte. *Merlin's Daughters: contemporary women writers of fantasy*. Westport, CT: Greenwood Press, 1987. 185 p.

On the transformation of mythology and Arthurian legend in the works of Andre Norton, Ursula LeGuin, Kathleen Kurtz, Mary Stewart, Evangeline Walton, Marion Zimmer Bradley, and others.

289. Spretnak, Charlene. "Knowing Gaia," *ReVision*, Winter 1987 (special issue on "Gaian Consciousness"), 9(2):69-73.

Spretnak describes the Gaia concept as a legacy from the Goddess-centered culture of Old Europe, aspects of which have survived the rise of patriarchal Classical religions. She acknowledges some problems with linking women with nature and in using Gaia imagery in ecological discourse, as this may falsely imply that Mom will always clean up after us.

290. Spretnak, Charlene. *The Spiritual Dimension of Green Politics*. Santa Fe: Bear and Co., 1986; originally published as *Green Politics: the spiritual dimension* (Great Barrington, MA: E. F. Schumacher Society of America, 1985). 95 p.

Building on the philosophy of her important anthology *The Politics of Women's Spirituality* (Anchor Books, 1982), Spretnak shows Green politics to be compatible with the holistic, earth-loving culture of ancient Goddess religion yet adaptable to the needs of modern industrialized society, offering a compassionate alternative to the patriarchal, power-over spirituality of the Religious Right.

291. Spretnak, Charlene. *States of Grace: spiritual grounding in the postmodern age*. San Francisco: HarperSanFrancisco, 1991. 337 p.

Spretnak writes about the necessity to recover a sense of meaning in our lives and the ways spiritual traditions may help. A practitioner of Vipassana meditation and active in Goddess spirituality, she shares what Buddhism, Native American religion, contemporary Goddess spirituality, and the Biblical traditions can teach us about fear, greed, violence, nature, sexuality and the body, and social justice.

292. Starck, Marcia. *Earth Mother Astrology: ancient healing wisdom*. St. Paul: Llewellyn Publications, 1989. 264 p.

A guide to using Goddess-centered astrology in ritual, in conjunction with crystals, and in holistic healing.

293. Starhawk and Jasper. "'Demeter, near in our grief...'," *Out and About* (Seattle), July 1982, p. 9.

A poem in memory of two women incarcerated at Purdy Prison who died because of medical neglect.

294. Starhawk. "From the Ground Up," *Creation*, Jan-Feb. 1988, 3(6):20-23.

On restructuring our civilization for future survival through the primary values of Earth-based religions—immanence, interconnectedness, and community—by which we can nurture non-coercive politics, sustainable economics, and a sense of celebration.

295. Starhawk. "Reclaiming the Dark: an interview with Starhawk," *The Sun* (Chapel Hill, NC), Aug. 1983, no. 93, p. 2-9.

A lively conversation with Howard Jay Rubin on politics, consciousness, feminism, and the need for women to reduce the energy we give to men.

296. Starhawk. *Truth or Dare: encounters with power, authority, and mystery.* San Francisco: Harper and Row, 1987. 370 p.

Drawing on theology and her own experiences with political activism, Starhawk has produced a major theoretical and practical text on power in society and personal relationships. Using poetry and re-membered history, weaving together rituals, meditations, and group exercises, she describes life in Inanna's Sumer, the rise of warlike, patriarchal city-states, how the Self-Hater and Censor within can cripple our lives and psyches, and how we can build a new paradigm of compassionate, responsible relations, particularly in the small-group setting.

297. Stein, Diane. *All Women Are Healers: a comprehensive guide to natural healing.* Freedom, CA: The Crossing Press, 1989. 286 p.

A survey of methods of alternative healing for women, with commentary on the effects that male-controlled health systems and the mechanistic model of the body have had on women's lives and psyches. Healing methods include crystals, Reiki, polarity therapy, Chinese medicine, reflexology, flower remedies, and homeopathy.

298. Stein, Diane. *Dreaming the Past, Dreaming the Future: a herstory of the earth.* Freedom, CA: The Crossing Press, 1991. 231 p.

Explores both women's past and our future, drawing upon matriarchal tradition and predictions of the near future and the New Age to come, which were received via several women channellers. With meditations and advice on how women can prepare ourselves for and bring about the coming world, this is a compelling book.

299. Stein, Diane. "The Goddess Who Laughs at Daddy," *Lesbian Contradiction,* Summer 1986, no. 16, p. 4-5.

"I don't so much worship the Goddess as I love her," Diane explains, as she tells of her struggle as a Jewish woman who rejected religious and familial patriarchy.

300. Stein, Diane. *Stroking the Python: women's psychic lives: awakening to the power within.* St. Paul: Llewellyn Publications, 1988. 355 p.

Organized according to the chakras and containing testimony from many women, this work is an introduction to parapsychology for women, with chapters on altered states of consciousness, auras and chakras, astral travel, past lives, dreams, healing, telepathy, divination, channelling and mediumship, and the near-death experience.

301. Stein, Diane. *The Women's Book of Healing: crystals and gemstones, auras and laying on of hands, chakras and colors.* St. Paul: Llewellyn Publications, 1987. 317 p.

A comprehensive guide to women's healing and the work women are doing in non-traditional medicine. The first half of the book covers theory and practice, the aura, chakras, meditation, and therapeutic touch; the second half is a detailed manual for using crystals and gemstones in healing, providing a major resource for crystal-work.

302. Stein, Diane. *The Women's Spirituality Book.* St. Paul: Llewellyn Publications, 1986. 262 p.

This was the first manual of feminist spirituality to be published since Hallie Iglehart's *Womanspirit* (Harper and Row, 1981), and it reflects the development of women's practice in the early 1980's. Diane summarizes the historical shift from matriarchy to patriarchy and the growth of women's spirituality in the seventies and eighties, then instructs the reader in using visualization, healing, crystals, Tarot, and the I Ching. A very useful handbook for the beginner.

303. Stein, Diane. "Writing *The Kwan Yin Book of Changes," Hot*

Wire, July 1987, 3(3):52-53.

Diane describes how she came to write the first feminist re-vision of the I Ching.

304. Steinfeld, Peter. "Teacher Fights School over Feminism and Beliefs," *New York Times,* May 10, 1989, p. A31.

Mary Daly, tenured professor at Boston College, a Catholic institution, charges that she has not been promoted to full professorship because of her radical feminism and ardent denunciation of the Church.

305. Stepanich, Kisma K. *An Act of Woman Power.* West Chester, PA: Whitford Press, 1989. 159 p.

A spiritual autobiography and guide to women's spirituality by a teacher of the ways of the Goddess. She suggests good centering meditations and menstrual rituals, but some readers may be turned off by her professed dislike for fat, "unfeminine" lesbians.

306. Stepanich, Kisma K. *The Gaia Tradition: celebrating the earth in her seasons.* St. Paul: Llewellyn Publications, 1991. 317 p.

Rituals to honor the Earth Mother and the Wheel of the Year.

307. Stone, Merlin. "Goddess Lifts Women's Spirits," *New Directions for Women*, Nov./Dec. 1986, 15(6):12-14.

An article on the contemporary Goddess movement, with comments from some of the women interviewed for the radio series *Return of the Goddess*, including Starhawk, Carter Heyward, Rabbi Lynn Gottlieb, and Shekhinah Mountainwater.

308. Stone, Merlin. *3000 Years of Racism: recurring patterns in racism.* New York: New Sibylline Books, 1981. 28 p.

Stone traces racism back to the appearance of stratified patriarchal cultures in Mesopotamia, finding a parallel with the rise of sexism and patriarchal religion.

309. Stone, Merlin. "When God Was a Woman," in: *At the Leading Edge: new visions of science, spirituality, and society,* compiled by Michael Toms (Burdett, NY: Larson Publi-

cations, 1991), p. 148-164.

An interview from Toms's National Public Radio program, "New Dimensions." Stone discusses the writing of her groundbreaking book *When God Was a Woman*, the response her work has received, and Goddess consciousness in daily life.

310. Stone, Merlin. "The Word of God on the ERA," *Sojourner,* Jan. 1981, 6(5):4, 27.

Stone defends women's spirituality against its feminist critics, reminding us that the Moral Majority knows quite well that religion is anything but irrelevant to politics.

311. Strachan, Elspeth and Gordon. *Freeing the Feminine.* Dunbar, East Lothian, Scotland: Labarum Publications, 1985. 208 p.

On the history of male dominance over nature and women, taking examples from the ancient Goddess religions, the I Ching, the Bible, the witch-hunts, and Jungian psychology.

312. Sunlight. *Being: guide to a new way.* Earth Books (Box 740, Redwood City, CA 95470), 1988. 79 p.

During the 1987 Harmonic Convergence an inner voice came to the author with advice on finding one's true path and living in the New Age with love. Meditations are interspersed throughout, and are available from the publisher on cassette.

313. Swan, Bonita L. *Thirteen Steps: an empowerment process for women.* San Francisco: Spinsters/Aunt Lute, 1989. 141 p.

The Twelve Steps of recovery adapted for feminists who reject the self-abnegation of conventional, Christian-based recovery programs. These thirteen steps (echoing the thirteen full moons in a year) can be used circularly and in any order necessary, for any program of shaking off old destructive patterns. Each copy of the book comes with a wallet-sized card imprinted with the thirteen steps.

314. Taylor, Dena. *Red Flower: rethinking menstruation.* Freedom, CA: The Crossing Press, 1988. 133 p.

A collection of women's poetry, stories, rituals, and personal experiences of menarche, bleeding, sexuality, and menopause, with additional information on remedies for cramps and PMS and research on tampons and sponges. The reader is guaranteed an utterly changed view of menstruation and its sacredness.

315. Thoele, Sue Patton. *The Woman's Book of Courage: meditations for empowerment and peace of mind.* Berkeley: Conari Press, 1991; dist. by Publishers Group West. 277 p.
    A purse-sized book of reflections and meditations, covering a full range of emotions.

316. Thomas, Elean. "In the Temple of Her Familiar," *Spare Rib*, Oct. 1989, no. 206, p. 6-10.
    An interview with Alice Walker, who talks about patriarchal religion, the Native American heritage she sought to acknowledge in her novel *The Temple of My Familiar*, and reclaiming colors, especially menstrual, matriarchal red.

317. Thompson, Margaret. "Women, Feminism, and the New Religious History: Catholic sisters as a case history," in: *Belief and Behavior: essays in the new religious history,* ed. Philip VanderMeer and Robert Swierenga (New Brunswick, NJ: Rutgers University Press, 1991), p. 137-163.
    Thompson shows that Catholic women's rebellion against male domination has a long history.

318. *A Time to Weep, a Time to Sing: faith journeys of women scholars of religion.* Ed. Mary Jo Meadows and Carole A. Rayburn. Minneapolis: Winston-Seabury Press, 1986. 250 p.
    Personal stories from Carol Christ, Christine Downing, Rita Gross, Kathryn Allen Rabuzzi, Ellen Umansky, and others from the Christian, Jewish, Buddhist, and Goddess traditions.

319. *To Be a Woman: the birth of the conscious feminine.* Ed. Connie Zweig. Los Angeles: Tarcher, 1990. 279 p.
    An anthology of Jungian-oriented articles by Riane Eisler, Deena Metzger, Merlin Stone, Marion Woodman, Jean Shinoda Bolen, Sylvia Perera and others on motherhood, the search for self, and woman-centered spirituality.

320. Toor, Djohariah. *The Road by the River: a healing journey for women.* San Francisco: Harper and Row, 1987. 227 p.
    Inspired by the ability of Native Americans to achieve

wholeness in spirituality and daily life, a therapist writes of women's road to wholeness, healing our relationships with our mothers and fathers, and finding the real woman inside.

321. "Toward a Nonsexist God," *Women & Language* (Urbana, Ill.), Winter 1986, 10(1):42-43.

322. Tucker, Janice. *The Way of the Rainbow Warrioress: a handbook of practical wisdom.* Santa Barbara: El Rancho Press, 1987. 96 p.
    A low-key manual of Native American-based women's spirituality, by a student of Lynn Andrews.

323. Ulanov, Ann Belford. *The Wisdom of the Psyche.* Cambridge, MA: Cowley Publications, 1988. 144 p.
    A call to honor the feminine face of God and the inner experience of the Divine. Ulanov "locates the feminine element in the Trinity in the mutual exchange of love in the inner life of God."

324. Van Dyke, Annette Joy. *Feminist Curing Ceremonies: the Goddess in contemporary spiritual traditions.* Ph.D. thesis, University of Minnesota, 1987. 215 p.
    On women's healing power in African-American, neo-Celtic, and Pueblo Indian traditions, with illustrations from women's fiction.

325. Vierzig, Siegfried. *Sehnsucht nach den Müttern: von der Renaissance des Weiblichen in der Religion [Longing for the Mothers: on the renaissance of the feminine in religion].* Stuttgart: Kohlhammer, 1991.
    On the women's spirituality movement, which incorporates elements of witchcraft, Eastern thought, and nature religion. The author believes that matriarchal religion will inevitably transform the religion of the Fathers.

326. Wadsworth, Cindy. "Kay Gardner: charms to soothe a savage breast," *Out!* (Madison, WI), Dec. 1983, p. 10.
    Kay discusses her research into ancient women's music and the healing power of music and sound.

327. Wagner, Kathleen. *Unlocking Secrets of the Feminine: the*

path beyond sexism. Kansas City: Sheed and Ward, 1986. 200 p.

Directed primarily at men and grounded in Jungian psychology and Christianity, the author writes that freeing the feminine within will transform not only the self, but all interactions in politics and business.

328. Walker, Barbara G. *The Crone: woman of age, wisdom, and power.* San Francisco: Harper and Row, 1985. 191 p.

The Crone is not just any old woman, but the powerful Wise Woman and Kali's dark forces. Walker muses on the Crone's mythological connection with the cauldrom of wisdom, the demonizing of the Wise Woman by the male powers of church and state, warning us to return to the wisdom of the Crone before we reach Doomsday.

329. Walker, Barbara G. *The I Ching of the Goddess.* San Francisco: Harper and Row, 1986. 114 p.

Walker discovered an alternate ordering of the Chinese hexagrams which is believed to be more ancient, and hence closer to the matriarchal period, than the commonly used system. She gives her own interpretations of the hexagrams plus corresponding illustrations of her own design, nearly half of which portray dark or demonic images.

330. Walker, Barbara G. *The Skeptical Feminist: discovering the Virgin, Mother, and Crone.* San Francisco: Harper and Row, 1987. 279 p.

Walker's spiritual autobiography, alternating between episodes in her life as she gradually rejected Christianity and the Bible in favor of women's spirituality, and her reflections on the history of Goddess religion and the oppression of women, chiefly by the Church.

331. Walker, Barbara G. *The Woman's Dictionary of Symbols and Sacred Objects.* San Francisco: Harper and Row, 1988. 563 p.

A Goddess-centered encyclopedia of symbols organized by shapes, sacred objects, emblems of the goddesses and gods, supernatural beings, animals and plants, and body parts. Good for quick reference.

332. Walter, Suzanne Danuta. "Caught in the Web: a critique of spiritual feminism," *Berkeley Journal of Sociology*, vol. 30 (1985), p. 15-40.

A Marxist scholar contends that women's spirituality does not challenge class society, and that forming an alternative women's culture merely allows women to drop out of the struggle for liberation for all. She rejects theories of ancient matriarchy and the popular identification of woman with nature, but admits that the Left has failed to reach people's souls as effectively as spirituality has.

333. Warrior, MaRa Heart. *Woman Warrior and the Art of Seeing*. Woman Warrior Press (Box 1825, Burlingame, CA, 94011), 1989. 189 p.

A former disciple of Da Free John, MaRa is an American guru who teaches women the warrior way, by which she means the way to claim our own power. In the first part of this book MaRa gives a brief guide to the spiritual life and tells her own story; the second part is written by her women students, who describe their training and the insights they have gained.

334. *Weaving the Visions: new patterns in feminist spirituality*. Ed. Judith Plaskow and Carol P. Christ. San Francisco: Harper and Row, 1989. 359 p.

A companion volume to the editors' landmark collection *Womanspirit Rising* (Harper and Row, 1979), featuring reprints of essays by Black, Hispanic, Jewish, Christian, and Goddess-oriented writers and scholars. Sections cover the heritage of the sacred feminine, female God-imagery, the transformation of the self, and spirituality combined with social action. Another essential text for the study of the feminist spirituality movement.

335. Weed, Susun. *Healing Wise*. Woodstock, NY: Ash Tree Publishing, 1989. 295 p.

An herbal based on the Wise Woman tradition of healing, which is woman-centered, non-dualistic, nourishing, honors our blood, and aims to make whole rather than to cure. Susun focuses on only the most important and readily available plant friends (e.g. burdock, dandelion, nettle, seaweed), providing specific directions for their use and the preparation of herbal remedies.

336. Weed, Susun. "Spotlight on Susun Weed," *Telewoman: a women's newsletter,* April 1984, p. [6-9].

Susun narrates her personal history and development as an herbalist and woman-loving woman, describing her seemingly idyllic lifestyle in Woodstock, N.Y., where she lives off the land while being physically close to "civilization." She gives the philosophy and worldview of the Green Witch and relates how she learned to honor women's power and ancient knowledge. She also did the artwork for the cover of this issue of *Telewoman*.

337. Weed, Susun. *Wise Woman Herbal for the Childbearing Year.* Woodstock, NY: Ash Tree Publishing, 1985. 171 p.

A handbook from the Wise-Woman/midwifery tradition, with herbal and other natural remedies for fertility, pregnancy, birth, neonatal care, nursing, and the post-partum period. Many remedies use food, movement, or meditation. Contains a comprehensive glossary and specific directions for using and preparing herbs.

338. Weintraub, Judith. "The New Theology—Sheology: mystical women's spiritual movements, gaining momentum... and adherents," *Washington Post,* April 28, 1991, Sec. F, pp. 1, 6.

On the feminist spirituality movement and women in Neo-Paganism, with comments by Margot Adler and a report on a workshop led by Starhawk.

339. Werthammer, Cynthia. "Feminist Spirituality Empowers," *New Directions for Women,* May-June, 1988, 17(3):5.

On the many strains of the growing feminist spirituality movement.

340. Werthammer, Cynthia. "Power Lies in the Stars and Ourselves," *New Directions for Women,* July/Aug. 1990, 18(4):8-9.

An interview with pioneer feminist astrologer Geraldine Thorsten.

341. Werthammer, Cynthia, and Robin Bennett. "Goddess Inspires Spiritual Community," *New Directions for Women,*

May/June 1989, 18(3):11.

On the building of women's culture through Goddess spirituality, featuring remarks by women participating in the 1989 New York City Goddess Festival, including Merlin Stone, Barbara Walker, Marion Weinstein, Susun Weed, and actress Olympia Dukakis.

342. West, Celeste, with the commentaries of Lady Clitoressa & her Circle. *A Lesbian Love Advisor: on the sweet & savory arts of Lesbian Courtship, sensualizing them with impeccable Bedside Manners, with sage advice on enjoying The Divine Lesbian Relationship in graceful gusto. How to manage* Faux Pas *with Finesse, Jealousy with Mercy and the Apples of Discord without war. Lesbian Rituals, Meta*Physicals, Sorcery & Ceremonies of Life elucidated.* Illustrated by Nicole Ferentz. Pittsburgh: Cleis Press, 1989. 190 p.

A whimsical yet practical guide to lesbian romance, sexuality, coupledom, and breaking up, with rituals in the Wiccan tradition for lesbian rites of passage: coming out, commitment, healing, breaking up, self-blessing. "Lady Clitoressa" is West's fond name for the late lesbian poet Elsa Gidlow, who was much loved in the West Coast lesbian community. Religious bookstores have shelves full of Christian guides to married life; *A Lesbian Love Advisor* is an entertaining, Goddess-based counterpart.

343. West, Karen Elaine. *Feminist Therapy, Feminist Spirituality: towards integration.* M.A. thesis, Pacific School of Religion, 1983. 91 p.

344. "When God Was a Woman," *Time*, May 6, 1991, p. 73.

It took the twentieth anniversary of Earth Day to spark the first article on feminist Goddess religion to appear in either of the major news magazines. Covers the revival of interest in the ancient goddesses, feminist spirituality's affinity with ecological awareness and feminist Christian theology, and quotes several skeptical women theologians.

345. Whitaker, Kay Cordell. *The Reluctant Shaman: a woman's first encounters with the unseen spirits of the earth.* San Francisco: HarperSanFrancisco, 1991. 296 p.

The story of an American housewife's apprenticeship to

South American shamans.

346. Willoughby, Linda Teal. *Mother Earth: ecofeminism from a Jungian perspective.* Ph.D. thesis, the Iliff School of Theology and University of Denver, 1990. 245 p.

Discusses the ecological philosophies of Starhawk, Rosemary Ruether, and Elizabeth Dodson Gray.

347. Wind, Wabun. *Woman of the Dawn: a spiritual odyssey.* New York: Prentice Hall Press, 1989. 224 p.

The spiritual autobiography of a white woman who for many years has worked with the Native American teacher Sun Bear and the interracial Bear Clan. She recounts her work as Sun Bear's medicine helper and the difficulties she had in getting Native Americans to accept her.

348. Wolfe, Amber. *In the Shadow of the Shaman: connecting with self, nature and spirit.* St. Paul: Llewellyn Publications, 1988. 357 p.

An intensive workbook/textbook of personal shamanism by a high priestess of Celtic Wicca who also received training from the clan mothers of the Seneca nation.

349. *Women as Healers: cross-cultural perspectives.* Ed. Carol Shepherd McClain. New Brunswick, NJ: Rutgers University Press, 1989. 274 p.

Articles on women healers in the Andes, Sri Lanka, Jamaica, Serbia, Korea, and Puerto Rico, on Christian Science practitioners, African shamanic mediums, and American lay midwives. Several contributors point out that anthropologists seldom pay sufficient attention to women healers.

350. *Women's Consciousness, Women's Conscience: a reader in feminist ethics.* Ed. Barbara H. Andolsen, et al. Minneapolis: Winston Press, 1985. 310 p.

Essays on peace, class, race, anti-Semitism, reproductive choice, sexuality, and socio-political ethics, by Starhawk, Judith Plaskow, Elisabeth Schüssler Fiorenza, Rosemary Ruether, Ada Maria Isasi-Diaz, June Jordan, Beverly Harrison, and others.

351. *Women's Religious Experience.* Ed. Pat Holden. Totowa,

NJ: Barnes and Noble, 1983. 205 p.

Essays on sexuality, ancient India, Judaism, the Greek Orthodox Church, Turkey, West Africa, and American spiritualism and theosophy.

352. Woodall, Diana. "Yoga and Lesbian Culture," *Lesbian Contradiction,* Winter 1990, no. 29, p. 13.

353. Woodman, Marion. *The Pregnant Virgin: a process of psychological transformation.* Toronto: Inner City Books, 1985. 204 p.

The pregnant virgin, the archetype of the ancient Virgin Goddess, is she who is one-in-herself, the woman who creates herself. Woodman looks at woman's creation of self via psychoanalytical studies, dreams, and the arts.

354. Ywahoo, Dhyani. *Voices of Our Ancestors: Cherokee teachings from the wisdom fire.* Ed. Barbara Du Bois. Boston: Shambhala Books, 1987. 294 p.

The teachings of the Tsalagi (Cherokee) people on finding our true path, listening to the wisdom of the ancients, living in right relationship with the Earth and each other. Includes meditations and guides to using crystals.

355. Zappone, Katherine. *Toward a Feminist Spirituality: the hope for wholeness.* Mystic, CT: Twenty-Third Publications, 1991.

A Christian feminist draws on many spiritual traditions.

The Goddess
Through Time and Space

In this section are listed works about historical goddesses from ancient times and surviving non-Western cultures; female deities and archetypes in mythology, literature, and psychology; and works about women's religious practices in traditional cultures. Writings about the non-specific Goddess of contemporary feminist spirituality will also be found in the previous section on women's spirituality.

356. Absher, Tom. *Men and the Goddess: feminine archetypes in Western literature.* Rochester, VT: Park Street Press, 1990. 157 p.

Absher examines several male literary characters who learn intuition, rebirth, and oneness with nature through their association with women, including Gawain, Macbeth, Gilgamesh, Ulysses, and Huck Finn (remember that part of his quest included dressing and living as a female).

357. Allen, Michael R. *The Cult of Kumari: virgin worship in Nepal.* Kathmandu, Nepal: Institute of Nepal and Asian Studies, Tribhuvan University, 1975. 67 p. 2nd ed.: Kathmandu: Madhab Lal Maharjan, dist. by Himalayan Booksellers, 1983. 114 p.

Kumari ("Daughter") is a virgin goddess worshipped by Nepalese Hindus. In several regions of Nepal a pre-menarchal girl is selected as a "living Kumari," leading a more or less ordinary life at home except during special festivals when she is publicly worshipped. If the girl develops any physical imperfection or begins menstruation, she ceases to be regarded as a goddess and a new Kumari is chosen. The text is illustrated with many photographs of little Kumaris.

358. Amstadt, Jakob. *Das Matriarchat bei den Germanen [Matriarchy among the Germanic peoples]*. Stuttgart: Kohlhammer, 1991.

Although the pagan Germanic tribes were essentially patriarchal, women had an important place in religion and served as diviners, wise women, and priestesses.

359. Anderson, William. *The Green Man: the archetype of our oneness with the earth.* Photography by Clive Hicks. San Francisco: HarperCollins, 1990. 176 p.

The Green Man is a ubiquitous pagan figure in the European Middle Ages, often simply shown as a male face wreathed in vegetation. Anderson analyzes him as the consort of the Goddess and spirit of the authentic masculine principle. Illustrated with dozens of photographs of the Green Man in mediaeval art and sculpture.

360. Antaya, Roger A. *The All-Night Festivals of the Greeks.* Ph.D. thesis, Johns Hopkins University, 1983. 157 p.

Many of these festivals were for women only, and women were always present at other festivals. These rites were dedicated to the Great Goddess or her son/consort and marked by religious ecstasy and free sexual expression.

361. Atre, Shubhangana. *The Archetypal Mother: a systemic approach to Harappan Religion.* Pune, India: Ravish Publishers, 1987. 229 p.

An archaeological work that classifies various elements of the religion of the 4,000-year-old Harappan civilization, which seems to have been dominated by female imagery and in particular by a Great Goddess who was Lady of the Beasts.

362. Austen, Hallie Iglehart [formerly known as Hallie Austen Iglehart; she has taken her mother's maiden name]. *The Heart of the Goddess: art, myth and meditations of the world's sacred feminine.* Foreword by Jean Shinoda Bolen. Berkeley: Wingbow Press, 1990. 174 p.

Beautiful images of the Goddess from ancient civilizations and contemporary artists, arranged by themes such as creation, fire, mothers, transformation, the erotic. Each full-page photograph is accompanied by a commentary on the goddess portrayed and a brief prayer or meditation, enabling the reader to live each goddess. Includes a substantial bibliography and a directory of organizations committed to protecting the environment and enacting social change.

363. Bacciega, Mario. *Dio Padre o Dea Madre? [Father God or Mother Goddess?].* Foggia, Italy: Bastogi, 1987; first published in 1976. 159 p.

On the Mother Goddess from Neolithic times to the Classical Age, as goddess of earth, water, moon, and Black Goddess. Explores what the Feminine means for Christian theology.

364. Baéz-Jorge, Félix. *Los oficios de las diosas: didáctica de la religiosidad popular en los grupos indios de México [The Functions of the Goddesses: didactics of popular religion in Mexican Indian groups].* Xalapa, Mexico: Universidad Veracruzana, 1988. 398 p.

On Mayan and Aztec goddesses: the Earth Mother and moon goddesses were transformed into aspects of the Virgin Mary and thereby survived the genocide wrought by conquistadores and Church.

365. Bandyopadhaya, Pranav. *Mother Goddess Durga.* Calcutta: Image India, 1987. 82 p.

366. Bandyopadhaya, Pranav. *The Goddess of Tantra.* Calcutta: Punthi Pustak, 1987. 129 p.

367. Bádéjò, Diedre L. "The Goddess Òṣun as a Paradigm for African Feminist Criticism," *Sage,* Summer 1989, 6(1):27-32.

The author considers Osun to be very different from white Western goddesses, as she simultaneously embodies power, femininity, strength, and courage. Her legacy is apparent in much of Black poetry celebrating women.

368. *Be Still My Beating Heart.* Ed. Benjamin Darling; introduction by Marija Gimbutas. Los Angeles: Tale Weaver Publishers, 1990. 63 p.

A collection of paintings and sculptures featuring women touching or holding their breasts, from the Venus of Willendorf to contemporary art and popular media. Published as a benefit for the Y-Me Breast Cancer Organization, which encourages us to examine our breasts.

369. Beckman, Gary M. *Hittite Birth Rituals.* 2nd rev. ed. Wiesbaden: Harrassowitz, 1983. 333 p.

Texts in English and transliterated Hittite on opposite pages, containing descriptions of ancient birthing practices, charms, and incantations to the gods which the midwife and birthing mother were instructed to recite. Each text is accompanied by a long scholarly commentary. If you can plow through the technical references, this book is a valuable resource for ancient rituals performed by women for the Goddess.

370. Bell, Robert E. *Women of Classical Mythology: a biographical dictionary.* Santa Barbara: ABC-Clio, 1991. 462 p.

A comprehensive dictionary of goddesses, mortal women, transsexuals, and female animals from Greek and Roman mythology.

371. Berkson, Carmel. *The Amazon and the Goddess: cognates of artistic form.* Bombay: Somaiya Publications, 1987. 53 p.

Using her own photographs, the author compares a 7th-century C.E. South Indian sculpture panel of the goddess Durga fighting demons, with a Battle-of-the-Amazons sarcophagus made in Hellenic Jerusalem five hundred years earlier, concluding that the Indian sculpture shows the influence of Greek myth. Includes material on the role of women in South Indian society and the popularity of the goddess Durga.

372. Berthier, Brigitte. *La Dame-du-Bord-de-l'Eau [The Lady of the Water's Edge].* Nanterre: Société d'Ethnologie, 1988. 311 p.

In South China and Taiwan there is a legend of a woman devoted to Kwan Yin, who refused marriage. After many adventures she apparently died after a self-induced abortion, her story serving to illustrate the conflicts between motherhood and shamanism. The shamaness was elevated to divine status, and is worshipped today.

373. Bharany, Chhote. *Images of Devi in Pahari Paintings.* New

Delhi: Clarion Books, 1984. 158 p.

A celebration of Hindu goddesses in 19th-century paintings, each accompanied by an ode to the goddess in English and Sanskrit and a commentary on the image in the painting. The aspects of the Goddess include Kali, Lakshmi, Durga, Sarasvati, and others.

374. Bhattacharyya, Kanilal. *Sarasvatī: a study on her concept and iconography.* Calcutta: Saraswat Library, 1983. 169 p., 51 plates.

On the goddess of music, poetry, and learning in Hinduism, Jainism, and Buddhism.

375. Birkhaüser-Oeri, Sibylle. *The Mother: archetypal image in fairy tales.* Edited by Marie-Louise von Franz. Toronto: Inner City Books, 1988. 172 p.

376. Blair, Nancy. *Invoking the Goddess: a personal passage way to the Feminine.* M.F.A. thesis in Visual Arts, Rutgers University, 1985. 22 p.

The author is one of the founders of Star River Productions, which creates and markets reproductions of ancient goddess sculptures and contemporary jewelry.

377. Bleibtrau-Ehrenberg, Gisela. *Der Weibmann: kultischer Geschlechtswechsel im Schamanismus: eine Studie zur Transvestition und Transsexualität bei Naturvölkern [The Female Man: cult sex-change in shamanism: a study of transvestism and transsexualism among nature peoples].* Frankfurt am Main: Fischer Taschenbuch Verlag, 1984. 200 p.

378. Boedecker, Deborah. "Hecate: a transfunctional goddess in the *Theogony*?" *Transactions of the American Philological Association,* 113 (1983): 79-93.

Hecate is usually thought of as the dark goddess of night and witchcraft originating in Central Asia, yet in Hesiod's *Theogony*, one of the chief sources for Classical Greek myth, she is so highly praised as a benevolent goddess that some scholars suspect that Hesiod himself was a devotee. The author examines the various functions of Hecate—warriors, athletes, and fisherfolk also prayed to her—and suggests that her multi-faceted nature is essentially Indo-European, not Asian.

379. Bonvin, Jacques. *Vierges Noires: la réponse vient de la terre [Black Virgins: the answer comes from the earth].* Paris: Dervy Livres, 1989. 302 p.

Statues of Black Virgins are venerated throughout Europe, and their origin has long been a mystery. Bonvin found that the siting of Black Virgins corresponds to leylines, solstice vantage points, and other sacred earth sites dating to the time of the Great Mother, and on closer inspection some "black" Virgins actually turn out to be red or green, or were painted black long after their construction. All are wooden and most are about three feet tall. An extensive list of European Black Virgins is appended.

380. Brouwer, H. H. J. *Bona Dea: the sources and a description of the cult.* Leiden; New York: Brill, 1989. 507 p.

The definitive work on the worship of the Roman goddess Bona Dea, often considered a lesbian goddess, as there are ancient reports of erotic, women-only rites. The author includes texts of all surviving literary references and inscriptions, showing Bona Dea to be a protective goddess, worshipped by Romans of both sexes and of varying social classes for hundreds of years.

381. Brown, Ardith F. *The Goddess Kâlî in Pahari Painting.* M.F.A. thesis, University of Florida, 1981. 130 p.

382. Brown, C. Mackenzie. *The Triumph of the Goddess: the canonical models and theological issues of the* Devī-Bhāgavata Purāna. Albany: State University of New York Press, 1990. 327 p.

The ancient authors of the *Puranas*, part of the Hindu sacred scriptures, reworked an older tradition, transforming Devi from a goddess of love and war into the compassionate World Mother who is ultimate reality itself.

383. Brüschweiler, Françoise. *Inanna: la déesse triomphant et vaincue dans la cosmologie sumerienne: recherche lexicographique [Inanna: the triumphant, conquered goddess in Sumerian cosmology: a lexicographic study].* Leuven, Belgium: Peeters, 1987. 233 p.

384. Buccellati, Giorgio. *The Descent of Inanna as a Ritual*

Journey to Kutha? and, Hempel, Wolfgang. *A Catalog of Near Eastern Venus Deities*. Malibu: Undena Publications, 1982. 22 p. (*Syro-Mesopotamian Studies*, Dec. 1982, v.4, no. 3).

In the first work the author wonders whether Inanna's descent, which involved passing though various Sumerian cities, might have elements of a ritual journey to the city of Kutha; in the second work, goddesses associated with the planet Venus are described: Inanna, Ishtar, Astarte, al-Uzza, Babylonian Nanay, and the Bedouin goddess Balthi.

385. Bulteau, Michel. *Mythologie des Filles des Eaux [Mythology of Water Maidens]*. Monaco: Éditions du Rocher, 1982. 187 p.

A poet writes about water goddesses: the Undines, Melusine, the Greek sirens, and the ladies of Arthurian legend.

386. Canan, Janine. *Her Magnificent Body: new & selected poems, 1968-1985*. San Francisco: ManRoot, 1986. 107 p.

Many poems to the Goddess.

387. Carlson, Kathie. *In Her Image: the unhealed daughter's search for her mother*. Boston: Shambhala Publications, 1989. 152 p.

A clearly written and jargon-free study of women's coming to terms with their mothers, with chapters on the positive and negative mother-experience, the importance of touch between mother and daughter, the pervasive fear of becoming one's mother, the healing of the inner child, and the Great Mother Goddess as life-source and archetype (for good or ill). Concludes with a case study of one of the author's patients, whose quest to heal the relationship with her mother led her to the practice of Goddess spirituality.

388. Castleden, Rodney. *The Knossos Labyrinth: a new view of the "Palace of Minos" at Knossos*. New York: Routledge, 1990. 205 p.

A very good guide to the palace and temple complex at Knossos, the seat of Minoan power. The author describes its layout and excavation, the Labyrinth, and the destruction and fall of the Palace and Minoan culture. Includes chapters on the sanctuaries of the Goddess within the Palace and on the Lady of the Labyrinth, the priestesses, and the bull-leaping rituals.

389. Chaudhuri, Dulal. *Goddess Durga, the Great Mother.* Calcutta: Mrimol Publishers, 1984. 66 p.
On the warrior goddess popular in India and Bangladesh.

390. Ching, Linda, and Bruce Shurley. *Hawaiian Goddesses.* Hawaiian Goddesses Pub. Co. (Box 25824, Honolulu, HI 96825), 1987. 118 p.
A book of color illustrations, photographed by Ching.

391. Clair, Jean. *Méduse: contribution à une anthropologie des arts du visuel [Medusa: contribution to an anthropology of the visual arts].* Paris: Gallimard, 1989. 243 p.
Medusa as the dark force within, the bearded woman, protector from the evil eye, and patroness of the artist, a deity who, unlike the Judeo-Christian God, is mutable and mortal.

392. Clark, Rosalind. *The Great Queens: Irish goddesses from the Morrigan to Cathleen ni Houlihan.* Savage, MD: Barnes and Noble Books, 1990. 260 p.
Based on her Ph.D. thesis (University of Massachusetts, 1985), *Goddess, Fairy Mistress, and Sovereignty: women of the Irish supernatural.*

393. Condren, Mary. *The Serpent and the Goddess: women, religion, and power in Celtic Ireland.* San Francisco: Harper and Row, 1989. 268 p.
Ireland was matricentric in pagan times, but even before christianization Irish literature betrayed signs of the patriarchal subjugation of women, often accomplished by rape. Sexism became codified in the Biblical identification of the serpent with Eve and the Fall, although the serpent had originally signified the life-giving goddess. In Ireland the goddess Brigid became a popular saint, while the mediaeval church's dual cult of motherhood and virginity has left its oppressive legacy on Irish women to this day.

394. Cornell, Portia, and Wilderness Starchild. "Goddess Puppets for Peace: using life-sized puppets to dramatize our connec-

tion to the earth," *In Context*, Spring 1985, no. 9, p. 49-51.

The authors describe the majestic puppets of Demeter, Persephone, and Hecate created by Anna Dembska and used in earth rituals and political marches to powerful effect. Illustrated.

395. Crane, Gregory R. *Calypso: stages of afterlife and immortality in the Odyssey.* Ph.D. thesis, Harvard University, 1985. 159 p.

On Calypso and Circe, and their connection with Persephone and the Underworld.

396. Crawford, O. G. S. *The Eye Goddess.* Oak Park, Ill.: Delphi Press, 1991. 168 p.

A reprint of a classic work on the goddess with bright, staring, protective eyes who appears throughout Neolithic and megalithic cultures. Introduction by Miriam Robbins Dexter, author of *Whence the Goddesses* (see below).

397. Day, Susie. *Mother Goddess Funnies.* Illus. by Jackie Urbanovic. [Minneapolis: the authors, 1983]. 22 p.

A collection of comic strips that ran in several feminist newspapers from 1982-1983: a broadly satirical tale of the Creatrix of All who comes to earth and has a run-in with a fundamentalist preacher.

398. De Giovanni, Neria. *Arianna: la signora del labirinto [Ariadne: the lady of the labyrinth].* Genoa: ECIG, 1990. 109 p.

399. *Dearest Goddess: translations from Latvian poetry.* [Compiled] by Eso Benjamins. Arlington, VA: Current Nine Publishing, 1985. 115 p.

A collection of over a hundred *dainas*—women's traditional folksongs, poems, and prayers to the pagan Goddess, reminiscent of Sappho's fragments. Two hundred thousand Lithuanian and nearly one million Latvian *dainas* have been gathered by scholars. The women sing of marriage, love, and what fate has dealt them.

400. Dehehjia, Vidya. *Yogini, Cult and Temples: a tantric tradition.* New Delhi: National Museum, 1986. 239 p.

Now all but forgotten, the Tantric cult of the Yoginis flourished in the 9th-12th centuries in North and Central India. The author reports that since Tantrism is a mystery religion it was very difficult for her to learn about it—in her travels people sometimes mistook her for a famous woman bandit. In Yoga "yogini" is the term used for a female adept, but these Yoginis are aspects of the Great Goddess herself, being the descendents of local village goddesses. In sculpture they are depicted as voluptuous, autonomous and powerful. Extensively illustrated with photos of manuscript illuminations and sculptures (a shocking number of which have literally been defaced, most likely by the Moslem Moghuls, who did not permit images).

401. Detienne, Marcel. "The Violence of Wellborn Ladies: women in the Thesmophoria," in: M. Detienne and Jean-Pierre Vernant, et al., *The Cuisine of Sacrifice Among the Greeks* (University of Chicago Press, 1989), p. 129-147.

Detienne points out that blood sacrifice was an anomaly among women in Greek religion, as it was considered inappropriate for pre-menopausal women to be covered with blood.

402. *Devi: the worship of the Goddess and its contribution to Indian pilgrimage: a report on a seminar and excursion.* Ed. Hans Bakker and Alan Entwhistle. Groningen, Neth.: Institute of Indian Studies, State University of Groningen, 1983. 133 p.

403. Dexter, Miriam Robbins [see also under Robbins, below]. *Whence the Goddesses: a source book.* New York: Pergamon Press, 1990. 280 p.

On the iconography of the Goddess, the Goddess in the ancient Near East, Eastern and Western Europe, India, Goddess-figures in patriarchal society, and woman-energy as reflected in the Goddess. Suitable for classroom use.

404. *The Divine Consort: Radha and the goddesses of India.* Ed. John Stratton Hawley and Donna Marie Wulff. Boston: Beacon Press, 1986 (reprint of 1982 ed.). 414 p.

Essays on Radha, Krishna's consort.

405. Doan, James E. *Women and Goddesses in Early Celtic History, Myth and Legend.* Boston: Northeastern University, Irish Studies Program, 1987. 106 p. (*Working Papers in Irish Studies,* 87-4/5)

406. *La Dona en l'Antiguitat [Woman in Antiquity].* Sabdell, Spain: AUSA, 1987. 141 p.

Proceedings of a conference held at the Universidad Internacional Menéndez Pelayo, Barcelona, 1985, entitled "Seminari Deesses i Heróines en les Mitologies Antigues" ("Seminar on Goddesses and Heroines in Ancient Mythologies"). Articles are on matriarchy and women in mythology and literature, in Spanish, Catalan, and Italian.

407. Donley, Barbara. *Arianrhod: a Welsh myth retold.* Art and illumination by Ken Ruffner. Stone Circle Press (Box 44, Oakland, CA 94604), 1987. 127 p.

The story of the Welsh sky goddess, retold from the *Mabinogion,* in a reconstruction of the original pre-patriarchal form.

408. Dourley, John Patrick. *The Goddess, Mother of the Trinity: a Jungian application.* Lewiston, NY: E. Mellen, 1988. 102 p.

The author is both a priest and a Jungian analyst, who writes that what Jung describes as the collective unconscious is "the basis of the experience of the Great Mother." He discusses Jung's interpretation of Biblical myth, Jung's mystical writings, and those of the medieval German mystic Meister Eckhart.

409. Dowden, Ken. *Death and the Maiden: girls' initiation rites in Greek mythology.* New York: Routledge, 1989. 257 p.

410. Downing, Christine. *Myths and Mysteries of Same-Sex Love.* New York: Continuum, 1989. 317 p.

On homosexuality in the writings of Freud and Jung, and in Greek society and myth. Chiefly on male homosexuality but with chapters on woman-loving women and female deities (Sappho, Demeter and Persephone, Artemis, Aphrodite).

411. Downing, Christine. *Psyche's Sisters: reimaging the meaning of sisterhood.* San Francisco: Harper and Row, 1988.

186 p.

Feminists speak of "sisterhood," but how is a feminist to regard biological sisterhood? In Greek mythology, which has so informed Downing's thought, there are actually very few goddesses who have sisters; instead, it is mortal women who have sisters. Downing writes about Psyche in particular, Ariadne the sister of the Minotaur, and sisters in Greek tragedy and European fairy tales.

412. Duerr, Hans Peter. *Sedna, oder, Die Liebe zum Leben [Sedna, or, the Love of Life]*. Frankfurt: Suhrkamp, 1990. 534 p.

A historian who has written on European paganism and mythology analyzes the rites of the Inuit goddess Sedna, the mistress of the sea animals, as reflecting an ecological religion.

413. Durdin-Robertson, Lawrence. *God the Mother: the creatress and giver of life*. Clonegal Castle, Enniscorthy, Eire: Cesara Publications, Anno Deae Cesarae 4332 [1984]. 86 p.

A treatise on the Goddess Creatrix as she appears in many cultures: Near Eastern, African, Asian, Siberian, and in the Western mystery tradition.

414. Durdin-Robertson, Lawrence. *The Year of the Goddess: a perpetual calendar celebrating the feminine principle*. London: Aquarian Publications, 1990. 240 p.

A calendar honoring goddesses and women saints.

415. Edwards, Carolyn McVickar. *The Storyteller's Goddess: tales of the Goddess and her wisdom from around the world*. San Francisco: HarperSanFrancisco, 1991. 224 p.

Retellings of thirty tales of goddesses from twenty different cultures, reworked into original stories which can be used to teach children about the Goddess. Includes material on the historical and cultural background of the tales.

416. *Encyclopedia of Religion*. Mircea Eliade, editor in chief. New York: Macmillan, 1987. 16 vols.

One of the last projects by the great historian of religion, this set contains many articles by important writers that are relevant to the study of women's spirituality and the Goddess. Rosemary Ruether contributes an article on

"Androcentrism," Christine Downing on the major Greek goddesses, Marija Gimbutas on "Doubleness," prehistoric religion, and several Slavic goddesses and gods, Rita Gross on "Birth" and "Couvade" (male imitation of birth), Kathryn A. Rabuzzi on "Family and Home," Anne Barstow on Joan of Arc, Carol Christ on the Lady of the Animals and the Virgin Goddess, Merlin Stone on "Goddess Worship in the Ancient Near East." While there is no article specifically on the feminist movement or the Pagan revival, other pertinent entries range from "Feminine Sacrality" to "Women's Studies."

417. Erndl, Kathleen Marie. *Victory to the Mother: the goddess cult of Northwest India.* Ph.D. thesis, University of Wisconsin-Madison, 1987. 377 p.

418. Estrada, Alvaro. *Maria Sabina: her life and chants.* Santa Barbara, CA: Ross-Erickson, 1981. 238 p.

The life of a Mexican Mazatec Indian shaman, her experiences with sacred mushrooms, and examples of the chants she used for healing. Preface by Jerome Rothenburg, poet and editor of *Technicians of the Sacred* (a collection of shamanic songs and invocations), and a retrospective essay by R. Gordon Wasson, the foremost authority on the ritual use of psychotropic drugs.

419. Farrar, Janet and Stewart. *The Witches' Goddess: the feminine principle of divinity.* London: R. Hale; Custer, WA: Phoenix Publishing, 1987. 319 p.

An overview of the Goddess as she was worshipped in the ancient Near East and Western Europe, followed by chapters on Celtic and Mediterranean goddesses with rituals to invoke each one, and a list of goddesses of the world.

420. Farrer, Claire R. "Singing for Life: the Mescalero Apache girl's puberty ceremony," in: *Southwestern Indian Ritual Drama,* ed. Charlotte J. Friskie (Albuquerque: Univ. of New Mexico Press, 1980), p. 125-59.

How the ceremony honors the role of women and its importance in the survival of the Mescalero people.

421. Fierz-David, Linda. *Women's Dionysian Initiation: the Villa of Mysteries in Pompeii.* Introduction by M. Esther Harding;

translated by Gladys Phelan. Dallas: Spring Publications, 1988 (first published in German, 1957). 149 p.

A study, done in the 1950's at Jung's Zurich Institute, which analyzes the mysterious, compelling, and beautiful frescoes portraying a woman's initiation into one of the mystery religions. Fierz-David interpreted the paintings as a series of dreams portraying Ariadne, Psyche, Medea, and Phaedra, symbolizing female psychological initiation and individuation.

422. Finn, Mary. "Isis in Ireland," *Ireland of the Welcomes,* Mar.-Apr. 1979, 28(2): 23-24.

A visit to the home of the Fellowship of the Goddess, which is led by Olivia Robertson, her brother Lawrence Durdin-Robertson, and his wife Pamela, in Clonegal, Ireland. The article describes them and the 13th-century castle where they live, worship, and receive visitors on Sundays.

423. Firestone, Homer L. *Pachamama en la cultura andina.* La Paz, Bolivia: Editorial Los Amigos del Libro, 1988. 135 p.
Pachamama was the Inca goddess of earth and moon.

424. Freedman, Jim. *Nyabingi: the social history of an African divinity.* Tervuren, Belgium: Musée Royal de l'Afrique Centrale, 1984. 119 p.

Nyabingi is worshipped in Uganda and Rwanda, where her followers were well known in the early twentieth century as resisters of British colonialism.

425. Frymer-Kensky, Tikva. *In the Wake of the Goddesses: women, culture, and the Biblical transformation of pagan myth.* New York: Free Press, 1992. 292 p.

A religious scholar traces the transition from Mesopotamian polytheism to Biblical monotheism, with parallel changes in attitudes towards women and sexuality.

426. Gadon, Elinor W. "The Goddess Tradition in Hinduism," *Creation* (Oakland, CA), Sept.-Oct. 1988, 4(4):13-14.
On the Goddess as Creator of the Universe, in her forms of Parvati, Lakshmi, Kali, Durga, Ganga.

427. Gadon, Elinor W. *The Once and Future Goddess: a symbol*

for our time. San Francisco: Harper and Row, 1989. 405 p.

A marvellously illustrated history of the Goddess, from Paleolithic caves to the Virgin Mary, the contemporary Goddess movement and imagery in women's art, Gaia and the earth as the body of the Goddess. A stunning tribute, to be lingered over.

428. Galland, China. *Longing for Darkness: Tara and the Black Madonna, a ten-year journey.* New York: Viking, 1990. 392 p.

The spiritual autobiography of a Catholic woman turned Buddhist. A serious illness drove her in search of Tara, the goddess of Tibetan Buddhism, the Hindu goddess Kali, and the European Black Madonna. Galland travelled throughout India, Nepal, Europe and the U.S., visiting the Dalai Lama several times. An intensely personal account of a woman facing and reclaiming the power of the dark.

429. Gatwood, Lynn E. *Devi and the Spouse Goddess: women, sexuality, and marriage in India.* Riverdale, MD: Riverdale Co., 1985. 206 p.

One of the few books available that discusses the Hindu goddesses from a feminist perspective. Covers women and the Goddess from the Indus Valley civilizations to Tantrism and Bhaktism. Two motifs are found in Indian goddess religion: Devi, the wild, pre-Hindu, lower-caste woman who expresses sexuality and power within marriage, and the more demure divine consort of upper-caste Hinduism, who is as domesticated as the traditional middle-class housewife.

430. Geminder, Kathleen Elaine. *Callisto: the recurrance and variations of her myth from Ovid to Atwood.* Ph.D. thesis, University of Manitoba, 1984. 333 p.

On the mythological theme of the girl who is raped in a wood and transformed into a bear. Many literary works employing the motif of the woman seduced/raped in the woods are analyzed from a feminist, Jungian perspective, including *Tess of the d'Urbervilles* and *Surfacing.*

431. George, Demetra, with Douglas Bloch. *Asteroid Goddesses: the mythology, psychology and astrology of the reemerging feminine.* New ed., expanded ephemeris. ACS Publications

(Box 16430, San Diego, CA 92116-0430), 1990 (first published 1986). 383 p.

Most of the major asteroids are named for goddesses, yet they are seldom figured into astrological charts, where they signify personal transformation rather than cosmic forces. George focuses on the largest asteroids (Ceres, Juno, Pallas, and Vesta), giving their mythological background and astrological significance, and other asteroids such as Lilith and Sappho.

432. Getty, Adele. *Goddess: mother of living nature*. New York: Thames and Hudson, 1990. 96 p.

A visual treasury of goddess imagery in painting and sculpture from Greece, the ancient Near East, China, Australia, and Native America. Prefaced with an essay on the myriad forms the Goddess has taken throughout history: the Creatrix, the Virgin Mary, Gaia as the soul of nature.

433. Gilchrist, Cherry. *The Circle of Nine: understanding the female psyche*. London: Dryad Press, 1988. 160 p.

Nine goddess images are presented as archetypes of the Feminine (nine has long been associated with the Triple Goddess): three Queens (Beauty, Night, and Earth); three Ladies (Light, Hearth, and Dance); and three Mothers (Weaving, Great Mother, and Just Mother). The text is accessible to women who do not practice women's spirituality.

434. Gill, Sam D. *Mother Earth: an American story*. Chicago: University of Chicago Press, 1987. 196 p.

According to Gill, a scholar of Native American religion, "Mother Earth" was never really a part of the traditional Native American pantheon, but was primarily a European concept imposed upon Native Americans. She does exist now as an important figure in Native spirituality, but is a deity that has been constructed or developed over time rather than a genuine part of indigenous culture.

435. Gimbutas, Marija. "Birds, Animals, Amphibians and Insects of the Old European Goddess of Death and Regeneration," in: World Archaeological Congress, Southampton, 1986. *Cultural Attitudes to Animals Including Birds, Fish, and Invertebrates* (London: Allen and Unwin, 1986), v. 2, p. 1-45.

436. Gimbutas, Marija. *The Civilization of the Goddess: the world of Old Europe.* San Francisco: HarperSanFrancisco, 1991. 529 p.

A masterpiece on the customs, art, daily life, and religious beliefs and practices of Neolithic Old Europe (eastern and southeastern Europe, 7000-3500 B.C.), with some 600 illustrations.

437. Gimbutas, Marija. "The Collision of Two Ideologies," in: *When Worlds Collide: the Indo-Europeans and the Pre-Indo-Europeans* (Ann Arbor: Karoma Publishers, 1990), p. 171-178.

Contrasts the cultures of Goddess-centered Neolithic Old Europe and the patriarchal Indo-Europeans who moved in during the early Bronze Age, with tables showing the differing functions of Old European goddesses and Indo-European gods.

438. Gimbutas, Marija. "The Image of Woman in Prehistoric Art," *The Quarterly Review of Archaeology*, Dec. 1981, p. 6-8.

439. Gimbutas, Marija. *The Language of the Goddess: unearthing the hidden symbols of western civilization.* Foreword by Joseph Campbell. San Francisco: HarperSanFrancisco, 1989. 388 p.

A visual compilation of Gimbutas's life work: a dictionary, as it were, of the symbols and goddess images of Old Europe. Her thesis is that the visual symbols and conventions in Neolithic art constitute pre-literate texts of a religion of creation, death, and rebirth, centered on the Great Goddess, which can be traced from prehistoric times well into the Christian era. With a glossary, chronologies, maps, and bibliography of archaeological and religious works in sixteen languages, making this a treasure-house of the lore of the Great Goddess.

440. Gimbutas, Marija. "The 'Monstrous Venus' of Prehistory or Goddess Creatrix," *Comparative Civilizations Review,* 1981, vol. 7, p. 1-26.

Part of the groundwork for *The Language of the Goddess* is laid here, where Gimbutas analyzes the pronounced breasts and buttocks of Paleolithic/Neolithic "Venus" figurines as illustrations of religious iconography rather than simple artistic license or erotic wishful thinking.

441. Gimbutas, Marija. "Pre-Indo-European Goddesses in Baltic Mythology," *Mankind Quarterly*, Fall-Winter 1985, 26(1/2):19-25.

The study of historical goddesses in the Baltic area (which was only Christianized in the 14th century) can shed light on the Goddess of Neolithic Old Europe. Examples are Laima, giver of all; Ragana (destruction, regeneration, magic), Žemyna (earth mother), and Austeja (bee goddess).

442. Gimbutas, Marija. "Rediscovering the Goddess: an interview with Marija Gimbutas," *Whole Earth Review,* Spring 1989, no. 62, p. 162-125.

Richard Nilsen and Lori Woolpert interview Gimbutas on the culture of Old Europe, the preponderance of female figurines, and goddess-centered folk customs which were still practiced during her girlhood in Lithuania.

443. Gimbutas, Marija. "Senosios Europos Deivės ir Dievai Lietuvių Mitologijoje [Old European Goddesses and Gods in Lithuanian Mythology]," *Metmenys* (New York), no. 48 (1984), p. 28-57.

444. Gimbutas, Marija. "Symbols and Sacred Images of Old Europe," in: *The Life of Symbols,* ed. Mary Lecron Foster and Lucy Jayne Botscharow (Boulder: Westview Press, 1990), p. 221-257.

Many illustrations of the Goddess from her *Goddesses and Gods of Old Europe* (Berkeley, 1982), portraying aspects of the Paleolithic Goddess as bird, snake, fertility deity, and death goddess.

445. Gimbutas, Marija. "Vulvas, Breasts, and Buttocks of the Goddess Creatress: commenting on the origins of art," in: *The Shape of the Past: studies in honor of Franklin D. Murphy,* ed. G. Buccellati and C. Speroni (Los Angeles: Institute of Archaeology and Office of the Chancellor, University of California, 1981), p. 15-42.

Was early art purely sexual in origin, as some (usually

male) scholars have supposed, or was it symbolic? Gimbutas believes that the ubiquitous imagery of female body parts symbolize a religion and philosophy of the Great Mother.

446. Gleason, Judith. *Oya: in praise of the Goddess*. Boston: Shambhala, 1987. 304 p.

A journey from dispassionate ethnography to the ardor of a devotee, as a white anthropologist becomes fascinated by the Yoruba goddess of nature, feminine charm, and masquerade. Oya is worshipped in West Africa, Brazil, and in North American Santería.

447. *The Goddess Hekate*. Ed. Stephen Ronan. London: Chthonios Press, 1989. 70 p.

448. *The Goddess Remembered*. Illus. by Melanie Lofland; ed. Shawn Evans. Freedom, CA: The Crossing Press, 1990. 128 p.

A blank book illustrated with resplendent goddess art, prayers, and spiritual quotations.

449. *The Goddess Within: a journal of awakening with quotes and space for notes*. Selected and compiled by Karen Scott Boates; ill. by Dennis Roberts. Philadelphia: Running Press, 1990. [179] p.

With an introduction by Boates on the contemporary re-awakening to the Goddess and a history of the Goddess-worshipping cultures of the Neolithic and ancient Eastern civilizations. The illustrations and designs are based on ancient sculptures and motifs; the quotations, by women and men, are on the Goddess, feminism, and the Spirit.

450. *Goddesses and Their Offspring: 19th and 20th century Eastern European embroideries*. Binghamton, NY: Roberson Center for the Arts and Sciences, 1986. 77 p.

Articles on motifs of the pagan fertility goddess and Lady of the Animals visible in Eastern European embroidery (chiefly in Russia and the Ukraine), and a catalogue of an exhibit held in 1987.

451. *Goddesses in Religions and Modern Debate*. Ed. Larry W. Hurtado. Atlanta: Scholars Press, 1990. 227 p.

Articles on Chinese goddesses, Tibetan Taras, Isis, Shakti, the Goddess in feminist thought, other topics.

452. Goodrich, Norma Lorre. *Priestesses.* New York: Franklin Watts, 1989. 428 p.

An important work on the priestess in the ancient world: the Hittites, Amazons, Egyptians, and Cretans, the Greek priestess and the goddesses she served, the Oracles of Delphi, priestesses in patriarchal Rome, and the Celtic priestesses as described by Roman conquerors. Includes many excerpts from ancient texts. The authority of the ancient priestesses points to a time when the power of all women was respected and granted sacred status, until it was overthrown both historically and mythologically by the male powers of heaven and earth.

453. Goswany, Karuna. *The Glory of the Great Goddess: an illustrated manuscript from Kashmir from the Alice Boner Collection in the Museum Rietberg, Zurich.* Zurich: the Museum, 1989. 105 p.

Illustrations and description of a manuscript of the *Devi Mahatmya*, a Sanskrit hymn to the Great Goddess praising her as Creatrix, Shakti, and protector.

454. Goux, Jean-Joseph. "Vesta, or the Place of Being," *Representations* (University of California at Berkeley), Feb. 1983, 1(1):91-107.

There are very few visual representations of the goddess Vesta/Hestia. Goux's explanation is that she is not only the goddess of the hearth, she *is* the hearth, and that her virginity is so all-encompassing that men cannot even look upon her face.

455. *Le Grandi Madri [The Great Mothers].* Ed. Tilde Giani Gallino. Milan: Feltrinelli, 1989. 262 p.

Proceedings of a conference in Turin, 1988. Articles (in Italian) on the Great Mother in Hinduism, protective goddesses, Mary and the witch, goddesses in the Kabbalah and Gnosticism, in the Greco-Roman world, and in psychoanalysis.

456. Gravelaine, Joëlle de. *Le Retour de Lilith: la lune noire [The*

Return of Lilith: the black moon]. Paris: L'Espace Bleu, 1988. 257 p.

On Lilith the Hebrew goddess, Lilith the asteroid, and her astrological influence on women.

457. Gray, William G. *Evoking the Primal Goddess: discovering the eternal feminine within*. St. Paul: Llewellyn Publications, 1989. 167 p.

Using rituals and meditations, the author invites the (male?) reader to return to the Goddess as an antidote to our crushingly masculine patriarchal culture.

458. "The Great Goddess," *New Internationalist*, June 1989, no. 196, p. 7.

A summary of the character and worship of the Great Mother from Paleolithic times, when the Goddess ruled the forces of birth and death, to the rise of male deities and the suppression of female power, with examples from African and Babylonian myth and Aztec ritual.

459. Grey, Morgan, and Julia Penelope. *Found Goddesses: Asphalta to Viscera*. Illus. by Allison Bechdel. Norwich, VT: New Victoria Publishers, 1988. 122 p.

A comic dictionary of the goddesses of lesbian culture, such as Euphoria, Chocolata, Paranoia...

460. Groupe de Recherches Interdisciplinaires d'Étude des Femmes (G.R.I.E.F.). *Générations de Vierges [Generations of Virgins]*. Toulouse: Presses Universitaires du Mirail, 1987. 99 p.

Studies of the virgin-figure in Greek religion (Artemis, Athena, Hestia), the cult of the Virgin Mary, and the political and ideological connotations of virginity. In French with one essay in English.

461. Gustafson, Fred. *The Black Madonna*. Boston: Sigo Press, 1990. 143 p.

On Black Virgins and their relation to other goddesses of the Dark (Lilith, Kali, Isis, Kore) and the feminine unconscious.

462. Harman, William. *The Sacred Marriage of a Hindu God-*

dess. Bloomington: Indiana University Press, 1989. 232 p.

On the South Indian goddess Minaksi, who is ritually married to Shiva. In this cult and its public rituals it is the goddess who is supreme. The author describes sacred marriages in several religious traditions, and how marriage is seen to function in the context of Hindu theology.

463. Harper, Jorjet. "Sappho and the Goddess Aphrodite," *Hot Wire: the journal of women's music and culture,* Nov. 1986, 3(1):16.

464. Harper, Katherine Anne. *The Iconography of the Saptamatrikas: seven Hindu goddesses of spiritual transformation.* Lewiston, NY: E. Mellen Press, 1989. 200 p., 120 p. of plates.

The Saptamatrikas ("Seven Little Mothers") are important aspects of Devi. Their worship dates to the Indus Valley civilizations.

465. Hendrix, Kathleen. "Goddesses and Goodness," *Los Angeles Times,* Aug. 21, 1989, Sec. V, p. 1.

An interview with Riane Eisler, who discusses the ancient Goddess cultures.

466. Higgins, Richard. "Goddesses and Worship: scholars turn to ancient cultures for a more feminine concept of the divine," *Boston Globe,* April 5, 1987, pp. 96, 98.

A thoughtful article on the resurgence of interest in ancient goddesses, touching upon the research of Elinor Gadon, Pamela Berger, Carol Christ, and Unitarian Elizabeth Anastos.

467. Hiltebeitel, Alf. *The Cult of Draupadi:* v. 1, *Mythologies;* v. 2, *On Hindu Ritual and the Goddess.* Chicago: University of Chicago Press, 1988—.

On the South Indian worship of Draupadi, the heroine of the Indian epic *Mahabharata* and Hindu goddess par excellence.

468. Hirsley, Michael. "Actress Puts God in Different Light," *Chicago Tribune,* April 19, 1991, Sec. 2C, p. 9.

Review of Carol Lynn Pearson's one-woman play "Mother Wove the Morning," whose theme is the historical primacy of the Goddess.

469. Hollis, Susan Tower. "Women of Ancient Egypt and the Sky Goddess Nut," *Journal of American Folklore,* Oct.-Dec. 1987, 100(398):496-503.

Egyptian mythology is unusual in that the sky deity, Nut, was female while the earth was male. Nut was the mother of the stars and the sun, as well as being a death goddess. In Egypt the power of the feminine was reflected by Egyptian women having considerable legal rights, if not actual equality with men.

470. Hubbs, Joanna. *Mother Russia; the feminine myth in Russian culture.* Bloomington: Indiana University Press, 1988. 302 p.

From the Paleolithic Lady of the Beasts to folk-art *matrioshka* dolls, from Baba Yaga to the passionate Orthodox devotion to the Virgin and "Mother Russia," the Goddess has had a long history in the Slavic realms.

471. *Images of Women in Antiquity.* Ed. Averil Cameron and Amélie Kuhrt. Detroit: Wayne State University Press, 1983. 323 p.

Relevant articles include: "Women and Witchcraft in Ancient Assyria" by Sue Rollin; "Hittite Birth Rituals" by Jackie Pringle; and the section on "Women in Religion and Cult" (Jezebel's worship of Asherah, Babylonian priestesses, Hellenic Jewish women, women in the Syrian Church).

472. *In All Her Names: explorations of the feminine in divinity.* Ed. Joseph Campbell and Charles Musès. San Francisco: HarperSanFrancisco, 1991. 177 p.

Four essays on the Goddess—"The Goddess of Nature and Spirituality" by Riane Eisler, "The Monstrous Venus" by Marija Gimbutas (see entry 440), "The Mystery Number of the Goddess" by Joseph Campbell, and "On Divine Pregnancy in Egypt and China" by Musès—followed by several odes to the Goddess from ancient and modern sources.

473. Ingham, Marion Frieda. *The Goddess Freyja and Other Female Figures in Germanic Mythology and Folklore.* Ph.D. thesis, Cornell University, 1985. 283 p.

Freyja was the Germanic and Norse goddess of nature

and love, and was also associated with the practice of magic and witchcraft.

474. International Conference on Archaeology of the Ancient Mediterranean (University of Malta, 1985). *Archaeology and Fertility Cult in the Ancient Mediterranean.* Ed. Anthony Bonanno. Amsterdam: B.R. Grüner, 1986. 356 p.

This interesting collection contains papers on Old Europe, the Near East, Thera, the Greco-Roman world, Phoenician goddesses, the issue of "fertility cult" vs. goddess religion, and several papers on the Maltese Great Goddess. Attendees included Christine Biaggi, Buffie Johnson, Mimi Lobell, Colin Renfrew, and Marija Gimbutas, who decided not to let her paper be published in the same volume as that of another, unnamed, participant (possibly Brian Hayden, whose paper criticizes Gimbutas's theories of Old European matriarchy).

475. Isenberg, Barbara. "The Art of Dressing a Goddess," *Los Angeles Times,* Mar. 30, 1988, Sec. V, p. 1.

On goddess imagery in clothing, art, and music, with a profile of Judy Chicago.

476. Ishbel. *The Secret Teachings of the Temple of Isis: a self-preparation for the New Age.* St. Paul: Llewellyn Publications, 1989. 322 p.

Seven-thousand-year-old teachings from the Inner Temple in Egypt, by a High Priestess of Isis.

477. Jayakar, Pupul. *The Earth Mother: legends, goddesses, and ritual arts of India.* New Delhi; New York: Penguin Books, 1989; San Francisco: Harper and Row, 1990 (a revised and updated edition of *The Earthen Drum: an introduction to the ritual arts of India* [New Delhi: National Museum, 1980]). 248 p.

On the ancient Mother whose worship originated long before Hinduism was codified into the patriarchal Vedas, and her presence in the Neolithic Harappan civilization, indigenous Dravidian (South Indian) culture, Tantric fertility rites, and survivals in rural religious traditions. With illustrations of goddess sculptures and folk symbols.

478. Jensen, Theadora. "The Bull of Heaven, or How the Goddess Was Destroyed," *New Catalyst* (Lillooet, BC), Winter 1987, no. 10, p. 4.

The herstory of civilization, from matriarchal Goddess culture to patriarchal oppression. Part of a special issue on "Women/Earth Speaking: feminism and ecology."

479. Johnson, Buffie. *Lady of the Beasts: ancient images of the Goddess and her sacred animals.* San Francisco: Harper and Row, 1988. 386 p.

A beautiful sourcebook on the ancient Goddess in her animal aspect and on her animal companions. From Paleolithic art to Christian symbolism, the Goddess has appeared as bird, serpent, lion, dog, butterfly, sheep, spider, scorpion, deer, fish, pig, cow, and bear. An outstanding resource of Goddess imagery, both scholarly and feminist, by an artist who has been fascinated by the Goddess for over forty years.

480. Johnson, Sally B. *The Cobra Goddess of Ancient Egypt: Predynastic, Early Dynastic and Old Kingdom Periods.* New York: Kegan Paul International, 1990. 276 p.

481. Johnston, Sarah. *Hekate Soteira: a study of Hekate's role in the Chaldean Oracles and related literature.* Atlanta: Scholars Press, 1990. 192 p.

On Hecate as mistress of magic, guide of souls, and moon goddess as she appears in Classical ceremonial magic. In the Chaldean Oracles, Hecate is not the goddess of witchcraft and dark forces, but the patron of the Cosmic Soul who mediates between human and divine, making her important to ancient Greek theurgists (ceremonial magicians). Based on the author's Ph.D. thesis (Cornell University, 1987): *The Development of Hekate's Archaic and Classical Roles in the Chaldean Oracles and Related Mystic Literature.*

482. Jones, Allen H. *Essenes: the elect of Israel and the priests of Artemis.* Lanham, MD: University Press of America, 1985. 146 p.

The author finds a possible connection between the Jewish sect of Essenes and another sect called Essenes who worshipped Artemis at Ephesus; not because both Jewish Essenes and Greek Artemis valued chastity, but because the

Ephesian Artemis was a mother goddess and queen bee, and there are many references to bees, milk, and honey in the texts of both groups.

483. Jones, Kathy. *The Goddess in Glastonbury.* Illustrations and photographs by Diana Griffiths. Glastonbury, Eng.: Ariadne, 1990. 52 p.
    The sacred hill of Glastonbury, long connected with Arthurian legend and the Holy Grail but with roots in pre-Christian times, has been associated by many scholars with the British Great Goddess.

484. Judd, Elizabeth. "The Myths of the Golden Age and the Fall: from matriarchy to patriarchy," in: *Views of Women's Lives in Western Tradition: frontiers of the past and the future,* ed. Frances Richardson Keller (Lewiston, NY: E. Mellen, 1990), p. 15-82.
    On the worldwide Golden Age as a time of peace, plenty, and harmony in ancient myth, to be distinguished from "civilization." Judd relates this myth to the transfer of worship from goddesses to gods and speculates on the likelihood of this reflecting matrifocal times.

485. Kahukiwa, Robyn. *Wahine Toa: women of Maori myth.* Paintings and drawings by Robyn Kahukiwa; text by Patricia Grace. Auckland, NZ: William Collins; dist. in the U.S. by Salem House, 1984. 80 p.
    A collection of portraits of important goddesses and foremothers in Maori myth, with explanatory text by Patricia Grace, a writer of Maori descent (I recommend her short stories). The paintings are brilliantly colored and full of power, reminiscent of the strong women of Sudie Rakusin and Monica Sjöö.

486. Kati-Ma [Kati Koppana]. *23 Cantos for the Goddess.* Iseum of the Star Goddess, c/o Sirius, Box 452, 00101 Helsinki, Finland, 1987; Loughborough, Eng.: Heart of Albion Press, 1991. 32 p.
    A book of Finnish Neo-Paganism, with poetry, songs, meditations, and rituals.

487. Kelen, Jacqueline. *Les Reines Noires: Didon: Salomé, la*

Reine de Saba [The Black Queens: Dido, Salome, the Queen of Sheba]. Paris: Albin Michel, 1987. 250 p.

"They are... initiates in that the most ancient traditions exist within them... embodying a femininity which has been forgotten in our time."

488. Keller, Catherine. "Psychocosmetics and the Underworld Connection," in: *Archetypal Process: self and divine in Whitehead, Jung, and Hillman,* ed. David Ray Griffin (Evanston, Ill.: Northwestern University Press, 1989), p. 133-155.

Jungian and Whiteheadian interpretations of Psyche's journey to the Underworld to fetch Persephone's cosmetic box, a task assigned to her by Aphrodite in order to win back Eros. Keller uses Daly's criticisms of Jungian interpretation of the Demeter-Persephone myth.

489. Kelly, Mary B. *Goddess Embroideries of Eastern Europe.* Winona, MN: Northland Press of Winona (Kings Mansion, Suite 412, 512 E. Fourth St., Winona, MN 55987), 1989. 215 p.

A brilliant contribution to art history, documenting the survival throughout Eastern Europe and Russia of Great Goddess motifs in embroidery and other folk arts. From Neolithic times to the present, images of the Goddess persist in the form of the Goddess with Upraised Arms, the Mother Goddess containing the daughter, and as a woman holding the reins of two horses. The book is carefully researched and wonderfully illustrated.

490. Kelly, Mary B. "Goddess Embroideries of Russia and the Ukraine," *Woman's Art Journal,* 1984, 4(2):10-13.

491. Kelly, Mary B. *Ten Goddesses to Embroider or Color.* [Dryden, NY]: Tompkins Cortland Community College, Liberal Arts Humanities Division, [1988]. 16 p.

Simplified black and white reproductions of goddess images in Slavic embroidery, with an introduction on the Slavic goddess heritage.

492. Kinsley, David. *The Goddesses' Mirror: visions of the divine from East and West.* Albany: State University of New York

Press, 1989. 320 p.

Essays on Durga, Kuan Yin, Lakshmi, Amaterasu, Sita, Inanna, Athena, Isis, Aphrodite, and Mary, illustrating the richness of the forms of the Goddess. Kinsley stresses that every goddess is multifaceted, and we should avoid affixing a single label onto any goddess, let alone "the" Goddess.

493. Kinsley, David. *Hindu Goddesses: visions of the divine feminine in the Hindu religious tradition.* Berkeley: University of California Press, 1986. 281 p.

This book is more accessible to the general reader than most texts on Indian goddesses. Chapters on goddesses in the Vedic literature, the goddesses Lakshmi, Parvati, Sarasvati, Sita (the heroine of the *Ramayana*), Radha, Durga, Kali, Mahadevi, the Matrikas, Tara, goddesses of the land, and local village deities.

494. Kisselgoff, Anna. "The Ancient Relationship of Goddesses and the Dance," *New York Times,* Dec. 14, 1986, Sec. H, pp. 18, 20.

A report on the Asia Society's two-day symposium on "the Universal Goddess." Indian, Korean, and African dances were performed.

495. Kleinbaum, Abby Wettan. "Amazon Legends and Misogynists: the women and civilization question," in: *Views of Women's Lives in Western Tradition: frontiers of the past and the future,* ed. Frances Richardson Keller (Lewiston, NY: E. Mellen, 1990), p. 83-109.

On Amazons as the pre-civilized woman—were they real or a mythic memory?—and their visionary appeal for lesbians.

496. Knepher, Tom. "The Goddess and the Green Man," *The Quest* (Wheaton, Ill.), Spring 1991, p. 60-66.

The Green Man is the quintessential Western European pagan god, the son-consort of the Great Mother, Lord of the Animals and the hunt, the Dying God, who has been known from Paleolithic times. His spirit is now being reborn in the worldwide environmental movement.

497. Koltuv, Barbara Black. *The Book of Lilith.* York Beach, ME:

Nicholas-Hays, Inc.; dist. by Samuel Weiser, 1986. 127 p.

"Lilith is that quality in a woman that refuses to be bound in a relationship." On Lilith's story in the Talmud and Jewish myth and folklore; Lilith as seductress and opposite of Eve/Mary; as demonic child-stealer; and as the dark and fascinating creature who resides deep within the feminine.

498. Kraemer, Ross Shepard. *Her Share of the Blessings: women's religions among Pagans, Jews, and Christians in the Greco-Roman world.* New York: Oxford University Press, 1992.

499. *Kuan Yin Opens the Door to the Golden Age: the path of the mystic East and West: the World Mother on love, karma, reincarnation, and the initiation of the soul.* Malibu, CA: Summit University Press, 1983-1984. 2 vols.

Channelled by Elizabeth Clare Prophet of the Summit Lighthouse; reprinted from their publication *Pearls of Wisdom,* v. 25, 1982.

500. Lacher, Irene. "She Worship," *Los Angeles Times,* Sept. 19, 1990, Sec. E, p. 1.

On feminist goddess religion.

501. LaDuke, Betty. "Susanne Wenger and Nigeria's Sacred Osun Grove," *Woman's Art Journal,* Spring/Summer 1989, 10(1):17-21.

An artist draws her inspiration from groves sacred to the goddess Osun.

502. Landucci Gattinoni, Franca. *Un culto celtico nella Gallia Cisalpina: le Matronae-Iunones a sud delle Alpi [A Celtic Cult in Cisalpine Gaul: the Matronae-Junos south of the Alps].* Milan: Jaca Book, 1986. 100 p.

On the worship of the Celtic Matronae or Triple Mother-Goddess, later merged with the Roman Juno, in the northernmost part of Italy.

503. Lassacher, Martina. *Auf der Suche nach der Grossen Mutter: zu einem Grundmuster der Weltliteratur [In Search of the Great Mother: towards a paradigm of world literature].* Frankfurt am Main; New York: Lang, 1987. 210 p.

On the Mother Goddess and nature divinities in literature.

504. Laut, Renate. *Weibliche Züge im Gottesbild Israelistisch-Jüdischer Religiosität [Feminine Elements in the God-Imagery of Israelite-Jewish Spirituality].* Köln: E. J. Brill, 1983. 96 p.

On the Semitic goddesses Astarte, Anat, and Asherah, Wisdom, Shekhinah, the Spirit, and the Sabbath Queen.

505. Lefkowitz, Mary R. *Women in Greek Myth.* Baltimore: Johns Hopkins University Press, 1986. 158 p.

On mortal, not divine, women in the myths; matriarchal theory and the Amazons; and other mythic women who live without men, such as Atalanta. She points out that while the myths are often misogynistic, female characters have a greater range of behavior than is commonly assumed.

506. Leslie, Jacques. "The Goddess Theory," *Los Angeles Times Magazine,* June 11, 1989, pp. 22-24, 26.

An interview with Marija Gimbutas and a discussion of her controversial theory of a peaceful matrifocal past. Emphasizes academic skepticism and negative reviews of her *The Goddesses and Gods of Old Europe* (Berkeley, 1982).

507. Lichtman, Susan A. *Life Stages of Woman's Heroic Journey: a study of the origins of the Great Goddess archetype.* Lewiston, NY: Edwin Mellen Press, 1991. 100 p.

Woman's heroic journey towards self-actualization, during which she must come to terms with the Maiden, Mother, and Crone within. Lichtman employs mythological goddess archetypes, literature, and popular culture.

508. Loon, Maurits N. van. *Anatolia in the Earlier First Millenium B.C.* Leiden: Brill, 1991. 49 p., 48 plates.

A comparison of the iconography of the Goddess among Hittites, Phrygians, Lydians, and others. These peoples worshipped Cybele (Kubaba) and other deities, but the Phrygians were "almost monotheistic" in their devotion to her.

509. Loon, Maurits N. van. *Anatolia in the Second Millenium B.C.* Leiden: Brill, 1985. 47 p., 46 plates.

On the Hittite goddess and her son, the Lord of the Hunt.

510. Loth, Heinrich. *Woman in Ancient Africa.* Trans. by Sheila

Marnie. Westport, CT: Lawrence Hill, 1987. 189 p.

A comprehensive if general study of women's social, legal, political, and cultural roles in traditional and pre-colonial Africa, with many illustrations. Loth has very old-fashioned views on "fetishism" and "primitive" religion, but he provides a great deal of background on a neglected area of women's religious experience.

511. *Maenads, Martyrs, Matrons, Monastics: a sourcebook on women's religion in the Greco-Roman world.* Ed. Ross S. Kraemer. Philadelphia: Fortress Press, 1988. 429 p.

A collection of Classical, Jewish, and early Christian texts on women's worship, rites to the Goddess, inscriptions, and biographies; intended for classroom use.

512. Maier, Walter A. *ʾAšerah: extrabiblical evidence.* Atlanta: Scholars Press, 1986. 260 p.

Asherah (Ashtoreth/Astarte) is well-known in the Old Testament as that "abomination" worshipped by the Hebrews, Canaanites, Phoenicians, Hittites, and other Near Eastern peoples for over 3,000 years. This book gives references to her in Ugaritic texts and in other texts and inscriptions found in the ancient Near East and Mediterranean cultures.

513. Maillot, Alphonse. *Eve, ma mère: la femme dans l'Ancien Testament et dans quelques civilisations proches [Eve, my mother: women in the Old Testament and some nearby civilizations].* Paris: Letouzey et Ané, 1989. 183 p.

514. Mascetti, Manuela Dunn. *The Song of Eve: mythology and symbols of the Goddess.* New York: Simon & Schuster, 1990. 239 p.

A lushly illustrated book on the archetypes of the Goddess and their meaning for women: the virgin, creatrix, terrible destroyer, the mother, lover, priestess, wise woman, and muse. Illustrated with artwork from ancient times to the early 20th century and contemporary photographs (unfortunately, most of the art is unidentified). A powerful visual experience.

515. Mathers, Jay. "Did Goddess Worship Mark Ancient Age of Peace?" *Washington Post,* Jan. 7, 1990, Sec. 1, p. 8.

On *The Language of the Goddess* by Marija Gimbutas.

516. *Matronen und verwandte Gottheiten [Matronae and Similar Deities].* Köln: R. Habelt, 1987. 254 p.

Proceedings of a conference on the Mother Goddess in Greece and pre-Christian Roman Europe, particularly among the Germans and Celts.

517. Matthews, Caitlín. *Arthur and the Sovereignty of Britain: king and goddess in the Mabinogion.* London: Arkana, 1989. 334 p.

The author has written several books on the Celtic tradition and the Western mystery ways. Here she examines the collection of Welsh romance-myths known as the *Mabinogion,* part of which include the Celtic versions of Arthurian legend. She uncovers the presence of Welsh goddesses, such as Morgan and the fairy women, Gwenhwyfar, and the Goddess of the Land, or Sovereignty (also important in Ireland), she whom the hero must marry in order to be the rightful King.

518. Matthews, Caitlín. *The Elements of the Goddess.* Shaftesbury, Eng.: Element Books, 1989. 130 p.

An introduction to the ancient goddess and Divine Feminine, with exercises and meditations designed to construct an Inner Temple to the Goddess. Includes addresses of goddess groups in the United Kingdom.

519. Matthews, Caitlín. *The Search for Rhiannon.* London: Hunting Raven Press, 1981.

520. Matthews, Caitlín. *Sophia, Goddess of Wisdom : the divine feminine from black goddess to world soul.* London: Unwin, 1990; Mandala, 1991. 378 p.

A thoroughly researched study of Sophia as Black Mistress, White Virgin, and Red Queen, primarily as the mystical presence of divine feminine Wisdom in Western religion, philosophy, and esoteric work, rather than in the Biblical context.

521. McClain, Jane C. "The Female Factor: when God became a man," *Creation,* Mar.-Apr. 1986, 2(1):34-35.

On the subsumation of Europe's goddess-centered, matrifocal civilization at the hands of Indo-European patriarchal invaders, and the shift in concept of God from immanent to transcendent in Classical Greece.

522. McKenna, Terence. *The Archaic Revival: speculations on psychedelic mushrooms, the Amazon, virtual reality, UFOs, evolution, shamanism, the rebirth of the Goddess, and the end of history.* San Francisco: HarperSanFrancisco, 1992.

523. McLean, Adam. *The Triple Goddess.* Edinburgh: Hermetic Research Series, 1983; Grand Rapids: Phanes Press, 1989. 76 p.

A study of the Triple Goddess in Greek mythology, as Maiden/Mother/Crone, the Fates, the Furies, etc., and other Triple Goddesses in Irish and Norse mythology.

524. Meador, Betty D. *The Descent of Inanna to the Underworld.* Inanna Institute (Box 11164, Oakland, CA 94611), n.d. 40 p.

A Jungian analyst's translation of the Sumerian myth into stately, rhythmic poetry.

525. Mellaart, James, Udo Hirsch, and Belkis Balpinar. *The Goddess from Anatolia.* Milan: Eskenazi, 1989. 4 v.

Mellaart wrote the classic archaeological works on Çatal Hüyük, an 8,000-year-old city in central Turkey (Anatolia), where the Goddess is clearly pre-eminent and which has been hypothesized to be a verifiably matriarchal state. The present work, like that of Mary Kelly (see above), reveals the presence of the Goddess in painting and especially in traditional weavings called *kilims,* in a heritage stretching from Neolithic times to the present. Motifs of the Great Goddess are shown in the many plates, with comparisons to painting and sculpture from Çatal Hüyük. An important resource for the archaeology of the Goddess.

526. *Merlin and Woman: the second Merlin Conference.* Ed. R. J. Stewart; illus. by Miranda Gray. London; New York: Blandford Press, 1983. 190 p.

A collection of essays by Stewart, Caitlín and John Matthews, Tarot author Rachel Pollack, poet Kathleen Raine, and ritualist Dolores Ashcroft-Nowicki on Merlin in Celtic myth, poetry, and later English literature. The most relevant essays are those by Stewart on the Tarot, a short story by Pollack, and "Merlin and the Mother Goddess" by Ashcroft-

Nowicki.

527. Metzger, Deena. "Re-Vamping the World: return of the holy prostitute," *Utne Reader,* Aug.-Sept. 1985, p. 120-124 (also in the anthology *To Be a Woman*; see item 319).

In the ancient Near East priestesses of the Goddess functioned as bodily "conduits to the divine," and prostitution in Her service was considered to be a method of healing the soul. Metzger suggests that women today might heal men by reviving the healing aspect of sexuality. This essay, which is not easy to understand, provoked a flood of letters to the *Utne Reader*, pro and con.

528. Meyer, Eveline. *Aṅkāḷaparamēcuvari: a goddess of Tamilnadu, her myths and cult.* Stuttgart: Steiner Verlag, 1986. 339 p.

Includes texts on the goddess in Tamil with English translation.

529. Miller, Casey, and Kate Swift. "Watch Your Words!" *New Directions for Women*, Sept./Oct. 1991, 20(5):24.

The authors of *The Handbook of Nonsexist Writing* question the use of the terms "priestess" and "Goddess," since the female forms literally signify "female priest" and "female God," thereby implying that "priest" and "God" are the (nonfemale) norm. (The Catholic Right loves to refer to hypothetical women priests as "priestesses," who are surely pagan.) The authors do not consider "the Goddess" to be equivalent to "the God," but they do not propose alternatives.

530. Misra, Om Prakash. *Mother Goddess in Central India.* Delhi: Agam Kala Prakashan, 1985. 192 p., 52 p. of plates.

Based on the author's Ph.D. thesis, Bhopal University, 1984 (*A Critical Study of Śakti Sculptures in the Museums of Madhya Pradesh*).

531. Monaghan, Patricia. *The Book of Goddesses & Heroines.* Revised and enlarged ed. St. Paul: Llewellyn Publications, 1990. 421 p.

A useful dictionary of goddesses and women in worldwide mythology. This edition is illustrated with photographs from the Field Museum of Natural History and lists additional goddesses from the Third World.

532. Mookerjee, Ajit. *Kali: the feminine force*. New York: Destiny Books, 1988. 112 p.

On the Hindu goddess of death and destruction who is also the Divine Mother. The author sees the resurgence of the feminine as a natural consequence of our living in the Kali Yuga or cosmic Age of Kali. Illustrated with many stunning photos of paintings and statues of Kali.

533. Mosich, S. Kathena. *Through the Eyes of the Goddess, or, How to Give Life to the Spirit of Aphrodite in You.* San Diego: Shapes of Spirit, Inc., 1990. 167 p., 23 p. of plates.

534. Naddair, Kaledon [J.A. Johnston]. *The Search for Awen: a quest for the Goddess in roots and relationships*. Edinburgh: Keltia Publications, 1985. 75 p.

Poetry by a priest of Druidic shamanism, with an introductory essay on the virtual eradication of Celtic culture in Scotland due to centuries of English Christian domination. Awen is a Welsh goddess of poetry and the mysteries; most of the poems in the book are about the loss of Celtic culture.

535. Nadyne, Fay. "The Mythology of Origins: Ancient Sumerian/ Babylonian perspectives," *Resources for Feminist Research,* Sept. 1989, 18(3):19-23.

A discussion of the Descent of Inanna to the Underworld. The author points out that although Inanna contains the powers of reproduction and sexuality of all kinds, in her myth she herself does not give birth.

536. Nagar, Shanti Lal. *The Universal Mother*. Delhi: Atma Ram & Son, 1989. 256 p.

A comprehensive survey of goddesses in Western, Northern, and Eastern Europe, Russia, Turkey, the Middle East, Africa, Asia and Australia. The second two-thirds of the book is on the goddesses of South Asia. This is a solid resource for the study of Indian goddesses which complements Gimbutas's work on Europe.

537. Nanda, Serena. *Neither Man Nor Woman: the hijras of India*. Belmont, CA: Wadsworth, 1990. 170 p.

An American anthropologist interviewed many *hijras*, members of an Indian sect of men who dress and live as women, worshipping the mother goddess Bahuchara Mata and assuming female ritual roles. They usually have themselves made into eunuchs and in traditional India are regarded as a sort of third gender.

538. Navarro, Virginia Sánchez. "Re-membering the Goddess: ecofeminism in Mexico," *New Catalyst* (Lillooet, BC), Spring 1989, no. 14, p. 6-7.

An activist in the Mexican eco-feminist movement sees the myth of the dismemberment of the Aztec moon goddess Coyolxauhqui as indicating the triumph of patriarchy over matriarchy. This goddess is being honored by women in public rituals in Mexico City as a re-membering of their pre-Columbian heritage.

539. Noble, Vicki. "Snake Goddess at Knossos," *East West,* Dec. 1990, p. 88.

A photograph by Irene Young of the Cretan snake goddess/priestess superimposed over a sacred walkway at Knossos; the text describes Young's spiritual vision of her art.

540. O'Flaherty, Wendy Doniger. *Women, Androgynes, and Other Mythical Beasts.* Chicago: University of Chicago Press, 1980. 382 p.

A complex journey through mythology and literature, encompassing sexuality and power in Indian mythology, the substratum of female primacy, Indo-European mare goddesses, and androgyny in myth.

541. Oda, Mayumi. *Goddesses.* Expanded edition. Volcano, CA: Volcano Press, 1988. 74 p.

Oda creates cheerful, unique serigraphs of Japanese Buddhist goddesses (some as female versions of traditionally male deities), and invents new goddesses as well. Accompanying the art is the story of her girlhood in Japan, her coming of age as an artist and mother, her Zen practice, and her awakening to the Goddess.

542. Olyan, Saul. *Asherah and the Cult of Yahweh in Israel.*

Atlanta: Scholars Press, 1988. 100 p.

On Asherah in the Bible and archaeological evidence of her worship. She was the consort of the Canaanite god Baal and apparently also of Yahweh, while "the asherah" was a sacred pillar, associated with the Tree of Life and the sacred serpent.

543. Orenstein, Gloria Feman. "Reclaiming the Great Mother: a feminist journey to madness and back in search of a Goddess heritage," *Symposium: a quarterly journal in modern foreign literatures,* Spring 1982, 36(1): 45-70.

Discusses five female French surrealist writers and artists, all of whom struggled with madness and whose works recreate the Great Mother and the creative force of the feminine.

544. Orme-Johnson, Rhoda Frances. *Psyche's Descent into the Underworld: the transcending pattern in myth and literature.* Ph.D. thesis, University of Maryland, 1982. 332 p.

Women's spiritual quest in six 20th-century novels, based on the myth of Psyche as related by Apuleius, a Roman novelist and initiate of Isis.

545. Ouguibenine, Boris. *La déesse Usas: recherches sur le sacrifice de la parole dans le Rig Veda [The Goddess Ushas: research into the sacrifice of the word in the Rig Veda].* Louvain: Peeters, 1988. 229 p.

Ushas was the ancient Hindu goddess of the dawn.

546. Pacsoo, Jo. "The Heritage of Sheila-na-Gig," *Everywoman* (London), August 1989, no. 53, p. 14.

The sheela-na-gig is the female figure who appears on many mediaeval churches and other sacred sites in the British Isles and France, grinning and holding her vulva wide. She represents the primordial power of the life-force, in stark contrast to the pervasive Christian view of women as unclean, particularly in our birthing activities. This pagan figure can help us reclaim the sacredness of the material world.

547. Paper, Jordan. "Through the Earth Darkly: the female spirit in Native North American religion," in: *Religion in Native North America,* ed. Christopher Vecsey (Moscow, ID: Uni-

versity of Idaho Press, 1990), p. 3-19.

548. Paris, Ginette. *Pagan Meditations: the worlds of Aphrodite, Artemis, and Hestia.* Dallas: Spring Publications, 1986. 204 p.
An enlightening work on three important goddess-archetypes: Aphrodite teaches us to face up to the erotic; Artemis represents the environment, the adolescent, chastity, solitude, and sacrifice—indeed, abortion may be seen as a sacrifice to Artemis; Hestia exemplifies the home, security, and stability. We cannot rightly live without any one of these goddesses.

549. Paris, Ginette. *La Renaissance d'Aphrodite.* Montreal: Boréal Express, 1985. 186 p.
Love and sexuality have been divorced from one another and trivialized in our culture. Aphrodite, a harsh mistress when ignored, can show us a way back to unity.

550. Patai, Raphael. *The Hebrew Goddess.* 3rd enlarged ed. Detroit: Wayne State University Press, 1990. 368 p.
In her foreword, Merlin Stone wishes she had known of Patai's work when she was researching her groundbreaking *When God Was a Woman.* She comments on the great explosion of Goddess research that has taken place in the past twenty years and the effect this has had on many areas of scholarship. In this edition, Patai adds material on the Shekhinah in the Kabbalah and Hasidism, and on the Goddess as spouse of God within Judaism.

551. Pettey, Richard J. *Asherah: goddess of Israel.* New York: P. Lang, 1990 (Ph.D. thesis, Marquette University, 1985). 231 p.

552. Powers, Marla N. "Mistress, Mother, Visionary Spirit: the Lakota culture heroine," in: *Religion in Native North America,* ed. Christopher Vecsey (Moscow, ID: University of Idaho Press, 1990), p. 36-48.

553. Pötscher, Walter. *Hera: ein Strukturanalyse im Vergleich mit Athena [Hera: a structural analysis in comparison with Athena]* Darmstadt: Wissenschaftliche Buchgesellschaft, 1987. 194 p.

554. *Proto-Indo-European: the archaeology of a linguistic pro-*

gram: studies in honor of Marija Gimbutas. Ed. Susan Nacev Skomal and Edgar C. Polomé. Washington, DC: Institute for the Study of Man, 1987. 396 p.

A festschrift, or collection of articles written expressly in honor of Gimbutas by her colleagues and former students. Includes her biography and a complete bibliography of her archaeological publications.

555. Rakusin, Sudie. *Dreams and Shadows: a journal.* The author (Box 88, Brooke, VA 22430), 1984. 224 p.

A large blank book illustrated with fifty drawings of goddesses and other powerful women of many races and body types.

556. Ramprasada Sena (Ramprasad Sen). *Grace and Mercy in Her Wild Hair: selected poems to the Mother Goddess.* Trans. Leonard Nathan and Clinton Seely. Boulder: Great Eastern, 1982. 73 p.

Poetry by an 18th-century Bengali poet who was a member of the Bhakti sect of Hinduism—a kind of mystical, ecstatic, quasi-pentecostal strain of Hinduism which seeks a direct relationship with a goddess or god. The poems are translated into blunt, colloquial English, directly addressing the Mother Goddess in her manifestation as Shakti and Kali.

557. Reis, Patricia. *Through the Goddess: a woman's way of healing.* New York: Continuum, 1991, 235p.

Women are psychologically healed by the pre-patriarchal goddess archetypes, which are more whole (containing the light and the dark, creation and destruction) than the conventional goddess images of patriarchal culture.

558. Ribner, Susan, and Christine Wade. "The Great Goddess Fights Back: resistance to patriarchy in ancient mythology," in: *Fight Back!: feminist resistance to male violence*, ed. Frédérique Delacoste and Felice Newman (Minneapolis: Cleis Press, 1981), p. 325-333.

On women's warrior heritage and tales of female vengeance in African, Sumerian, and Celtic myth and history.

559. Riedel, Ingrid. *Demeters Suche: Mütter und Töchter [Demeter's Search: mothers and daughters].* Zurich: Kreuz,

1986. 166 p.

560. Robb, Christina. "Listening for the Goddess," *Boston Globe,* April 13, 1991, p. 8.

On the use of the Feminine Divine by psychotherapists.

561. Robbins, Kittye Delle. "Tiamat and Her Children: an inquiry into the persistence of mythic archetypes of woman as monster/villainess/victim," in: *Face to Face: fathers, mothers, masters, monsters—essays for a nonsexist future,* ed. Meg McGavran Murray (Westport, CT: Greenwood Press, 1983), p. 47-69.

The earliest depictions of women are positive, yet become demonized in Biblical and Near Eastern myth as well as in the myths of some indigenous peoples, who tell of a time when men took power from women by force.

562. Robbins, Miriam [see also under Dexter, above]. "The Assimilation of Pre-Indo-European Goddesses into Indo-European Society," *Journal of Indo-European Studies,* Spring-Summer 1980, 8(1-2):19-29.

The invading Indo-Europeans had few goddesses, mainly nature deities. Powerful goddesses in Indo-European mythology (Danu, Anahita, the Celtic horse goddesses, the Greek goddesses) reflect pre-Indo-European religion, while the deities of sovereignty and war derive from the victory of one culture over the other.

563. Robertson, Olivia. *Sophia: cosmic consciousness of the Goddess.* Clonegal Castle, Enniscorthy, Eire: Cesara Publications.

564. Rosser, Phyllis. "Ann McCoy Uses Goddess Symbols to Heal and Renew in Painting and Sculpture," *New Directions for Women,* July/Aug. 1989, (18(4):11.

565. Rufus, Anneli S., and Kristan Lawson. *Goddess Sites: Europe: discover places where the Goddess has been celebrated throughout time.* Marija Gimbutas, consulting editor. San Francisco: HarperSanFrancisco, 1991. 319 p.

A much-needed travel guide to places where the Goddess has been worshipped, extending from the Neolithic Era to the

Middle Ages, and from Ireland to Crete. The authors, who are travel writers, retell the myths associated with the goddess of each site and provide complete information on how to get there.

566. Rüttner-Cova, Sonja. *Frau Holle, die gestürzte Göttin: Märchen, Mythen, Matriarchat [Mother Holle, the Dethroned Goddess: fairy tales, myths, matriarchy]*. Basel, Switz.: Sphinx Verlag, 1986. 203 p.

On the ancient German mother goddess, who survives in Grimms' fairy tales as "Mother Hulla."

567. Rüttner-Cova, Sonja. *Der Matriarch: die gespaltene Liebe des Mannes [The Matriarch: man's cleft love]*. Basel: Sphinx, 1988. 240 p.

On the legacy of matriarchy in the psyches of women and men. Patriarchal separation of the feminine and masculine principles is responsible for the division of women and men into rigid psychological, as well as social, roles. The rejection of the Goddess also results in men's rejection of the feminine within. Illustrated with examples from Greek myth, German literature, and Bachofen's theory of matriarchy.

568. Salmonson, Jessica Amanda. *The Encyclopedia of Amazons: women warriors from antiquity to the modern era*. New York: Paragon House, 1991. 290 p.

A dictionary of Amazons, warrior queens, pirates, women soldiers and women who served in the military disguised as men, with over a thousand entries.

569. Saul, Donallen, with Jean Napali. "Goddess Worship: toxic niceness?" *New Directions for Women*, July/Aug. 1991, 20(4):4.

"The Goddess fad is, in effect, just feminism drunk on disembodied nostalgia, ritualistic pretence, and New Age ideology."

570. Sawyerr, Harry. "The Earth-Goddess: a study of a mythical concept which directs the life of many ethnic groups in Africa," *Studia Missionalia*, 33 (1984), p. 29-64.

Despite the obvious assumption of the superiority of Christianity, this is an informative essay on the West African concept of the Earth as origin of the people and home of the ancestors.

571. Schauffler, Robert Haven, ed., and Susan Tracy Rice, comp. *Mothers' Day: its history, origin, celebration, spirit, and significance as related in prose and verse.* Detroit: Omnigraphics, 1990 (reprint of 1927 ed.). 363 p.
A history of the honoring of mothers, from the prehistoric Mother Goddess to the rites of many 20th-century cultures.

572. Scott, David. "The Return of the Goddess," *Bangalore Theological Forum,* Oct.-Dec. 1987, 19(4): 253-279.
A careful defense of the restoration of feminine imagery to conventional theology. Suggests Christians should re-appraise the Hindu goddesses, who have survived more intact than those of the Near East, for their strength, motherhood, and combination of creative and destructive powers.

573. *Sexual Archetypes, East and West.* Ed. Bina Gupta. New York: Paragon House, 1987. 233 p.
Articles on the divine feminine in the Trinity, in Hinduism, Yoga, Tantra, and mediaeval mysticism, and women and sexuality in the Unification Church.

574. Sfameni Gasparro, Giulia. *Misteri e culti mistici di Demetra [Mysteries and Mystical Cults of Demeter].* Rome: L'Erma di Bretschneider, 1986. 371 p.
Scholarly work on Demeter, Persephone, the Eleusinian mysteries, and the Thesmophoria.

575. Sfameni Gasparro, Giulia. *Soteriology and Mystic Aspects in the Cult of Cybele and Attis.* Leiden: E.J. Brill, 1985. 142 p.
Soteriology, or salvation, is a frequent theme in mystery religions, which in essence are religions of the transformation of the soul. Here the author examines the worship of Cybele among the Phrygians and Greeks.

576. *She Rises Like the Sun: invocations of the Goddess by contemporary American women poets.* Ed. Janine Canan; illustrated by Mayumi Oda; foreword by Jean Shinoda Bolen. Freedom, CA: The Crossing Press, 1989. 226 p.

Poetry to the Goddess in her many aspects, by Paula Gunn Allen, Diane Di Prima, Elsa Gidlow, Linda Hogan, Carolyn Kizer, Denise Levertov, Audre Lorde, Marge Piercy, May Sarton, Ntozake Shange, Diane Wakoski, Anne Waldman, and many others.

577. Singh, Niddy-Guninder Kaur. *The Feminine Principle in the Sikh Vision of the Transcendent.* Ph.D. thesis, Temple University, 1987. 382 p.

578. Sissa, Giulia. *Greek Virginity.* Cambridge, MA: Harvard University Press, 1990. 240 p.
On virginity and female celibacy in Greek religion and myth; translated from the French.

579. Sjöö, Monica. "The Goddess/es of the Northern Peoples, Part I and II," *Arachne* (London), 1985 (Part II is in *Arachne,* 1985, p. 13-19).
A good source of information on Scandinavian, Anglo-Saxon, and Germanic goddesses and their myths, and folk survivals such as veneration of holy wells throughout Northern Europe.

580. Sjöö, Monica, and Barbara Mor. *The Great Cosmic Mother: rediscovering the religion of the earth.* San Francisco: Harper and Row, 1987; 2nd edition: HarperSanFrancisco, 1991 (reprint with a new introduction). 501 p.
A vastly enlarged edition of Sjöö's *Ancient Religion of the Great Cosmic Mother of All* (Trondheim, Norway, 1975) and an important history of the worship of the Great Goddess in Paleolithic and Neolithic times, with chapters on the images and symbols of the Goddess, the megalithic cultures of Britain and Malta, the moon and blood mysteries, and the Goddess-centered civilization of Bronze Age Crete. The second half traces the origins of patriarchal religion, the rejection of the worship of the Mother and hence the life force, which led to the subjugation of women, the rise of class society, the witch-hunts, and more recently, economic exploitation and global militarism. A comprehensive study of the contrasts between gynocentric and androcentric religious and social systems, extensively illustrated with Goddess imagery and Sjöö's matriarchal art.

581. Skelton, Robin, and Margaret Blackwood, comps. *Earth, Air, Fire, Water: pre-Christian and pagan elements in British songs, rhymes and ballads.* London; New York: Arkana, 1990. 324 p.

A collection of poems, charms, songs, and nursery rhymes celebrating the Goddess and the fairy-folk, as well as those that praise (or revile) witches. Included are spells and charms in verse, blessings and curses, songs of pagan origin such as "Under the Greenwood Tree" and "John Barleycorn," and poems by William Blake, Robert Herrick, and the most famous woman poet of all time, Anonymous. Blackwood is a Canadian poet; Skelton is a respected British poet and initiated pagan priest.

582. Smith, W.L. *The One-Eyed Goddess: a study of the Manasa Mangal.* Stockholm: Almqvist and Wiksell International, 1980. 208 p.

On Manasa, a popular snake goddess; a revision of the author's Ph.D. thesis (University of Stockholm, 1976).

583. Sobel, Hildegard. *Hygieia: die Göttin der Gesundheit [Hygieia: the goddess of health].* Darmstadt: Wissenschaftliche Buchgesellschaft, 1990. 136 p., many illustrations.

584. Sourvinou-Inwood, Christiane. *Studies in Girls' Transitions: aspects of the arkteia and age representation in Attic iconography.* Athens: Kardamitsa, 1988. 159 p.

The *arkteia* was the ancient Greek institution of sending young girls to sanctuaries of Artemis, where they served her as priestesses called *arktoi* ("bears"—Artemis means "bear"). The girls generally served as *arktoi* from the ages of five to ten; the author speculates that they may have been little priestesses up until menarche.

585. Spaeth, Barbette Stanley. *The Goddess Ceres: a study in Roman religious ideology.* Ph.D. thesis, Johns Hopkins University, 1987. 260 p.

586. Spitz, Ellen Handler. "Mothers and Daughters: ancient and modern myths," *Journal of Aesthetics and Art Criticism,* Fall 1990, p. 411-420.

On the Demeter-Persephone myth and its echo in contemporary novels such as Jamaica Kincaid's *Annie John*. Part of a special issue on "Feminism and Traditional Aesthetics."

587. Springborg, Patricia. *Royal Persons: patriarchal monarchy and the feminine principle*. Boston: Unwin Hyman, 1990. 256 p.

The patriarchal power of kings in the Egyptian, Babylonian, and Hittite civilizations essentially imitated the creative female force residing in the goddesses Isis, Tiamat, and Anat. We know that Pharoahs often married their sisters because the right to rule ultimately came from the female line.

588. Springer, Christina. "Whose Goddesses Are They?" *New Directions for Women,* July/Aug. 1990, 18(4):4.

Black women speak up about the neglect of African heritage and the co-opting of African motifs and goddesses by the white feminist spirituality movement; with a sidebar on the Yoruba goddess Oya, goddess of transformation.

589. Springer, Judy. "Goddesses Unite: the making of a mural," *Canadian Woman Studies,* Spring 1990, 11(1):97-98.

A lesbian artist describes her creation of a ceramic mural, "Goddesses Unite," celebrating women's power. The process of making the mural was empowering for the artist, who at the time was struggling with homophobia and with the sense of herself as Other.

590. Stambaugh, Sara. *The Witch and the Goddess in the Stories of Isak Dinesen: a feminist reading*. Ann Arbor: UMI Research Press, 1988. 139 p.

Stambaugh sees Dinesen's witch-figures as symbolic of the free woman.

591. Stein, Diane. *The Goddess Book of Days: a perpetual 366 day engagement calendar*. St. Paul: Llewellyn Publications, 1988. 280 p.

Contains notes for each day on goddess rites and women's festivals from past and present world cultures. Can be used as a datebook, but it's too beautifully illustrated to write in!

592. Stein, Rolf Alfred. *Grottes-Matrices et Lieux Saints de la Déesse en Asie Orientale [Grotto-Matrices and Holy Places of the Goddess in East Asia]*. Paris: École Française d'Extrême Orient, 1988. 106 p.

Throughout China, India, Tibet, and Japan there are caves dedicated to the Buddhist goddess Tara, where worshippers enter naked and emerge reborn and cleansed of their sins.

593. Steinbart, Hiltrud. *Im Angfang war die Frau: die Frau, Ursprung der Religionen [In the Beginning Was Woman: woman, origin of religion]*. Frankfurt: R.G. Fischer, 1983. 223 p.

594. Steinfels, Peter. "Idyllic Theory of Goddesses Creates Storm: was a peaceful matriarchal world shattered by patriarchal invaders?" *New York Times,* Feb. 11, 1990, Sec. C, pp. 1, 12.

On the matriarchal research being done by Marija Gimbutas, Riane Eisler, and Elinor Gadon and their somewhat chilly reception in the scholarly world.

595. Stepanich, Kisma K. "The Goddess," *Fate*, Oct. 1989, p. 59.

596. Sterckx, Claude. *Éléments de Cosmogonie Celtique [Elements of Celtic Cosmogony]*. Brussels: Éditions de l'Université de Bruxelles, 1986. 127 p.

On the pre-Christian Celtic religion of the Continent and the British Isles, focusing particularly on the goddesses Epona, Rhiannon, and Boann and showing parallels between Celtic and Indian Vedic mythology.

597. Stone, Merlin. *Ancient Mirrors of Womanhood: a treasury of goddess and heroine lore from around the world.* Boston: Beacon Press, 1990. 425 p.

A reprint of the original 1981 edition, with a new preface.

598. Sweeney, Patricia Ann. *Healing the Earth Through an Awareness of the Goddess.* M.A. thesis, California Institute for Integral Studies, 1990. 102 p.

599. Swinton, Nelda. *The Inuit Sea Goddess.* M.A. thesis, Concordia University, 1985. 129 p.

600. Tapia Adler, Ana Maria. *Inanna-Ishtar: origen y evolución de una figura religiosa [Inanna-Ishtar: origin and evolution of a religious figure].* Santiago: Universidad de Chile, Facultad de Filosofia, Humanidades y Educación, Centro de Estudios de Cultura Judaica, 1984. 135 p.

601. Tewari, Laxmi. *A Splendor of Worship: women's fasts, rituals, stories and art.* Riverdale, MD: Riverdale Co., 1990. 150 p.

602. Thinley, Norbu. *Magic Dance: the display of the self-nature of the five Wisdom Dakinis.* 2nd ed. New York: Jewel Publishing House, 1985. 166 p.

603. Thorsten, Geraldine. *The Goddess in Your Stars.* New York: Simon and Schuster, 1989. 272 p.
    A revision of her *God Herself: the feminine roots of astrology* (New York: Avon Books, 1980), which was the first feminist, Goddess-centered astrology book, from which the author has reproduced much of the personality interpretations for each zodiac sign, dropped the herstorical/matriarchal material, and added suggestions for visualizations of goddesses appropriate for each sign. With a lunar ephemeris for the 1990's.

604. Tiwari, Jagdith Narain. *Goddess Cults in Ancient India (with special reference to the first seven centuries A.D.).* Delhi: Sundeep Prakashan, 1985. 271 p.
    Based on the author's Ph.D. thesis (Australian National University, 1971), a good source for research on Indian goddesses. Chapters on the proliferation of goddess cults throughout India, the mother goddesses, and the frequent depictions of the goddess in birthing/sexual positions. With a 25-page bibliography.

605. Troy, Lana. *Patterns of Queenship in Ancient Egyptian Myth and History.* Stockholm: Almquist & Wiksell International, 1986. 236 p.
    On the goddesses Isis, Nephthys, Nut, and Hathor, and the role of priestesses, queens and queenship symbolism; includes a list of all known Egyptian queens from the First Dynasty to Cleopatra.

606. Turner, Hernan (Buckwheat Turner). *Tales of a Womanspirited Traveler*. 4th ed. The author (Box 20024, Oakland, CA 94620-0024), 1985. 130 p.

A collection of essays, several reprinted from *WomanSpirit* magazine, on the author's travels alone and with her lover to goddess sites in England, Ireland, the Southwest, and Mexico, including a guide to goddess artifacts in the Metropolitan Museum of Art and the American Museum of Natural History in New York City, and a visit to the Silver Sisterhood (the Madrians), a contemporary matriarchal community in Ireland.

607. "The Ultimate Mother," *New York Times*, May 12, 1981, Sec. 4, p. 16.

An editorial sympathetic to goddess religion.

608. *Voices of the Goddess: a chorus of sibyls*. Ed. Caitlín Matthews. Wellingborough, Eng.: Aquarian Press, 1990. 240 p.

Essays, art, and rituals by priestesses of the Goddess: Matthews, Olivia Robertson of the Fellowship of Isis, Monica Sjöö, Diana Paxson, and others write about witchcraft, the sun goddess, Irish and Welsh goddesses, death, the light and the dark. These are moving, personal stories of rebirth and service to the Lady. Includes a list of resources and addresses of organizations in the British Isles and the U.S. which offer training for priestesses.

609. Vycinas, Vincent. *The Great Goddess and the Aistian Mythical World*. New York: P. Lang, 1990. 275 p.

"Aistians" are what Vycinas calls the oldest Indo-Europeans, whom he identifies with the Balts and the goddess-worshipping Old Europeans as described by Marija Gimbutas. Following her work, he compares Old European cosmology of the Great Mother with Heidegger's philosophy of Being, the prehistoric consciousness being one of wholeness and being-in-nature. The author lived in pre-Soviet Lithuania, and seems to regard the Balts as the true inheritors of Old Europe. He blames the Slavs for destroying the matriarchal Old European culture, suggesting that the Communist quest for world domination is an essentially Slavic trait.

610. Weigle, Marta. *Creation and Procreation: feminist reflections on mythologies of cosmogony and parturition.* Philadelphia: University of Pennsylvania Press, 1989. 292 p.

The mythology of conception and birth in Native American religion and Christian iconography. Includes texts of myths, chiefly Native American.

611. Weir, Anthony, and James Jerman. *Images of Lust: sexual carvings on medieval churches.* London: Batsford, 1986. 166 p.

A re-assessment of the sheela-na-gigs and other explicit sexual figures found on Romanesque (early medieval) churches chiefly in Ireland, France, and Spain. The authors believe that rather than being pre-Christian fertility deities, these carvings were in fact Christian images—misogynistic, anti-sex propaganda—although they do retain elements of the Cretan Snake Goddess, Lady of the Beasts, and Baubo, the female exhibitionist of the Demeter-Persephone myth. Illustrated with many amazing photographs and drawings of the carvings; fascinating, whatever one's conclusions.

612. White, Marjorie. *Papers.* At the Schlesinger Library of Women's History, Radcliffe College, Cambridge, MA.

One hundred notebooks kept from ca. 1930-1970, containing clippings, articles, essays, photographs and notes on women's history, from prehistoric times to the 20th century. Contains material on woman as priestess and founder of civilization, and the transition from matriarchy to patriarchy.

613. Willson, Martin, comp. and trans. *In Praise of Tārā: songs to the Saviouress: source texts from India and Tibet on Buddhism's Great Goddess.* London: Wisdom Publications, 1986. 487 p.

Texts on Tara's rituals and worship compiled by a British Buddhist monk, with a comprehensive glossary of Buddhist terminology.

614. Wilson, Brian Alden. *Power to the Powerless: shamanism and the Korean woman.* Ph.D. thesis, University of Wisconsin, 1985. 282 p.

Korean women are still socially oppressed, but the practice of traditional shamanism allows them some measure of power.

615. Woodman, Marion. *Addiction to Perfection: the still unravished bride: a psychological study.* Toronto: Inner City Books, 1982. 204 p.

A tour through women's psyche, examining dreams, eating disorders, and sexuality in the language of the Great Mother, with the Medusa/witch as Shadow self.

616. Wolkstein, Diane. *The First Love Stories: from Isis and Osiris to Tristan and Iseult.* New York: HarperCollins, 1991. 270 p.

Wolkstein retells the stories of divine lovers, including Inanna and Dumuzi, Shiva and Sati, the lovers in the Song of Songs, Psyche and Eros, and Layla and Majnun.

617. Wolkstein, Diane. "Inanna as a Woman of Power," *The Quest* (Wheaton, Ill.), Spring 1990, p. 58-63.

An interview conducted by Regina Ress, in which Wolkstein describes her collaboration with Samuel Kramer in turning the myth of Inanna into a book with a coherent story. Inanna's descent to the underworld symbolizes the finding, retention, and use of power.

618. *Women in the World's Religions, Past and Present.* Ed. Ursula King. New York: Paragon House, 1986. 261 p.

A collection of essays on women in sacred scriptures, feminine symbols, and women's religious experience in Christianity, Judaism, Buddhism, and African and new religions. Contributors include Rose Horman Arthur on the Biblical Wisdom goddess; Anne Bancroft on Buddhism; Ursula King on "Goddesses, Witches, Androgyny and Beyond?"

619. Woolger, Jennifer Barker and Roger J. *The Goddess Within: a guide to the eternal myths that shape women's lives.* New York: Fawcett/Columbine, 1989. 482 p.

Described by one reviewer as "the *Sun Signs* of the Goddess movement," the psychologist-authors discuss Athena, Artemis, Aphrodite, Hera, Persephone, and Demeter as archetypes for women's psyche. A brief questionnaire enables the reader to find which goddess she is ruled by, and there is a chapter for men on living with the goddess/woman in their lives. Also includes a list of Hollywood films which portray goddess archetypes (e.g. *Eleni* as Demeter, Marilyn Monroe as Aphroditc).

620. Zabkar, Louis V. *Hymns to Isis in Her Temple at Philae.* Hanover, NH: Published for Brandeis University Press by the University Press of New England, 1988. 203 p.

621. Zak, Nancy C. "The Earth Mother Figure of Native North America," *ReVision,* Winter 1988, 10(3): 27-36.

A scholar of Inuit descent writes on goddesses of the Inuit and Native Americans of the Northwest, Northeast, Southwest, Plains, and Cherokee peoples and their sacred connection with the people and the earth. She concludes with a myth of the creator-goddess of the Keres (Pueblo) people, whose culture she regards as truly matriarchal.

Witchcraft:
Traditional Europe and
Feminist Wicca

Here are entered books and articles on traditional European witch-craft of the mediaeval and early modern period (the period of the witch-hunts); the revival of European paganism in 20th-century witchcraft, often referred to as Wicca (the feminine form in Anglo-Saxon is Wicce, which is used by some writers when speaking of women's practice); and the contemporary re-visioning of witch-craft as ancient female wisdom.

622. Adler, Margot. *Drawing Down the Moon: witches, Druids, goddess-worshippers, and other pagans in America today.* Rev. and expanded ed. Boston: Beacon Press, 1986 (first published 1979). 595 p.

Adler, radio journalist and Wiccan priestess, has updated her classic text with new chapters on men's spirituality and the revival of Norse Paganism, adding observations on the impact feminism has had on the Craft and vice versa. Contains a new resource guide listing pagan festivals and gather-ings, which have become important means of communication among Neo-Pagans, and a comprehensive list of Neo-Pagan periodicals and organizations that are either nature-revering or sympathetic to Pagan values, such as the ACLU and the Green Party. *Drawing Down the Moon* remains *the* authorita-tive source on Neo-Paganism, and coincidently but conve-niently, all revised passages are in a slightly different type-face. An article on Margot appeared in the *New York Times,* Halloween 1991, pp. C1, C5.

623. Amber K. *Beginning True Magick.* Moonstone Publications (Box 176, Blue Mounds, WI 53517), 1985. 48 p.

Revised and expanded into *True Magick* (see below); also

reprinted in: "Neo-Paganism and Wicca," vol. 23 of *Cults and New Religions,* edited by J. Gordon Melton (Garland Publications, 1990).

624. Amber K. *How to Organize a Coven or Magickal Study Group.* Madison, WI: Circle Publications, 1983; Blue Mounds, WI: Moonstone Publications, 1985. 24 p.

Explains the difference between a study group and a formal coven, how to find like-minded people, and coven organization and ethics.

625. Amber K. *Lithomancy: divination with stones within an astrological structure.* Blue Mounds, WI: Moonstone Publications, 1985. Booklet, board and set of stones.

A method of divination by casting stones depicting zodiac signs.

626. Amber K. *Paganspoof.* Blue Mounds, WI: Moonstone Publications, 1984. 32 p.

A hilarious one-time parody of Pagan periodicals, featuring cartoons, useful advice such as "Never invoke anyone you can't banish," "Occult Uses of French Fries," and ways to celebrate that little-known Pagan festival, Moosemas, sacred to Bullwinkle.

627. Amber K. *True Magick: a beginner's guide.* St. Paul: Llewellyn Publications, 1990. 252 p.

A solid, sensible introduction to working magic: what magic(k) is and is not, how to obtain instruction, how magic works, the varieties of practice (e.g. Pagan, Shamanic, Afro-Hispanic), appropriate lifestyle, devising and using rituals, a selection of spells, and ethical guidelines. Includes a glossary and tables of correspondences. The most useful $5 paperback an occultist can own.

628. Aswynn, Freya. *Leaves of Yggdrasil: a synthesis of runes, gods, magic, feminine mysteries, and folklore.* St. Paul: Llewellyn Publications, 1990 (first edition self-published, London, 1988). 260 p.

Frisian/Dutch magic, with an emphasis on the feminine principle, by a Dutch-born rune mistress and Volva (Germanic shamaness). Llewellyn also offers her *Songs of*

Yggdrasil, an audio-cassette of poetry and myths.

629. Barker, Janet. "Witchcraft: modern witch tries to dispel spooky myths," *The Daily Breeze* (Los Angeles), Religion section, Apr. 16, 1983.
    An interview with Starhawk.

630. Barstow, Anne. "Women as Healers, Women as Witches," *Old Westbury Review*, Fall 1986, no. 2, p. 121.

631. Bass, Dave. "Drawing Down the Moon," *Christianity Today,* Apr. 29, 1991 (cover story).
    On Neo-Paganism in the United States; critical, but not sensationalistic, though the author does try to link Witchcraft with Satanism.

632. Beth, Rae. *Hedge Witch: letters on solitary witchcraft.* London: Hale, 1990. 189 p.
    A guide to the wisdom of the "hedge witch" or traditional English wise woman, written as letters to her apprentices.

633. Bilotti, Nicole. "A Witch of Uncommon Definition," *Out!* (Madison, WI), Jan. 1984, p. 9.
    An interview with Starhawk, who discusses political activism, re-valuing non-reproductive sexuality, and how gay and lesbian sexuality threatens the patriarchal order.

634. Bog, Rosmarie. *Die Hexe: schön wie der Mond, hässlich wie die Nacht [The Witch: beautiful as the moon, ugly as night].* Zurich: Kreuz Verlag, 1987. 176 p.

635. Brandenberg, Sandra, and Debora Hill. "Fallingstar: a witch in time," *New Directions for Women*, July/Aug. 1990, 20(4):7.
    A profile of feminist witch and novelist Cerridwen Fallingstar, who tells of her memories of a past life during the Burning Times.

636. Budapest, Zsuzsanna (Z). "Glimmerings of the Goddess: campaign of a religious revolutionary," *Magical Blend,* Jan. 1991, no. 29, pp. 38-42, 97.
    An interview in which she describes her folk/pagan roots as a girl in Hungary, the origins of the American feminist

witchcraft movement in the 1970's, Europeans' pagan and shamanic heritage, and the power of collective consciousness to change the world.

637. Budapest, Zsuzsanna. *Grandmother Moon: lunar magic in our lives— spells, rituals, goddesses, legends, and emotions under the moon.* San Francisco: HarperSanFrancisco, 1991. 288 p.

Following the Wheel of the year, each chapter corresponds to one of the thirteen lunations, with lunar holidays, magic, the effect of the moon on women's health, spells, myths, and stories from Z's life.

638. Budapest, Zsuzsanna. *The Grandmother of Time: a woman's book of celebrations, spells, and sacred objects for every month of the year.* San Francisco: Harper & Row, 1989. 261 p. Also available from Harper & Row as a 60 min. audiocassette read by Z.

A lighthearted, woman-proud trip through the year. For each month a different goddess speaks and there are special spells and meditations for the season and a calendar of women's holydays, mainly from European cultures, with tips on how we moderns might observe the spirit of the day, followed by a story from Z's own life: her personal journey from Hungarian student, wife and mother, to feminist witch, leader of the women's spirituality movement, and respected teacher. Any visit with Z is a delight.

639. Budapest, Zsuzsanna. *The Holy Book of Women's Mysteries.* Rev. ed. Oakland, CA: Susan B. Anthony Coven No. 1, 1986. [First published as *The Feminist Book of Lights and Shadows*, 1976; expanded to the 2 vol. *Holy Book*, 1979-80].

Volume 1 only was published in this edition, which is completely revised and has a foreword by Phyllis Chesler, a new introduction, expanded rituals, and additional sections on the history of the feminist witchcraft movement and Pan as the male principle in paganism.

640. Budapest, Zsuzsanna. *The Holy Book of Women's Mysteries (complete in one volume): feminist witchcraft, Goddess rituals, spell casting, and other womanly arts...* Berkeley: Wingbow Press, 1989. 308 p.

Essentially the revised edition of volume 1 (see above) plus material from the original part 2, somewhat re-arranged. The chapter on herbal remedies from volume 1 has been deleted; new materials include additional rituals, observations on coven politics, and the history of European shamanism. Retains all the exuberance of the early feminist witchcraft movement, and essential for anyone who has never acquired the earlier editions.

641. Burmeister, Elizabeth. *Was die Hexen singt: die Lieder der schwarzen Rosa [What the Witches Sing: the songs of the black rose].* Münster: Frauen-Verlag, 1985. 73 p.

642. Cabot, Laurie, with Tom Cowan. *Power of the Witch.* New York: Delacorte Press, 1989. 310 p.
   An introduction to Wicca by a woman who lives openly as a witch in Salem, Mass.

643. Campanelli, Pauline. *Wheel of the Year: living the magickal life.* St. Paul: Llewellyn Publications, 1989. 159 p.
   Wiccan rituals for every day.

644. Cedar. "Hagrites," *Out and About,* Dec. 1981, p. 25.
   On Pagan holidays.

645. Cedar. "What is Wicce?" *Out and About,* Nov. 1981, p.13.

646. Cobra. "Hallomas," *Out and About,* Oct. 1981, p.15.
   Cobra is active in the Seattle feminist witchcraft community and a frequent contributor to the periodical *Goddess Rising.*

647. Crowley, Vivianne. *Wicca: the Old Religion in the New Age.* Wellingborough, Eng.: Aquarian Publications, 1989. 268 p.

648. Dahlsgard, Inga. "Witch-hunts and Absolutism in Ancient Denmark," in: *Women—From Witch-Hunt to Politics: selection of articles reproduced from cultures—dialogue between the peoples of the world* (Paris: Unesco, 1985), p. 38-46.
   An appreciation of the witch-hunts as oppression of women. The entire volume is illustrated with remarkable and wonderful traditional art from many cultures.

649. Daly, Tom. "Facing the Witch: the masks of the inner feminine, part I," *Wingspan: journal of the male spirit,* July-Sept. 1991, pp. 1, 12.

A man active in the men's movement recounts his personal confrontation with the witch-figure, whom for years he projected onto any aggressive woman who came his way. Through artwork he learned how to find the witch in himself.

650. de Combray, Natalie. "In Search of Witches: in which our intrepid reporter casts myths aside and boldly goes where few reporters have gone before," *Ithaca Times* (Ithaca, NY), Aug. 14, 1986, pp. 1, 7.

An interview with two witches and a male wizard, who explain the Pagan worldview, the philosophy of magic, the importance of living in harmony with nature, and the history of the Western image of the witch.

651. Donner, Florinda. *The Witch's Dream.* Foreword by Carlos Castaneda. New York: Simon and Schuster, 1985. 287 p.

Like Castaneda's Don Juan books, this is a fictionalized narrative by an anthropology student who was apprenticed to a Venezuelan woman healer.

652. Dragonfly. "From Mormonism to Womon Witchcraft," *Lesbian Contradition,* Winter 1987, no. 17, p. 4-5.

A lesbian feminist witch describes her youth as a sexually abused Mormon, and her break with the church and its oppressive structure.

653. Draaisma, Muriel. "Witches on Celluloid," *Herizons* (Winnipeg), July 1986, 4(5): 44-45.

A review of Laurie Meeker's film *Remember the Witches* (see the Audio-Visual section), and an interview with her. The reviewer considers the film flawed but a valuable contribution to feminist cinema.

654. Dubie, Francesca. *Her Winged Silence: a shaman's notebook.* [San Francisco: the author], 1989; available from Old Wives' Tales Bookstore, 1009 Valencia St., San Francisco, CA 94110. 51 p.

Poetry, meditations, and excerpts from the notebooks of a Wiccan priestess and student of Victor Anderson (priest of the Faery Tradition of Wicca and Starhawk's teacher).

655. Dunwich, Gerina. *Wicca Craft: the book of herbs, magick, and dreams.* Secaucus, NJ: Carol Pub. Group, 1991. 160 p.
A basic manual of Wicca, well-illustrated, with emphasis on healing, the magical properties of herbs, and the Pagan love for the earth.

656. Eaton, S. "The Female Craft: an interview with Deborah Bender," *Pentalpha Journal,* 1980, p. 6-8.
Bender was one of the early theorists of feminist witchcraft in the 1970's and is still active in the Neo-Pagan community.

657. Eclipse. *The Moon in Hand: a mystical passage.* Portland, ME: Astarte Shell Press, 1991. 151 p.
A guide to the ancient mysteries of the Goddess, earth spirituality, and Native American wisdom by an Earth-witch who did her own illustrations and paintings for the book. Arranged by the four directions, each with rituals, meditations, stories, invocations. Very attractively produced, written for women but usable by men or groups, and a good resource for ritual work.

658. Egnell, Helene. "The Goddess Within Us," *Connexions,* 1988-89, no. 28, p. 24-25.
Translation of "The Search for a Lost Religion"(in Swedish), first published in *Kvinnobullitinen,* June 1983: an interview with three Swedish feminist witches who discuss ritual and the process of creating a woman-centered religion.

659. Erickson, L. "Womanspirit," *Simply Living* (Terry Hills, NSW, Australia), 1988, 3(6):23.

660. Farrar, Janet and Stewart. *Eight Sabbats for Witches, and Rites for Birth, Marriage, and Death.* London: Robert Hale, 1981, 192p.
Includes photos of rituals being performed.

661. Farrar, Janet and Stewart. *The Life & Times of a Modern Witch.* London: Piatkus, 1987. 208 p.

662. Farrar, Janet and Stewart. *A Witches' Bible.* New York: Magickal Childe, 1984. 2 vols. (First published in England as *The Witches' Way: principles, rituals and beliefs of modern witchcraft* [London: R. Hale, 1981]; not to be confused with *The Witches' Bible* by Gavin and Yvonne Frost); also issued in a one-volume edition entitled *A Witches Bible Compleat* (Magickal Childe, 1984).

The most complete selection of rituals from the Gardnerian and Alexandrian traditions of the Craft.

663. Fitch, Ed, and Janine Renée. *Magical Rites from the Crystal Well.* St. Paul: Llewellyn Publications, 1984. 147 p.

A collection of Wiccan rituals by two noted Pagan ritualists; *The Crystal Well* was a Pagan periodical published by Fitch. Includes seasonal and moon rituals, rites of passage, the "Paganing" (as opposed to a christening) of a baby, and a ritual to be performed for the spirit of an animal killed in traffic.

664. Forfreedom, Ann. "Feminist Witchcraft in Today's World," *On the Issues: the journal of substance for progressive women,* 1987, v. 7, p. 7.

665. Forfreedom, Ann. "The 'Wise Woman' in Feminist Witchcraft," *Broomstick,* July-Aug. 1988, 10(4):3-5.

666. Fox, Matthew. "Earth Spirituality: a common ground where priest and witch meet," *Creation,* Nov.-Dec. 1985, 1(5):11-13.

Fox, a Dominican priest, received a great deal of criticism, not to mention hate mail, from self-styled "ecumenical" Christians when he engaged Starhawk to teach at his Institute of Culture and Creation Spirituality at Holy Names College in Oakland, California. In this article he defends his work with her, not only because he admires her as a spiritual person and defender of the earth, but because it is un-Christian (and un-Catholic, at least officially) to harrass anyone because of their religion.

667. Gannon, Tom. "Out of the Broom Closet," *Boston Globe,* Dec. 25, 1988, p. 73.

An interview with Rhode Island high priestess Joyce

Siegrist.

668. Gaylor, Annie Laurie. "Exploring the Legacy of the Witch Trials," *Feminist Connection* (Madison, WI), Jan. 1985, p.19.

An article on Wisconsin novelist Kay Nolte Smith, who researched the Burning Times for one of her books. She relates in grim detail the horrors of accusation, torture, and execution that uncounted numbers of women suffered at the hands of the Church.

669. Ginzburg, Carlo. *Ecstasies: deciphering the witches' sabbath.* New York: Pantheon, 1991. 339 p.

In their confessions, European witches often described their rituals as including flying, sex, and cannibalism, and it has long been controversial as to how much this testimony can be relied upon, since it was usually obtained under torture or threat thereof. Ginzburg has studied the pagan elements of European witchcraft for many years and has concluded that the descriptions of the witches' sabbaths reflect shamanistic "journeyings" and that the supposed Devil was, as some have suspected, an echo of a prehistoric animal-god.

670. Glass-Koentop, Pattalee. *Year of Moons, Season of Trees: mysteries & rites of Celtic tree magic.* St. Paul: Llewellyn Publications, 1991. 242 p.

The Wheel of the Year, dedicated to the goddess of Wicca, with lunar and tree lore.

671. Golowin, Sergius. *Die Weisen Frauen: die Hexen und ihr Heilwissen [Wise Women: witches and their healing knowledge].* Basel: Sphinx Verlag, 1982. 405 p.

The legacy of witchcraft and the Wise Woman, and the pervasive fear of the Other in 20th-century Europe. Far more than a history, this is a cultural kaleidoscope, rocketing back and forth from the Middle Ages to California hippies, a book which deserves to be translated into English. The author has also written on shamanism and the Tarot.

672. Green, Marian. *A Witch Alone: thirteen moons to master ritual magic.* Hammersmith, Eng.: The Aquarian Press, 1991. 192 p.

A general handbook of paganism, providing exercises

and sensible advice (e.g. practitioners of nature religion should spend more time with nature and less with books).

673. Guiley, Rosemary Ellen. *The Encyclopedia of Witches and Witchcraft.* New York: Facts on File, 1989. 488 p.

Over 500 entries on Neo-Paganism, traditional and modern witchcraft, and perhaps the best source on the important personalities of the Craft. (Did you know that Anodea Judith is comedian Martin Mull's sister?) Articles on Margot Adler, Z Budapest, Starhawk, Marion Zimmer Bradley, Selena Fox, Otter and Morning Glory Zell, features of the Craft such as initiation, "cakes and wine," the Burning Times, Voodoo, Santería, powwowing. An essential addition to collections on the Craft.

674. Hawthorne, Nan. *Loving the Goddess Within: sex magick for women.* Oak Park, Ill.: Delphi Press, 1991. 171 p.

A guide to re-discovering the beauty and sacredness of sexuality, however the reader chooses to love. Most texts on sex magic concentrate on using sexual energy as a tool in working magic or as a means for attaining enlightenment, but Hawthorne urges us to reclaim sexuality simply as an integral part of spiritual practice, whether or not one has a partner. She provides meditations for loving one's body, suggestions for incorporating sexuality into private ritual and sexual imagery into Wiccan gatherings (without group or promiscuous sex), all in a loving manner and with the objective of recognizing the Goddess and God in one's self.

675. Hennginsen, Gustav. *Fra Heksejagt til Heksekult, 1484-1984 [From Witch-Hunt to Witch Cult].* Copenhagen: Gyldendal, 1984. 139 p.

A history of the witch-hunts, especially in Denmark (where, apart from the early 17th century, there were few trials), the traditional image of the witch, and the 20th-century revival of witchcraft.

676. Herron, Patricia. *The Spinning Cross: a women's dance play,* in: "Neo-Paganism and Wicca," v. 23 of *Cults and New Religions,* ed. J. Gordon Melton (Garland Publications, 1990); first published by the author in 1977.

677. Hurley, Karen. "Coming Out in Spirit and in Flesh," in: *Bi Any Other Name: bisexual people speak out,* ed. Loraine Hutchins and Lani Kaahumanu (Boston: Alyson Publications, 1990), p. 94-98.

A feminist witch chronicles her transformation from Catholic girl to wife, to lover of women and the Goddess. She believes that an understanding of the cosmic rhythms celebrated in Wiccan ritual enables us to accept and love our own sexual rhythms.

678. Jade. *To Know: a guide to women's magic and spirituality.* Oak Park: Delphi Press, 1990. 174 p.

Not a handbook of specifics but "a guide for those who want to live as spiritual women" and an introduction to the witchcraft branch of the feminist spirituality movement. The author, a Wiccan priestess and co-publisher of the periodical *Of a Like Mind*, outlines the thealogy of women's spirituality, the various forms of contemporary Wicca, Neo-Paganism, and shamanism, ritual and divination, the culture and networks of women's spirituality and Paganism, and lists contact groups and periodicals. This book will also be useful as background information for researching the feminist spirituality movement.

679. "Jade: practicing what she preaches," *Hag Rag*, Nov.-Dec. 1990, 5(3):22.

680. Jannberg, Judith (Gerlinde Adia Schilcher). *Ich bin ein Hexe: Erfahrungen und Gedanken [I am a Witch: experiences and thoughts]* . Bonn: Edition die Maus, 1983. 160 p.

A German feminist witch writes of women's witch consciousness re-emerging after centuries of slumber, the witch being the autonomous woman.

681. Jensen, Theadora. "Season of the Witch: uncovering women's past," *This Magazine,* Aug. 1985; reprinted in the *Utne Reader,* Oct. 1986, no. 18, p. 118-125.

Jensen travelled to the French Basque country to research a historical novel on the witch-hunts, in the process experiencing a powerful re-membering of the holocaust of women.

682. Karlsen, Carol F. *The Devil in the Shape of a Woman:*

witchcraft in colonial New England. New York: Norton, 1987. 360 p.

Based on the author's Ph.D. thesis (Yale, 1980), this is a closely documented study of patterns of witch accusations for the period. She found that the accused witches were often unmarried (thus independent of men), owned property which neighbors or family members felt entitled to, and frequently were rebellious or otherwise unpopular with their accusers.

683. Kirkpatrick, R. George, et al. "An Empirical Study of Wiccan Religion in Postindustrial Society," *Free Inquiry in Creative Sociology,* 1986, 14(1):33-38.

An ethnographic study of 144 Pagans finds that Wiccans tend to be "normless" and feel powerless in society, "under-rewarded status discontents who care little for money and much for knowledge and balance of nature." With a table of demographic characteristics such as age, education, income, politics.

684. Klaits, Joseph. *Servants of Satan: the age of the witch hunts.* Bloomington: Indiana University Press, 1985. 212 p.

This study of the European witch craze pays special attention to the role of gender in patterns of accusations. One chapter is devoted to the beggar and the midwife, two typical categories of victims.

685. Klaniczay, Gábor. *The Uses of Supernatural Power: the transformation of popular religion in medieval and early-modern Europe.* Princeton: Princeton University Press, 1990. 259 p.

Of most interest is Chapter 8, "Shamanistic Elements in Central European Witchcraft." Following are chapters on the witch-hunts in Hungary and belief in witches and vampires in 18th-century Central Europe.

686. Larner, Christina. *Witchcraft and Religion: the politics of popular belief.* Edited and with a foreword by Alan McFarland. New York: Blackwell, 1984. 172 p.

Larner examines the political aspects of the witch-hunts, discusses the role of women as witches, and compares the European Burning Times to 20th-century political terror in Latin America. She does not consider modern witchcraft to be anything but foolishness.

687. Lit(wo)man, Jane. "On Being a Jewish Witch," *Genesis 2*, Spring 1988, 19(1):2, 42.

A response to Starhawk's essay of the same title (see below), in which she chides Starhawk for turning to paganism for spiritual validation of her womanhood instead of seeking out the feminist reconstructions and revivals of women's spirituality within Judaism. Starhawk's reply is appended.

688. Ludeke, Joan Carole. *Wicca as a Revitalization Movement Among Post-Industrial, Urban, American Women.* Ph.D. thesis, Iliff School of Theology and the University of Denver, 1989. 171 p.

689. Luhrmann, T. M. *Persuasions of the Witch's Craft: ritual magic and witchcraft in present-day England.* Oxford: Basil Blackwell, 1988; Cambridge, MA: Harvard University Press, 1989. 382 p.

Tanya Luhrmann went to England to study the witchcraft community for her Ph.D. thesis in anthropology, in order to understand how middle-class Westerners could adopt a magical worldview. For a year she worked with a coven and immersed herself in Wiccan culture, where the subjective and objective are not distinguished and reality exists on many planes. Discarding scholarly detachment, she acknowledges that she was profoundly affected by what she experienced.

690. Mach, Teri. "Out of the Broom Closet: a tale of two witches," *Twin Cities Reader,* Oct. 30, 1985, p. 12-13.

An interview with two witches: Antiga (Mary Lee George), a ritualist and frequent contributor to women's spirituality publications, and a male witch. They explain witchcraft as a nature religion, its use of magic, the holidays, and the symbols of broom, cat, cauldron, and pointed hat.

691. Manarelli, María Emma. *Inquisición y Mujeres: las hechiceras en el Peru durante el siglo XVII [Inquisition and Women: sorceresses in Peru during the 17th century].* Lima: CENDON-Mujer, Centro de Documentacion Sobre la Mujer, 1987. 24 p.

692. McLachlan, Hugh V., and J.K. Swales. "Witchcraft and Anti-Feminism," *Scottish Journal of Sociology,* 1980, v. 4, p. 141-158.

Using evidence from Scottish witch-accusations, the authors find that while the overwhelming majority of the accused were women, accusations tended to be initiated through neighborly disputes rather than by the legal establishment. They see little evidence that the witch-hunts were deliberately used as a means of suppressing midwives and women herbalists, although they concede that practicing witchcraft may have been a form of rebellion for women.

693. Medici, Marina. *Good Magic.* London: Macmillan, 1988. 249 p.

An illustrated handbook by a English witch.

694. "'Meet a Witch' Plan Brews Up Parent Protest," *Los Angeles Times*, July 10, 1986, part I, p. 25.

Brief article on the controversy over Z Budapest's lecture at the San Jose, Cal., Public Library (see item 708). "We all have different religions," said a mother, "but let's not get strange."

695. Mertens, Heidi. "State Control vs. Birth Control: the politics of the witchhunt in Europe," *Spare Rib*, July 1986, no. 168, p. 38-42.

Mertens reads the witch-hunts as stemming in part from the State's wish to keep women producing workers. She detects a definite campaign against midwives, herbalists, and contraception (103 forms of contraception were known in mediaeval Europe).

696. Miesel, Sandra. "The 'Craft' and Feminism," *National Catholic Register,* Aug. 6, 1989, pp. 1, 7.

On feminist witchcraft and the revival of Goddess religion, a generally factual report but with many exaggerations and oversimplifications.

697. Miesel, Sandra. "Witches Today: what they are, what they aren't," *National Catholic Register,* July 30, 1989, pp. 1, 6.

A less sensational summary of the beliefs and practices of Wicca, based on *Drawing Down the Moon.*

698. Morgan, Ffiona. *Wild Witches Don't Get the Blues: astrology, rituals & healing.* Daughters of the Moon Publishing (Box 357, Rio Nido, CA 95471), 1991. 284 p.

A solid handbook of feminist witchcraft, with chapters on astrology, Tarot, healing, rituals, lunar and seasonal rites. Illustrated with images from the Daughters of the Moon Tarot deck. If you have no other recent manual and are drawn to astrology, this would be a good purchase.

699. Morris, Katherine Sue. *Early Medieval Witchcraft: characteristics of the feminine witch figure.* Ph.D. thesis, University of Texas-Austin, 1985. 218 p.

700. Morrissey, Mary. "Being a Neo-Pagan Isn't Easy," *Sojourner*, Dec. 1986, 12(4):8.

A lesbian-feminist Neo-Pagan priestess describes how Pagans celebrate the Winter Solstice, and how Neo-Paganism pushes the boundaries of spirituality, its adherents encountering opposition on the Left as well as the Right.

701. Morrissey, Mary. "Roll Over Jehovah and Tell St. Nick the News," *Gay Community News,* Dec. 14, 1988, 14 (22):5.

On Neo-Paganism.

702. Mountainwater, Shekhinah. *Ariadne's Thread: a workbook of Goddess magic.* Freedom, CA: The Crossing Press, 1991. 382 p.

Shekhinah is a font of women's wisdom, having been involved with the feminist spirituality movement from its inception. This is her first book, a manual which is full of the Goddess and feminist Wicca. Information is given on the sacred elements, the Goddess as Maiden-Mother-Crone, the moon, rituals, magic, herbs, divination, group formation and practice, and the vocation of priestess.

703. *Neo-Paganism: a feminist search for religious alternatives.* Ed. Mary Ellen Brown. Bloomington: Women's Studies Program, Indiana University, 1988. (Its *Occasional Series,* no. 3) 127 p.

704. Paxson, Diana L. *The Liturgy of the Lady: the Fellowship of the Spiral Path.* MZB Enterprises, Box 72, Berkeley, CA

94701.

This popular author of science fiction and fantasy novels is also a priestess of the Goddess. Her book is the liturgy used by her spiritual group.

705. Perrone, Bobette, H. Henrietta Stockel, and Victoria Krueger. *Medicine Women, Curanderas, and Women Doctors.* Norman, OK: University of Oklahoma Press, 1989. 252 p.

The authors interviewed Native American healers (a Navajo medicine woman, an Apache woman, and Cherokee spiritual teacher Dhyani Ywahoo), Hispanic *curanderas* (traditional spiritual healers), and white women physicians. They found a distinct contrast between the medical organic model of disease and the traditional concept of spiritual imbalance, and believe that women physicians generally take a more holistic approach toward healing than male doctors. The authors add their own perspectives on women and healing: that the unknown is frightening to many people, that medical doctors need to learn an entirely new set of ethics. Includes chapters on witchcraft as "the dark side of healing," and witchcraft accusations among Native Americans. Altogether a fascinating and important book.

706. Perry, Deborah L. "Ancient Rituals Celebrate Women's Lives," *New Directions for Women,* Nov. 1986, 15(6):14.

A "hedgewitch" describes a typical Wiccan handfasting, or marriage ceremony.

707. Pittman, Rebecca. "Witches, ACLU Foil Helms, Casting Off Evil Curse," *Washington Magazine*, Jan. 1986, p. 15.

The notorious Senator Jesse Helms of North Carolina, in direct violation of several tenets of the Constitution, introduced a bill into Congress which would deny tax-exempt status to any religion which promoted witchcraft or Satanism. After considerable pressure from Pagans and others, the bill died a swift death.

708. "Protestors Try to Nix Witch Talk," *American Libraries,* July/Aug. 1986, 17(7):503-504.

Z Budapest gave a talk on Wicca and its ancient roots at the San Jose Public Library amid a storm of protests by right-wing Christians. She ended up with 500 people in the audience and 800 demonstrating outside, pro and con.

709. Quaife, G. R. *Godly Zeal and Furious Rage: the witch in early modern Europe.* New York: St. Martin's Press, 1987. 235 p.
A history of witch beliefs and persecutions, focusing on the relationship of mediaeval misogyny to the rise of witch accusations in the late Middle Ages and thereafter. The author also looks at the motivations behind accusations and the survival of paganism in rural areas.

710. Raven. *The Teachings of the Holy Strega.* Moon Dragon Publications. Available from Magickal Childe, 35 W. 19th St., New York, NY 10011.
A handbook of Italian witchcraft, based on the legend of the goddess Aradia, who taught magic and rebellion to mediaeval Italian peasants.

711. Reed, Ellen Cannon. *The Witches' Qabalah: Book 1: The Goddess and the Tree* [also published as *The Goddess and the Tree*]. St. Paul: Llewellyn Publications, 1985. 160 p.
Much of modern Pagan ceremony and symbolism comes from the Kabbalah, yet few people study this rich mystical system in any depth. This book is a basic introduction to the Tree of Life and the Goddess symbolism of each *sephir* or sphere, with meditations, exercises, and magical correspondences.

712. Reed, Ellen Cannon. *The Witches Tarot.* St. Paul: Llewellyn Publications, 1989. 293 p. (Book 2 of *The Witches' Qabalah*).
A text to accompany her Tarot deck.

713. Rufus, Sharon. "Who Are the Witches?" *Fate*, May 1986, p.59-64.

714. Rufus, Sharon. "Witches in Oakland: Great Goddess!" *Out and Out: the East Bay's gay and lesbian monthly*, April 1982, 1(7):6-8.
On the feminist witchcraft community in Oakland, California.

715. Rulseh, Ellen. "Prudent Priestess: meet Selena Fox, Wiccan wise woman," *Wisconsin Woman,* Oct. 1989, 3(7):12-13.

Selena Fox is a healer, the director of Circle, a Pagan retreat and networking organization, the publisher of the Wiccan/Neo-Pagan periodical *Circle Network News*, and a legally ordained minister of the Wiccan religion.

716. Ryall, Rhiannon. *West Country Wicca: a journal of the Old Religion.* Custer, WA: Phoenix Publications, 1989. 93 p.

A memoir of the traditional English Craft as it was practiced in the 1940's before the public revival of witchcraft led by Gerald Gardner: a charming collection of Wiccan practice, folk magic, herbal recipes, and divination, in an elegantly designed volume printed in English Country style.

717. Sell, Ingrid. "Seizing Power to Regenerate the Earth," *New Directions for Women,* July/Aug. 1990, 20(4):3.

On the phenomenon of feminist witchcraft, with comments by Starhawk, Z Budapest, Eclipse, and other feminist witches.

718. Starhawk. "Bending the Energy: an interview with Starhawk," *New Catalyst* (Lillooet, BC), Winter 1978/88, p.12-13.

Starhawk talks about restructuring power-relationships, feminist politics, the Green movement and spirituality, and the importance of a feminist perspective on ecology.

719. Starhawk. *Dreaming the Dark: magic, sex & politics.* New ed. Boston: Beacon Press, 1988 (first published 1982). 242 p.

In her introduction to this edition, Starhawk re-evaluates her analysis of the psychology of control and explains how her Jewish identity has been strengthened over the years, notes that the AIDS epidemic has altered the field of the erotic, and assesses changes in politics, society and religion, as well as her own life changes.

720. Starhawk. "Essential Starhawk," *Yoga Journal,* Nov./Dec. 1989, no. 89, pp. 68-74, 109.

An interview by Frederick Levine, in which she gives her current political philosophy and view of Wicca, criticizes New Age ideology and the "new shamanism," and suggests that practicing European Wicca may be more appropriate for white people than imitating Native Americans.

721. Starhawk. "Introduction" to *Rainbow Nation Without Borders: toward an ecotopian millenium*, by Alberto Ruz Buenfil (Santa Fe: Bear & Co., 1991), p. xi-xviii.

As a preface to this "catalog of countercultural experiments in the Americas and Europe all linked by the symbol of the rainbow," Starhawk outlines the tenets of Neo-Pagan thought, especially with respect to the environment and the global community. She reminds the reader that activists in the U.S. still have much to learn from European and Third World people about the work being done to create a peaceful future, and that Americans have much to offer with respect to feminism and gay liberation.

722. Starhawk. "On Being a Jewish Witch," *Genesis 2,* Winter 1987, 18(4):29-30, 38-39.

With an introduction by Jewish theologian Ellen Umansky. Starhawk writes about her Jewish identity and religious practice, the elements of Judaic heritage that inform her Wiccan spirituality, and how Pagan theology differs from Judaism. Her article elicited a response from Jane Litwoman (see above).

723. Starhawk. *The Spiral Dance: a rebirth of the ancient religion of the Great Goddess.* 10th anniversary edition, with new introduction and chapter by chapter commentary. San Francisco: Harper and Row, 1989. 288 p.

The book which has sent thousands of women and men on the path of the Goddess: an eloquent exposition of Craft thealogy coupled with exercises, meditations, rituals, and spells, constituting one of the first textbooks of Goddess spirituality. The text for this edition is virtually unchanged, with discreet asterisks directing the reader to notes in the back, where Starhawk muses on the evolution of the Craft in the last ten years and the development of her thealogy and politics. She adds an introduction placing the book in the context of her life as it was when she wrote it, commenting on the growth of the Craft, feminist spirituality, and her own understanding.

724. Starhawk. "We Are the Turning of the Tide," *Peace Newsletter* (Syracuse, NY), May 1984, 5(7):17.

An interview in which she discusses witchcraft, power, and directing energy in political as well as spiritual work.

725. Starhawk. "Witchcraft & the Religion of the Great Goddess," *Yoga Journal,* no. 68, May/June 1986, pp. 38-42, 56, 58-59.

On the history of goddess-worship and its survival in witchcraft, its form today, how its philosophy differs from Western and Eastern religions, and what it can offer women.

726. Steichen, Donna. "From Convent to Coven: Catholic Neo-Pagans at the Witches' Sabbath," *Fidelity* (South Bend, IN), Dec. 1985, 5(1):27-37 (also printed in *Epiphany* [San Francisco], Summer 1988).

A report on the Fourth Annual Conference on Woman and Spirituality held at Mankato State University, Minnesota in October 1985, with special attention given to the participation in Wiccan rituals by practicing and ex-Catholics. In attendance were Lynnie Levy and Jade from the feminist witchcraft periodical *Of a Like Mind* and Christian theologian Rosemary Ruether. Although the author is openly hostile to feminist spirituality and witchcraft, the article appears to be accurately reported. Other articles in this issue of *Fidelity*, a conservative Catholic periodical, attack Christian feminism, female ordination, inclusive language in liturgy, and the book *Lesbian Nuns.*

727. Stein, Diane. *Casting the Circle: a women's book of ritual.* Freedom, CA: The Crossing Press, 1990. 260 p.

A guide to feminist Wiccan spiritual practice: the role of the cycles of the Moon and Earth in women's lives; how to design a successful ritual and keep a coven going; rituals for life passages, candle magic, and an appendix on women in contemporary witchcraft. A solid companion to her *Women's Spirituality Book.*

728. Talbert, Linda Lee. *Witchcraft in Contemporary Feminist Literature.* Ph.D. thesis, University of Southern California, 1979. 198 p.

Witchcraft as women's rebellion in the poetry of Adrienne Rich, Diane Wakoski, Ntozake Shange, and Anne Sexton, and African witchcraft and Voodoo in the works of African and West Indian women writers (Ama Ata Aidoo, Jean Rhys, Bessie Head).

729. Ulanov, Ann and Barry. *The Witch and the Clown: two archetypes of human sexuality.* Wilmette, Ill.: Chiron Publications, 1986. 337 p.

In the first part of the book, the image of the Witch is explored in terms of the dark side of women and men, sexuality, and ways the hag figure may be reclaimed. The second half deals with the Clown as an archetype and the Clown within women.

730. Ungar, Rusty. "Oh, Goddess!: feminists and witches create a new religion from ancient myths and magic," *New York*, June 4, 1990, p. 40-46.

The author writes of feminist rejection of male-dominated religion in favor of Wicca and nature-religion, interviewing writer and performer Donna Wilshire, Margot Adler, Susun Weed, Gardnerian witch Judy Harrow, the women of Star River Productions, and others. While the women are allowed to speak for themselves, the article is marred by the inevitable snickering at ritual activities and spiritual excesses, and by the author's intrusive comments on the appearance and attractiveness of every woman interviewed.

731. Valiente, Doreen. *The Rebirth of Witchcraft.* Custer, WA: Phoenix Publishing, 1989. 236 p.

A valuable history of the 20th-century revival of witchcraft by the work of Gerald Gardner in 1930's England, the popularization of the Craft in the sixties, and the birth of feminist witchcraft, of which Valiente heartily approves.

732. Valiente, Doreen, and Evan John Jones. *Witchcraft: a tradition renewed.* Custer, WA: Phoenix Publications, 1990. 203 p.

Another handbook of Wicca, chiefly written by Jones, Valiente's co-covener from the 1960's. This book emphasizes Wicca's heritage as the Old Religion which originated in prehistoric times, contributing specialized information on the Craft, coven structure, ritual tools (knife, wand, etc.) which may not be found elsewhere, and rituals for the cross-quarter days. A useful source of information on traditional Wiccan practice.

733. *Voices from the Circle: the heritage of Western paganism.*
Ed. Prudence Jones and Caitlín Matthews. London: Aquarian
Press, 1900. 222 p.

Contributions by a variety of priestesses, shamans,
Wiccans, Druids, Goddess-worshippers, and other spiritual
teachers.

734. Wagar, Sam. "Witch Way," *Kick It Over* (Toronto), Feb.
1985, no. 11, p. 7.

A succinct summary of the basic tenets of witchcraft by a
Pagan: the nature of the Goddess, the interconnection of all
things, and an outline of a typical ritual.

735. Walker, Barbara. *Women's Rituals: a sourcebook.* San
Francisco: Harper and Row, 1990. 230 p.

A guide to forming groups and conducting rituals, with
information on the use of ritual tools, seasonal and life-
passage rituals, and the texts of many original and creative
rituals and meditations.

736. Warren-Clarke, Ly. *The Way of the Goddess: a manual for
Wiccen initiation.* Bridport, Eng.: Prism; Garden City, N.Y.:
distributed by the Avery Publishing Group, 1987. 140 p.

An introduction to contemporary Wiccan (female form,
Wiccen) practice.

737. Weinstein, Marion. *Earth Magic: a Dianic book of shadows.*
Rev. and expanded ed. Custer, WA: Phoenix Publishing,
1986. 101 p.

A down-to-earth handbook of Wiccan beliefs and practice: ritual tools, coven traditions, Sabbats and moon rituals,
the use of familiars, magic for protecting the home and for
transformation of the self.

738. Wenzel, Lynn. "Witchcraft in History," *New Directions for
Women,* July/Aug. 1990, 20(4):3.

Brief article on the rediscovery of women's power within
witchcraft and women's sacred history.

739. "Witch Under Fire," *National Catholic Reporter,* Nov. 11,
1988, 25(4):1, 5.

An interview with Starhawk, who describes the tenets of traditional witchcraft and contemporary goddess religion, explains how it is possible for witches to co-exist with Christians, and defends the work of Fr. Matthew Fox, who had just been put under an order of silence by the Vatican.

740. "'Witches' Brouhaha," *Christian Century*, Aug. 22-29, 1990, p. 760-761.

At a Methodist church in Dallas, a ceremony led by a witch was held during Women's Week, which was sponsored by the Perkins School of Theology. Some conservative Christians felt that this was highly inappropriate for a Christian seminary.

741. Worth, Valerie. *The Crone's Book of Wisdom*. St. Paul: Llewellyn Publications, 1988. 168 p.

Charms and herbal lore in verse.

Christianity and Judaism:
Woman-Centered Re-Visioning

Listed below are books, dissertations, articles, and liturgies which reflect a woman-centered spirituality. Also included are works on feminine God-imagery and inclusive language, and feminist Christian and Jewish liturgies, which are often eclectic and multicultural. Ritualists drink from many wells, and a typical Woman-Church or Rosh Chodesh service might begin with a Wiccan-style calling of the four directions, contain readings from the Bible in praise of the earth, and culminate in the participants weaving a communal web. These worship celebrations can easily serve as resources for rituals of other women's spirituality circles. May we continue to learn from one another.

Christian and Jewish feminist literature—and the reaction to women's greater visibility—is vast, and I could not possibly give equal treatment to it within the scope of this bibliography. For this reason the writings of some important feminist theologians, such as Elisabeth Schüssler Fiorenza and Letty Russell, are not included here. To do justice to the corpus of writings in feminist theology alone would have produced a volume several times the length of the present one; happily, a comprehensive bibliography of Christian feminism has finally been compiled by Shelley Davis Finson (see the Bibliography section).

742. *The Absent Mother: restoring the Goddess to Judaism and Christianity*. Ed. Alix Pirani. San Francisco: HarperSanFrancisco, 1991. 256 p.

A powerful anthology by women and men on the presence of the Goddess and the Feminine Divine within Judaism and Christianity. Particularly strong on woman-centered Judaism, with several pieces on Lilith, the Shekhinah, and the Hebrew Goddess.

743. Ackerman, Susan. "'And the Women Knead Dough': the worship of the Queen of Heaven in sixth-century Judah," in: *Gender and Difference in Ancient Israel,* ed. Peggy L. Day (Minneapolis: Fortress Press, 1989), p. 109-124.

Denounced by the prophet Jeremiah, the Biblical Queen of Heaven may have been a combination of Astarte and Ishtar.

744. Adelman, Penina V. *Miriam's Well: rituals for Jewish women around the year.* Fresh Meadows, NY: Biblio Press, 1986; 2nd ed., 1990. 143 p.

A year's worth of Rosh Chodesh (New Moon) ceremonies and rituals—in the Jewish calendar the month begins with the New Moon, and the custom of women's Rosh Chodesh ceremonies is most likely pre-Biblical. Here the rituals are based on traditional Jewish holydays but are re-interpreted for woman-centered meaning. Each ceremony includes an outline of the ritual, a Biblical reading, stories, songs, menu, and a *kavannah* or intention for the ritual. There are rituals for menarche, menopause, death, naming. Adelman also gives advice on starting a Rosh Chodesh group.

745. Angelou, Matia, and Hanna Bandes. "Jewish Women Reclaim Rituals," *New Directions for Women,* July/Aug. 1989, 18(4):8.

How Rosh Chodesh groups are reclaiming the Shekhinah as image of God, creating women's rituals, and celebrating female life passages within a Jewish context.

746. Armstrong, Karen. *The Gospel According to Woman: Christianity's creation of the sex war in the West.* Garden City, NY: Anchor Press, 1986 (first published in Great Britain, 1986). 366 p.

A history of how almost from its inception Christianity has oppressed women: since women have been identified with the body and sexuality we have been categorized as either sinful Eves or saintly Virgins. The witch being a symbol of the powerful, sexual woman, the "destroyer" of men, the witch-hunts served as a "Final Solution," while even the Church's approval of holy virgins indicates its misogyny, given the emphasis on gory martyrdom and bodily mortifications.

747. Arnold, Patrick M. *Wildmen, Warriors, and Kings: masculine spirituality and the Bible*. New York: Crossroad, 1991.

On the masculine principle in the Bible; written from the standpoint of the contemporary men's movement as propounded by Robert Bly, but opposing feminist theology and Goddess religion.

748. Arnoldi, Harriet Jerusha. *Haggadah Shella; Her Haggadah*. N.p.: Arnoldi, 1981. 55 p.

A feminist Passover Haggadah in English, Hebrew, and Yiddish. Copy at Harvard University Library.

749. Ashe, Kaye. "God, Our Heavenly Mother," in: *God and Me*, ed. Candida Lund (Chicago: Thomas More Press, 1988), p. 58-78.

A Dominican nun describes her lifelong, everchanging relationship with God, who evolved from the invisible male being of Catholic teaching, to medieval mystic Julian of Norwich's Immanent Presence, to the Divine Mother who participates in our lives and whom women can recognize in ourselves.

750. Bankson, Marjory Zoet. *Braided Streams: Esther and a woman's way of growing*. San Diego: LuraMedia, 1985. 179 p.

Using the Biblical story of Esther—a woman coming to power by discovering her own potential—a religious educator shows how we can integrate our own braided streams of identity (sexual, vocational, and spiritual). *Braided Streams: leader's guide*, by Lura Jane Geiger and Pat Backman, is also available from LuraMedia. It supports a ten-session course based on the book, using guided imagery, journal-keeping, and other tools.

751. Bankson, Marjory Zoet. *Seasons of Friendship: Naomi and Ruth as a pattern*. San Diego: LuraMedia, 1987. 139 p.

In this gentle book Bankson takes the relationship between Naomi and Ruth—one of the clearest Biblical examples of women's bonding—as a model for friendship between women and our relationship with God. Like the four seasons, friends help us grow, allow us to change, accept our accomplishments, and grant us needed solitude. Includes study questions and journal exercises.

752. Barz, Monika, et al. *Hättest du gedacht, dass wir so viele sind: Lesbische Frauen in der Kirche [Would You Have Thought That We Were So Many?: lesbian women in the church].* Stuttgart: Kreuz Verlag, 1987. 236 p.

753. Bloom, Harold, and David Rosenberg. *The Book of J.* Translated from the Hebrew by Rosenberg; interpreted by Bloom. New York: Grove Weidenfeld, 1990. 340 p.

There are several hypothetical original texts upon which Biblical scholars believe the Bible to have been based (e.g. the Synoptic Gospels of Matthew, Mark and Luke are said to derive from a single text known as the Q Document). The authors conjecture that much of the first five books of the Bible (the J Document) was the work of a member of Solomon's court, possibly a woman, perhaps one of Solomon's daughters. Thus they suggest that the earliest part of the Bible is a novel by a woman author and reflects a female perspective.

754. *Border Regions of Faith: an anthology of religion and social change.* Ed. Kenneth Aman. Maryknoll, NY: Orbis Books, 1987. 528 p.

An anthology of Christian writings on feminism, Black and Chicano theology, the Third World, economics, peace, and the New Right. The feminist section contains previously printed articles by Carol Christ, Mary Daly, Elizabeth Schüssler Fiorenza, Elaine Pagels, Kay Turner, and others, on women in the Christian tradition, the Virgin Mary, women in ministry and the Catholic Church, and feminist rituals.

755. Bührig, Marga. *Die unsichtbare Frau und der Gott der Väter: eine Einführung in die feministische Theologie [The Invisible Woman and the God of the Fathers: an introduction to feminist theology].* 2nd ed. Stuttgart: Kreuz Verlag, 1987. 135 p.

756. Burns, Camilla. *The Heroine With a Thousand Faces: Woman Wisdom in Proverbs 1-9.* Ph.D. thesis, Graduate Theological Union, 1990. 204 p.

757. Cady, Susan, Marian Ronan, and Hal Taussig. *Sophia: the future of feminist spirituality*. San Francisco: Harper and Row, 1986. 103 p.

Three ministers write that women in the Church need not reject the Biblical tradition in order to find the feminine face of God, for She has been there all along in the Wisdom literature of the Hebrew Bible (chiefly in the Books of Proverbs, Wisdom, Ecclesiasticus, and Baruch), where Wisdom ("Sophia" in Greek) is personified as a female companion or aspect of God. They present an introduction to Sophia's presence in the Old and New Testament and in post-Biblical Christian and mystical literature, and advise that when traditional church congregations try to include a feminine aspect of God in weekly worship, Sophia is far more palatable to any churchgoers than most feminist re-visionings of the Divine.

758. Cady, Susan, Marian Ronan, and Hal Taussig. *Wisdom's Feast: Sophia in study and celebration*. San Francisco: Harper and Row, 1989. 228 p.

In this edition most of the text of the above book has been reprinted, with the addition of a comprehensive guide to performing Wisdom-centered rituals and conducting Bible study of the Wisdom texts with church groups. The rituals/ services are creative and can be adapted for use by most woman-identified circles, as well as by groups unfamiliar with—and perhaps distrustful of—feminist spirituality.

759. Camp, Claudia V. *Wisdom and the Feminine in the Book of Proverbs*. Decatur, GA: Almond Press, 1985. 352 p.

On the imagery of Wisdom as wife, lover, harlot, and wise woman.

760. Caprio, Betsy. *The Woman Sealed in the Tower: being a view of feminine spirituality as revealed by the legend of St. Barbara*. New York: Paulist Press, 1982. 105 p.

St. Barbara is said to have been a Roman pagan whose father shut her up in a tower, like Rapunzel and Danaë. While imprisoned she converted to Christianity and was killed by her father. Caprio takes this legend of martyrdom and uses it to explore the four Jungian female archetypes, arranging them by the four ancient elements (earth, air, fire and water). An unusual blend of paganism and Catholicism, with meditations and study questions to be used with an unsophisticated audience.

761. Carmody, Denise Lardner. *Feminism and Christianity: a two-way reflection.* Nashville: Abingdon Press, 1982; Lanham, MD: University Press of America, 1990. 188 p.
    See Chapter 1, "The New Focus on the Goddess," and Chapter 8, "Feminist Theory of Nature."

762. Chalmer, Judith, and Fran Solin. "Turning Twelve: becoming a woman," *Lilith*, Fall 1988, no. 21, p. 17.

763. Clanton, Jann Aldredge. *In Which Image?: God and gender.* Bloomington: Meyer-Stone Books, 1989. 135 p.
    On the femininity of God.

764. Clark, Linda, et al. *Image-Breaking/Image Building: a handbook for creative worship with women of Christian tradition.* New York: Pilgrim, 1981. 144 p.
    Exercises and woman-centered liturgies.

765. Craighead, Meinrad. *The Litany of the Great River.* New York: Paulist Press, 1991. 76 p.
    Craighead is an artist living in New Mexico. Remembering the rich Catholic culture of the traditional Church, she has composed litanies to the sacred earth, each accompanied by a reflective text and and one of her powerful paintings. Her art is in earth tones and often depicts women who seem to be made from the Earth herself. A former contemplative nun, her spirituality is now nourished by Catholicism, Native American wisdom, and the strength of the Mother.

766. Daly, Mary. *The Church and the Second Sex* [first pub. 1968]*: with the feminist postchristian introduction* [1975] *and new archaic afterwords by the author.* Boston: Beacon Press, 1985. 231 p.
    Daly's first book, a brilliantly trenchant yet hopeful critique of the Catholic Church and patriarchal theology, is by no means irrelevant to contemporary religious discourse, even if the author now regards it as a quaint document from a bygone era. Her "New Archaic Afterwords" are written in the language of the Spinsters which she devised at the time of

Gyn/Ecology: Muse-ings on the courage to leave the church and the dead zone of patriarchy, the courage to live in the not-yet post-patriarchal world of the 1980's. To the reader she stresses that by now she and many feminists have journeyed light-years beyond her original reformism.

767. Daum, Annette. "Blaming the Jews for the Death of the Goddess," *Lilith*, no. 7, 1980/5741, p. 11-13; also in: *Nice Jewish Girls: a lesbian anthology,* ed. Evelyn Torton Beck (Trumansburg, NY: The Crossing Press, 1982; rev. and updated ed., Boston: Beacon Press, 1989), p. 255-261.

Daum objects to the inadequate scholarship and negative perspective of some feminist writers, especially Christians, who claim that the attitudes of Christianity, and Jesus in particular, were a liberation for women from the heritage of the Hebrew Bible. Critics of the Judaic tradition are as "selectively judgmental" about sexist or brutal practices among the Hebrews as they are about the Jews' Goddess-worshipping neighbors.

768. Dietrich, Gabriele. "Perspectives of a Feminist Theology: towards the full humanity of women and men," in: "God, Women, and the Bible," special issue of *Logos*, Oct. 1983, 22(3):1-51.

769. Dillon, Bonny Kay. *Contributions of Selected Feminist Theologians and Feminist Psychoanalytic Theorists to Pastoral Psychotherapy.* Ph.D. thesis, Southern Baptist Theological Seminary, 1987. 170 p.

770. Ellis, Ronald F. *The Feminine Principle in Biblical, Theological, and Psychological Perspective.* D.Min. thesis, Drew University, 1985. 229 p.

771. *A Faith of One's Own: explorations by Catholic lesbians.* Ed. Barbara Zanotti. Trumansburg, NY: The Crossing Press, 1986. 202 p.

Catholic and lesbian may seem to be mutually exclusive categories, yet for reasons unknown, a disproportionate number of lesbians were brought up Catholic, and Catholicism is a heritage not lightly abandoned. The personal stories gathered here are by a variety of women: some are still in the Church, some have left, some are former nuns, some have found the Goddess. Contributors include poet Martha Courtot, literary scholar Margaret Cruikshank, theologian Mary E. Hunt, writers Gloria Anzaldúa and Valerie Miner, and many unknowns.

772. *Feminist Theology: a reader*. Ed. Ann Loades. Louisville: Westminster/John Knox Press, 1990. 324 p.

This collection, ideal for course use, includes Mary Daly, Beverly Wildung Harrison, Elisabeth Schüssler Fiorenza, Ursula King, Sallie McFague, Rosemary Ruether, Letty Russell, Phyllis Trible, and others.

773. *La Femme, son Corps, la Religion: approches pluridisciplinaires I [Woman, Her Body, Religion: interdisciplinary approaches]*. Ed. Élisabeth J. Lacelle. Montreal: Éditions Bellarmin, 1983. 246 p.

French and English articles written 1977-81 by the Groupe d'Études Interdisciplinaires sur la Femme et la Religion du Canada, of the University of Ottawa Religious Science Department. With a general bibliography and a bibliography of Rosemary Ruether's dozens of books and articles.

774. Ferreira, Cornelia R. "The Emerging Feminist Religion," *Homiletic and Pastoral Review,* May 1989, p. 10ff.

A hostile critique of (and call to arms against) the feminist movement within the Christian, especially Catholic, Church. Ferreira regards feminist theology as mere ideology, not true theology, grounded in secular humanism. She characterizes Christian feminism as an idolatrous, Gnostic heresy.

775. Ferreira, Cornelia R. "The Feminist Agenda Within the Church," *Homiletic and Pastoral Review*, May 1987, p. 10-21 (also published as a pamphlet [Toronto: Life Ethics Centre, 1987]).

An anti-feminist but well-researched review of Christian feminism and the feminist spirituality movement, occasioned when the author was asked to critique a kit of discussion papers on "Women in the Church" distributed by the Canadian Conference of Catholic Bishops. The bibliography of the kit made her uncomfortably aware of the extent of feminist criticism within the church from women theologians like Rosemary Ruether, and she was alarmed by the influence of

Goddess-religionists such as Starhawk and Hallie Iglehart.

776. Fine, Irene. *Midlife—a rite of passage; The Wise Woman—a celebration.* San Diego: Women's Institute for Continuing Jewish Education, 1988. 72 p.

Two rituals for Jewish women, with commentary. Fine has done a great deal of interesting work on re-visioning a woman-centered Judaism and nurturing Jewish feminist spirituality.

777. Finson, Shelley Davis. *On the Other Side of Silence: patriarchy, consciousness and spirituality: some women's experiences of theological education.* D.Min. thesis, Boston University, 1985. 274 p.

On women seminarians' experiences of sexism in Canadian seminaries, by a minister in the United Church of Christ.

778. Fischer, Kathleen R. *Women at the Well: feminist perspectives on spiritual direction.* New York: Paulist Press, 1988. 215 p.

A handbook of feminist spiritual direction for women who remain in the church, advising directors to reject the role of objective expert in favor of forming circles for empowerment. With exercises, meditations, and discussion questions on issues such as violence, Scripture, prayer, and family legacy.

779. Frankiel, Tamar. *The Voice of Sarah: feminine spirituality and traditional Judaism.* San Francisco: HarperSanFrancisco, 1990. 140 p.

A feminist Orthodox Jew writes that Judaism is not oppressively patriarchal but in fact celebrates feminine experience through women's rituals mirroring body rhythms and in the traditional seasonal holidays. She embraces the paradox that traditional Jewish life, when lived with full consciousness, can be fulfilling for so many women. Thought-provoking and beautifully expressed.

780. Frye, Roland Mushat. *Language for God and Feminist Language: problems and principles.* Princeton: Center of Theological Inquiry, 1988. 26 p.

781. Gelpi, Donald L. *The Divine Mother: a trinitarian theology*

of the Holy Spirit. Lanham, MD: University Press of America, 1984. 245 p.

A priest writes about the importance of envisioning the Holy Spirit as the feminine face of God, as She was briefly regarded during the early history of the Church.

782. Goldman, June Parker. "Are Church Feminists Tilting Toward Witchcraft?" *United Methodist Reporter*, Aug. 29, 1986.
The author thinks so, and she doesn't like it.

783. Goldstein, Elyse. "Who *Has* Made Me a Woman," *Lilith*, Spring 1990, p. 32.
A feminist rabbi reclaims menstruation by reciting, at the onset of each period, a variation on the prayer Orthodox men recite, thanking God for not making them women: "Blessed art Thou, Lord our God, Ruler of the Universe, who *has* made me a woman."

784. Good, Deirdre J. *Reconstructing the Tradition of Sophia in Gnostic Literature.* Atlanta: Scholars Press, 1987. 103 p.
On Sophia (Wisdom) in early Gnostic and orthodox Christianity. In surviving Gnostic texts Sophia appears as Genitrix, Mother, and Consort.

785. Gritz, Sharon Hodgin. *Paul, Women Teachers, and the Mother Goddess at Ephesus: a study of 1 Timothy 2:9-15 in light of the religious and cultural milieu of the first century.* Lanham, MD: University Press of America, 1991. 198 p.
The Bible verses referred to are Paul's notorious instructions to women to be modest, silent, and submissive. Gritz describes the Hellenic city of Ephesus, in Biblical times still a major center of worship of Artemis as Great Mother, women's social position of the time, goddess-worship and the role of women among the Jews, and the attitudes of Jesus and Paul towards women.

786. Hammett, Jenny Yates. *Woman's Transformations: a psychological theology.* Lewiston, NY: Edwin Mellen Press, 1982. 120 p.
Brief essays grounded in depth psychology on the gender of God, women in Christian theology, and goddesses and the Holy Spirit as symbols of feminine consciousness.

787. Hampson, Daphne. *Theology and Feminism.* Cambridge, MA: Basil Blackwell, 1990. 188 p.

A Christian theologian's long hard look at Christianity led her to conclude that feminism presents such a serious challenge to Christianity that the religion with which we are familiar is in fact "neither true nor moral," yet may eventually be transformed into a more nourishing spirituality.

788. Hardesty, Nancy. *Inclusive Language in the Church.* Atlanta: John Knox Press, 1987. 114 p.

789. Hebblethwaite, Margaret. *Motherhood and God.* London: Geoffrey Chapman, 1988. 147 p.

Personal insights on the presence of God in motherhood and the motherhood of God.

790. Heschel, Susannah. "Women Before the Law," *New Traditions: explorations in Judaism,* Spring 1984, no. 1, p. 45-54.

On the position of women in Judaism and feminist criticism. Mentions Jewish thealogians such as Starhawk and Naomi Goldenberg and poses the question: can a feminist Judaism be said to be Judaism at all?

791. Hoeffel, Roseanne. "From Feminist Parables to Woman-Church," *The Women's Studies Review* (Columbus: Ohio State Univ. Center for Women's Studies), Autumn 1987, 9(4):17-18.

792. Howell, Alice O. *The Dove in the Stone: finding the sacred in the commonplace.* Wheaton, Ill.: Theosophical Publishing House, 1988. 199 p.

A Jungian psychologist travels to Iona with her husband and becomes powerfully aware of the ancient wisdom to be found in Celtic Christianity, the wisdom that comes from Sophia. An unusual and intriguing journey.

793. Hunke, Sigrid. *Am Anfang waren Mann und Frau: Vorbilder und Wandlungen der Geschlechterbeziehungen [In the Beginning Were Man and Woman: models and transformations of relations between the sexes].* 3rd ed. Hildesheim: Olms, 1987. 324 p.

On Adam and Eve, and Eve's connections with the ancient mother goddesses.

794. Ingram, Kristen. "The Goddess: can we bring her into the Church?" *Spirituality Today,* 1987, 39:39-55.
     Ingram is decidedly negative towards any feminizing of Christianity.

795. Kirk, Martha Ann. *Celebrations of Biblical Women's Stories: tears, milk, and honey.* Kansas City: Sheed and Ward, 1987. 113 p.
     A collection of prayer services/rituals dedicated to Biblical women, incorporating song, dance, and prayer.

796. Kirk, Martha Ann. *The Prophetess Led Them in Praise: women's stories in ritual.* Th.D. thesis, Graduate Theological Union, 1986. 524 p. and cassette of music.

797. Lang, Bernard. *Wisdom and the Book of Proverbs: a Hebrew goddess redefined.* New York: Pilgrim Press, 1986. 192 p.
     On Wisdom as teacher, goddess, Lady Wisdom vs. Folly the harlot. Addresses the thorny problem of Hebrew polytheism.

798. *Lesbian Nuns: breaking silence.* Ed. Rosemary Curb and Nancy Monahan. Tallahassee: Naiad Press, 1985. 383 p.
     First-person accounts by fifty lesbians who have been (and in some cases still are) nuns. Most discovered their lesbianism after they left the convent, some are still active in the Church, while a dozen now practice feminist spirituality or feminist witchcraft. Contributors include Hannah Blue Heron, a frequent contributor to *WomanSpirit* magazine, and Kevyn Lutton, a member of one of Starhawk's covens and the designer of the cover of the first edition of *The Spiral Dance.*

799. *Liberating Liturgies.* Women's Ordination Conference (Box 269, Suite 11, Fairfax Circle Center, 9653 Lee Highway, Fairfax, VA 22031-2693), 1989. 91 p.
     A "vernacular" collection of liturgies, many written by nuns, for celebrating summer, Candlemas, Pentecost, naming a new baby, and empowering women, using Biblical texts and selections from women's spirituality authors. Includes music

for some of the songs.

800. Litwoman, Jane. "Reclaiming the Shekhinah," *New Directions for Women,* July/Aug. 1990, pp. 1, 21.
   On the multiplicity of Jewish feminisms; part of *NDFW*'s annual spirituality issue.

801. Maeckelberghe, E. "Vanuit de Ervaring: recente ontwikkelingen in de feministische theologie van de Vereinigte Staaten [From Experience: recent developments in feminist theology in the United States]," *Tijdschrift voor Theologie,* 1986, 26(4):392-405.
   A bibliographic essay on feminist biblical interpretation, feminist ethics, women's challenges to traditional theology, and the work of Mary Daly.

802. *Mainstreaming: feminist research for teaching religious studies.* Ed. Arlene Swidler and Walter E. Conn. Lanham, MD: University Press of America, 1985. 83 p.
   Contributors, chiefly women, include such important feminist theologians as Swidler, Denise Lardner Carmody, Elisabeth Schüssler Fiorenza, and Rosemary Rader.

803. *Mariologie und Feminismus [Mariology and Feminism].* Ed. Walter Schöpsdau. Göttingen: Vandenhoeck & Ruprecht, 1985. 143 p.

804. Marriage, Alwyn. *Life-Giving Spirit: responding to the feminine in God.* London: SPCK, 1989. 133 p.

805. McFague, Sallie. *Models of God: theology for an ecological, nuclear age.* Philadelphia: Fortress Press, 1987. 224 p.
   A Protestant theologian contends that the traditional male God-image is idolatrous and is leading us towards global destruction. She rejects power as domination and calls for a return to metaphor in God-language, suggesting God as mother, lover, friend, and imaging the Earth as God's body.

806. McGrew Bennett, Anne. *From Woman-Pain to Woman-Vision: writings in feminist theology.* Ed. Mary E. Hunt. Minneapolis, Fortress Press, 1989. 180 p.

807. Mitchell, Rosemary Catalano, and Gail Anderson Ricciuti.

Birthings and Blessings: liberating worship services for the inclusive church. New York: Crossroad, 1991. 191 p.

808. Mollenkott, Virgina R. "Female God-Imagery and Wholistic [sic] Social Consciousness," *Studies in Formative Spirituality,* Nov. 1984, 5(3):345-354.

The use of exclusively male imagery when speaking of the Divine turns women and our experience into "the Other," which, in a dualistic theology, separates women from God and from the world of spirit. Mollenkott has also written on the female imagery of God in the Bible.

809. Moore, Mary Elizabeth Mullino. "Feminist Theology and Education," in: *Theological Approaches to Christian Education,* ed. by Jack L. Simpson and Donald Eugene Miller (Nashville: Abingdon Press, 1990), p. 63-80.

Written for Christian theologians, this essay explains what feminist theology is (a theology in which women's experience and perspective are central) and the issues raised by feminists from Catholic, Protestant, Orthodox, Jewish, and Black traditions: How to speak of God? How does God relate to creation? What is sin? Sexuality? Ethics?

810. Morton, Nelle. *The Journey Is Home.* Boston: Beacon Press, 1985. 255 p.

A collection of essays from the nineteen-seventies and eighties by a Presbyterian theologian, recounting her journey through a deeper awareness of women's oppression within Christianity and her own growing appreciation of the power of the Goddess.

811. *Motherhood: experience, institution, theology.* Ed. Anne Carr and Elizabeth Schüssler Fiorenza. Edinburgh: T. & T. Clark, 1989. (*Concilium,* 206) 128 p.

A thoughtful collection of articles: mothers confronting the military, eco-feminism, poverty, God as mother, Mary, and problems of mothers worldwide. Contributors include Sallie McFague, Ursula King, Marcy Amba Oduyoye, Ivone Gebara.

812. Mulack, Christa. *"Im Anfang war die Weisheit" : feministische Kritik des mannlichen Gottesbildes [In the Beginning Was*

Wisdom: feminist criticism of the masculine image of God].
Stuttgart: Kreuz, 1988. 119 p.

813. Mulack, Christa. *Maria: die geheime Göttin im Christentum
[Mary: the secret goddess in Christianity].* Stuttgart: Kreuz,
1985. 246 p.

It is well-known that the Virgin Mary retains many of the
features of pre-Christian goddesses, as Mother of God, sor-
rowing mother, Queen of Heaven, Mother of All, Mother
Church.

814. Muto, Susan. *Womanspirit: reclaiming the deep feminine in
our human spirituality.* New York: Crossroad, 1991. 179 p.

Women's experience of the sacred as expressed by Catholic
women. The author, who works for the National Council of
Bishops, reminds us that women have much to offer in the
spiritual life.

815. Neu, Diann, and Ronnie Levin. *A Seder of the Sisters of
Sarah: a Holy Thursday and Passover feminist liturgy.*
Women's Alliance for Theology, Ethics, and Ritual (8035
13th St., Silver Spring, MD 20910), 1986. 20 p.

816. Neu, Diann. *Women Church Celebrations: feminist liturgies
for the Lenten season.* Women's Alliance for Theology,
Ethics and Ritual (8035 13th St., Silver Spring, MD 20910),
1985. 70 p.; 2nd ed., Silver Spring: Waterworks, 1989. 49 p.

Liturgies for the Christian holydays from Ash Wednes-
day through Easter Sunday, with readings, poetry, and music.

817. Neu, Diann. *Women Church Liturgies of Solidarity.* Women's
Alliance for Theology, Ethics, and Ritual (8035 13th St.,
Silver Spring, MD 20910), 1987.

818. *New Eyes for Reading: Biblical and theological reflections
by women from the Third World.* Ed. John S. Pobee and
Bärbel von Wartenberg-Potter. Yorktown Heights, NY:
Meyer-Stone Books, 1987 (first published: Geneva: World
Council of Churches, 1986). 108 p.

Perspectives from African, Asian, and Latin American
women.

819. Oddie, William. *What Will Happen to God?: feminism and the reconstruction of Christian belief.* London: SPCK, 1984; San Francisco: Ignatius Press, 1988. 159 p.

An especially mean-spirited attack on all forms of feminist criticism of traditional Christianity, stridently anti-feminist and pro-God-the-Father. The author characterizes women scholars who question traditional assumptions about theology and Biblical scholarship as neurotics who are obsessed with their "particular" concerns. As Mary Daly might put it, it's a-mazing how the boys persist in their phallacies. The cover has a photograph of "Christa," Edwina Hawkes' sculpture of a female crucified Christ.

820. Peay, Patricia. "Making the Invisible Visible," *Common Boundary,* Nov./Dec. 1990, p. 16-23.

An interview with artist and mystic Meinrad Craighead, a former Benedictine nun, who creates intense earthy images of God the Mother, rooted as much in her personal childhood experience of the Feminine Divine as in the Catholic image of the Blessed Mother.

821. Plaskow, Judith. "Blaming Jews for Inventing Patriarchy," *Lilith,* no. 7, 1980/5741, p. 11-12 (also in *Nice Jewish Girls: a lesbian anthology,* ed. Evelyn Torton Beck, Crossing Press, 1982, p. 250-254).

Plaskow accuses Christian feminist theologians of anti-Judaism and careless historiography in their assumptions that Christian misogyny comes directly from Judaism and that Jesus's feminism was a significant break with the Jewish past. She rejects the notion that the Hebrews were wholly responsible for the suppression of goddess-worship.

822. Plaskow, Judith. *Standing Again at Sinai: Judaism from a feminist perspective.* San Francisco: Harper and Row, 1990. 282 p.

Plaskow struggles to combine Judaism, Jewishness, and feminism, determined to claim Jewish and Biblical history, the good and the bad. She urges Judaism to develop a new theology of sexuality, the erotic, and social justice.

823. Proctor-Smith, Marjorie. *In Her Own Rite: constructing feminist liturgical tradition.* Nashville: Abingdon Press, 1990.

189 p.

The theory behind feminist liturgy. Designers of liturgy need to reach out to women's experience, change male-centered language, create multi-cultural images of God, re-vision baptism and the eucharist, and assume the name feminist with pride.

824. Rae, Eleanor, and Bernice Marie-Daly. *Created in Her Image: models of the feminine divine.* New York: Crossroad, 1990. 157 p.

Two Christian theologians explore how the loss of female God-imagery damages women's psyches and sense of self and has contributed to a general unbalance in modern society, where aggression and domination are rewarded. The authors find the Virgin Mary to be inadequate as a form of the Divine, the Goddess being a more whole image; and wholeness is what is needed today in our vision of God and the world.

825. Riley, Maria. *In God's Image.* Washington: Center of Concern.

A feminist nun leads a six-session workshop for women to study women-as-Church, the femininity of God, and the work of women, drawing upon scripture readings, prayers, and discussions. Based on Riley's book of the same title (published by Sheed and Ward, 1985).

826. Riley, Maria. *Wisdom Seeks Her Way: liberating the power of women's spirituality.* Washington: Center of Concern, 1987. 86 p.

The guidebook for another six-session workshop on women's spirituality, focusing on wholeness, the body, and relationships.

827. "Rosemary Radford Ruether: retrospective," *Religious Studies Review,* Jan. 1989, 15(1):1-12.

Three essays: "The Development of My Theology," by Ruether; "The Socialist Feminist Vision of Rosemary Radford Ruether: a challenge to liberal feminism," by Kathryn Allen Rabuzzi; "Seeing and Naming the World Anew: the works of Rosemary Radford Ruether," by Rebecca S. Chopp.

828. Ruether, Rosemary Radford. "Feminist Theology in the

Academy: how not to reinvent the wheel," *Christianity and Crisis*, Mar. 4, 1985, p. 57-62.

Feminist theology must be pluralistic and must attack the idea that "male" equals "normal," while simultaneously utilizing the alternative tradition of liberation which is still visible in the Scriptures. She insists that if we are ever to transform theology, we must work within existing academic institutions.

829. Ruether, Rosemary Radford. "Sex: Female; Religion: Catholic; Forecast: Fair," *U.S. Catholic*, April 1985, p. 19-26.

Ruether explains how she came to feminism, why she remains in the Catholic Church, and how the Church is quite capable of rejecting centuries of sexism. As always, she responds smartly to the editors' obtuse and negative questions.

830. Ruether, Rosemary Radford. *Women-Church: theology and practice of feminist liturgical communities.* San Francisco: Harper and Row, 1985. 306 p.

Participants in the woman-centered movement within Christianity, or Women-Church, believe that egalitarianism is a return to authentic Biblical tradition, not a rejection of it. Ruether gives the history of women in the church, the role of woman-centered liturgy and the theory and theology behind it, and a broad collection of non-sexist liturgies and rituals, primarily from the Christian and Jewish traditions but also deriving from contemporary Goddess religion and Neo-Paganism. There are liturgies for marriage, baptism, etc., as well as ceremonies for menarche, moving house, coming out as a lesbian, remembering Hiroshima, and healing psychologically from abortion or other tragedies of women's lives.

831. Rupp, Joyce. *The Star in My Heart: experiencing Sophia, inner wisdom.* San Diego: LuraMedia, 1990. 77 p.

A handbook for working with the Biblical Sophia, for transforming the self and healing the past.

832. Schneiders, Sandra M. *Women and the Word: the gender of God in the New Testament and the spirituality of women.* New York: Paulist Press, 1986. 81 p.

---

833. Schulenberg, Andrea. *Feministische Spiritualität: Exodus in eine befreiende Kirche? [Feminist Spirituality: exodus into a liberated church].* Stuttgart: Kohlhammer, 1991.

The feminist exit from the patriarchal church is also an entrance into a new church of liberation and equality.

834. Sears, Marge. *Life-Cycle Celebrations for Women.* Mystic, CT: Twenty-Third Publications, 1989. 77 p.

835. Snyder, Mary Hembrow. *The Christology of Rosemary Radford Ruether: a critical introduction.* Mystic, CT: Twenty-third Publications, 1988. 152 p.

Ruether has an understanding of the Christ as not absolutely identical with the man Jesus: that the Christ is a way of being to which any human can aspire.

836. Sölle, Dorothee. *Und ist noch nicht erschienen, was wir sein werden: Stationen feministischer Theologie [And it is not yet apparent what we shall become: stations of feminist theology].* Munich: Deutscher Taschenbuch Verlag, 1987. 185 p.

Sölle is one of the outstanding thinkers in contemporary Christian theology, many of whose books on feminism and the place of social justice within the Church have been translated into English. In this book she writes that the religion of the Mother is Utopia, which can only be attained through and with women.

837. Steichen, Donna. *Ungodly Rage: the hidden face of Catholic feminism.* San Francisco: Ignatius Press, 1991. 420 p.

An exposé of feminist activities within the Catholic Church: Steichen denounces Catholic feminism as born of a loss of faith and fueled by a "vengeful rage" (I can't imagine why). She is particularly appalled by feminist Catholics' alliance with Goddess religion and feminist witchcraft.

838. Stein, Judith. *A Jewish Lesbian Chanukah: prayers for lighting Chanukah candles.* Bobbeh Meisehs Press (137 Tremont St., Cambridge, MA 02139), 1979. 8 p.

Blessings for each of the eight days of Chanukah, celebrating women's strength while acknowledging darkness and struggle. May also be used by non-lesbians.

839. Stein, Judith. *The Purim Megillah: a feminist retelling.*
Bobbeh Meisehs Press (137 Tremont St., Cambridge, MA
02139), 1986. 14 p.
A dialogue among Vashti, Esther, and Zeresh (Haman's
wife), recounting the story of Purim and showing the struggle
of women against men's brutal oppression.

840. Tardiff, Mary. "Bibliography: Rosemary Radford Ruether,"
The Modern Churchman, 1988, 30(1):50-55.

841. Taussig, Hal. *The Lady of the Dance.* Austin: The Sharing
Co., 1981. 24 p.
A pamphlet on using dance and Biblical texts on Sophia
in creative worship services.

842. Terrenus, Aurora, comp. *Sophia of the Bible: the spirit of
wisdom.* Santa Cruz, CA: Celestial Communications, 1988.
78 p.
A compilation of Biblical verses from the Old and New
Testaments, most referring to Sophia (Biblical Wisdom) and
the feminine spirit of God, adapted into beautiful poetry.

843. Terrenus, Aurora. *The Shroud of Sophia. from the myths of
Omikros.* Santa Cruz: Celestial Communications, 1988. 133 p.
Described as "a transforming myth of magic, love, and
renewal."

844. Teubal, Savina J. *Hagar the Egyptian: the lost tradition of
the matriarchs.* San Francisco: Harper and Row, 1990. 226 p.
Hagar is usually referred to as Abraham's concubine, but
in reality she was Sarah's servant and thus had closer ties to
her mistress than to Abraham (in the Hebrew Bible virtually
any woman who is not a wife is called a "concubine.") With
meticulous documentation, Teubal connects Hagar to the
Near Eastern goddess religions, showing that she certainly
followed the customs of non-Hebrew peoples and perhaps
even their religion.

845. Thomas, Trudelle. "Ancient Rite for Today," *New Directions for Women,* July/Aug. 1989, p. 9.
A review of "The Tallit" (the *tallit* is the Jewish prayer
shawl), a ritual/dance performance by the group Growth in

Motion. The piece includes audience participation and a ritualized birth, and was created by Fanchon Schur, who has also choreographed a woman's dance performance called "Rosh Chodesh."

846. *The Tribe of Dina: a Jewish women's anthology.* Ed. Melanie Kaye/Kantrowicz and Irene Klepfisz; associate editor, Esther F. Hyneman. Rev. and expanded ed. Boston: Beacon Press, 1989. 360 p.

This fine collection of Jewish feminism contains essays and poetry on Jewish history and culture, Jewish foremothers, religious issues, Israel, and the Jewish heritage of working toward social justice. First published as an issue of *Sinister Wisdom* in 1986; for this edition the editors have added material in reponse to the Palestinian Intifada, pieces by Israeli women, Sephardic women, and working class women.

847. Trible, Phyllis. *Texts of Terror: literary-feminist readings of Biblical narratives.* Philadelphia: Fortress Press, 1984. 128 p.

With thorough scriptural documentation, Trible takes four Biblical women as models of women's oppression under patriarchal religion and society: Hagar, Sarah's handmaiden; Tamar, King David's daughter who was raped by her brother; the raped and murdered concubine of Judges 19; and Jephthah's sacrificed daughter. She does not paint a pretty picture.

848. Umansky, Ellen. "(Re)Imaging the Divine," *Response* (New York), 1982, no. 41-42, p. 110-119.

On the femininity of God in Judaism.

849. *Verdrängte Vergangenheit, die uns bedrängt: feministische Theologie in der Verantwortung für die Geschichte [A Repressed Past Which Oppresses Us: feminist theology taking responsibility for history].* Ed. Leonore Siegele-Wenschkewitz. Munich: Kaiser, 1988. 280 p.

A German conference on the tendency in Christian feminism, noticed by both Jewish and Christian women, towards anti-Judaism; contributors include Marie-Theres Wacker and Jewish feminist Susannah Heschel.

850. Voss-Goldstein, Christel. *Aus Ägypten rief ich meine Töchter: feministische Theologie praktisch [From Egypt I Called My*

Daughters: practical feminist theology]. Düsseldorf: Patmos Verlag, 1988. 117 p.

A handbook for forming a feminist theology group.

851. Vuola, Elina. *Uusi Nainen, Uusi Maa: Rosemary Radford Ruetherin feministinen teologia [New Women, New Earth: Rosemary Radford Ruether's feminist theology].* Helsinki: Tasa-arvoasiain neuvottelukunta, 1987. 145 p.

With a summary in Swedish.

852. Watkins, Keith. *Faithful and Fair: transcending sexist language in worship.* Nashville: Abingdon Press, 1981. 128 p.

A guide for seminaries on planning liturgy, with redactions of some of the Psalms in inclusive language.

853. Weber, Christin Lore. *Blessings: living a WomanChrist spirituality.* San Francisco: Harper and Row, 1989. 256 p.

Feminist theology, patterned after the Beatitudes.

854. Weber, Christin Lore. *WomanChrist: a new vision of feminist spirituality.* San Francisco: Harper and Row, 1987. 178 p.

Weber is a former nun who has experienced the profound power of the Goddess and the Great Mother while maintaining her ties to Christianity. Some readers may take issue with her rejection of the "masculine" within women, but this is a sincere book on the healing power of the Divine Feminine. Includes examples of woman-centered rituals and meditations.

855. Weems, Renita J. *Just a Sister Away: a womanist vision of women's relationships in the Bible.* San Diego: LuraMedia, 1988. 145 p.

A Black feminist discusses several Biblical women—e.g. Naomi and Ruth, Sarah and Hagar, Jephthah's sacrificed daughter—in ways that are relevant to Black women's experience. With study/disussion questions on ways to minister to the women in our lives.

856. Weiler, Gerda. *Ich verwerfe im Lande die Kriege: das verborgene Matriarchat im Alten Testament. [I Reject Wars in this Land: the hidden matriarchy of the Old Testament].*

2nd ed. Munich: Frauenoffensive, 1986. 422 p.

Like Raphael Patai, Weiler dispells the notion that the religion of the Hebrews was completely monotheistic and patriarchal. She discusses the matriarchal Queen of Heaven and her consort who are concealed in the Old Testament, the polytheistic nature of the religion of the early Hebrews, Mesopotamian influences in the Scriptures, the Biblical matriarchs, and the literal demonizing of non-Hebrew matriarchal peoples. "All war begins with the battle between the sexes," she warns.

857. Weiler, Gerda. *Das Matriarchat im Alten Israel.* Stuttgart: Kohlhammer, 1989. 368 p.

Essentially a revised edition of the above work, with a new afterword on the anti-Judaism that is apparent in some feminist theology.

858. Wilcox, Linda P. "The Mormon Concept of a Mother in Heaven," in: *Sisters in Spirit: Mormon women in historical and cultural perspective,* ed. Maureen U. Beecher and Lavina F. Anderson (Urbana: University of Illinois Press, 1987), p. 64-77.

859. Winter, Miriam Therese. *WomanPrayer, WomanSong: resources for ritual.* Oak Park, Ill.: Meyer Stone Books, 1987. 254 p.

Christian-based rituals and songs celebrating creation, liberation, transformation; illustrated by Meinrad Craighead. The music is available on cassette from Ladyslipper (see Resources section).

860. Winter, Miriam Therese. *WomanWisdom: a feminist lectionary and psalter: women of the Hebrew Scriptures, part one.* Illus. by Meinrad Craighead. New York: Crossroad, 1991. 367 p.

Divided into Matriarchs, Wives and Concubines, and Memorable Women (e.g. the Witch of Endor, Huldah the prophetess). The selection for each woman contains a biography and commentary, a Bible reading, points for discussion, and original psalms and prayers. Includes both well-known figures and women whom the texts barely mention—for example, the wives of Cain and Samson. This is a treasure trove for feminist Bible study.

861. Winter, Mirian Therese. *WomanWitness: a feminist lectionary and psalter: women of the Hebrew Scriptures, part two.* Illus. by Meinrad Craighead. New York: Crossroad, 1992.
Additional readings and psalms dedicated to women in the Old Testament.

862. Winter, Miriam Therese. *WomanWord: a feminist lectionary and psalter: women of the New Testament.* New York: Crossroad, 1990. 319 p.
Readings, commentary, psalms and prayers inspired by women of the New Testament, both famous and obscure.

863. *Women's Issues in Religious Education.* Ed. Fern M. Giltner. Birmingham, AL: Religious Education Press, 1985. 190 p.
Essays on herstory (or "Woman-story"), the needs of young women, sexuality, re-visioning religious develoment, and feminist perspectives on peace.

864. Wren, Brian. "Meeting the Awesome She," *Christian Century,* Feb. 17, 1988, p. 159.
While in the throes of sexual desire, Wren had an intense and vivid vision of God as female. He is strongly in favor of using feminine imagery of God as a way to re-value women and to see God in the humble.

865. Wren, Brian. *What Language Shall I Borrow?: God-talk in worship: a male response to feminist theology.* New York: Crossroad, 1989. 264 p.
On sexism in liturgical language, supportive of feminist goals in the use of inclusive terminology.

866. Zagano, Phyllis. "In Whose Image— feminist theology at the crossroads," *This World* (New York), Fall 1986, p.78-86.
Strongly critical of Ruether and the Women-Church movement, the author believes that focusing on the feminine will completely undermine Christianity.

Fiction and Fantasy Literature

In addition to feminist and mainstream fiction there is a huge body of fantasy and historical fiction featuring all sorts of witches, Amazon warriors, healers, and wise women. Included below is a broad selection of works that are inspired by or relevant to the feminist spirituality and feminist witchcraft movements.

867. Anderson, Poul and Karen. *Roma Mater*. New York: Baen Books, dist. by Simon and Schuster, 1986. (Book 1 of *The King of Ys*.) 461 p.

     The first novel in a series set in Roman-occupied Armorica (Brittany), about a man who is a member of the Mithraic religion and for political reasons is ritually married to the Gallicenae, nine priestess-queens who serve the Celtic goddess. The authors strove for as much authenticity as fiction would allow: besides several maps of the Celtic realms and the Roman Empire, the novel contains over 40 pages of notes on the history and culture of Rome and the Celts. The subsequent titles in the series are: *The Gallicenae, Dahut,* and *The Dog and the Wolf.*

868. Arthur, Elizabeth. *Binding Spell*. New York: Doubleday, 1988. 372 p.

     A novel set in rural Indiana about a young woman who is teaching herself witchcraft from *The Spiral Dance*, with an old Hungarian herbalist, a cast of other quirky characters and a lot of dogs. Witty, affectionate, and recommended.

869. Badenoch, Lindsay. *The Daughter of the Runes*. London; New York: Arkana, 1988. 229 p.

     A young pagan woman in 7th-century England is studying traditional Saxon magic at a time when Christian Northumberland is waging war across Britain. Written by an archaeologist who incorporates actual Anglo-Saxon poetry and charms into the text.

870. Baudino, Gael. *Strands of Starlight.* New York: Signet, 1989. 371 p.
A woman with healing powers fights persecution by the Inquisition with the help of pagan witches, Christians, and Elves.

871. Béguin, ReBecca. *Her Voice in the Drum (my name is womon).* Lichen Publications (Box 616, Hanover, NH 03755; printed by New Victoria Printers, New Lebanon, NH, now in Norwich, VT), 1980. 75 p.
A novella in the form of a prose-poem, written largely as a love letter to the author's lover by a woman who loves the Goddess and loves women.

872. Bogus, S. Diane Adams. *The Chant of the Women of Magdalena,* and *The Magdalena Poems.* San Francisco: Women in the Moon Publications, 1990. 120 p.
A narrative poem about an international group of women who escape from a 17th-century English jail and form a community called the Women of Magdalena, named after a healer among them. Also available on audio-cassette.

873. Bradley, Marion Zimmer. *The Firebrand.* New York: Simon and Schuster, 1987. 608 p.
A retelling of the *Iliad* from the point of view of Kassandra, daughter of Hecuba the Amazon Queen. After being educated by the Amazons, Kassandra assumes the duties of priestess of Apollo and witnesses the Trojan War (in this version she is not killed by Clytemnestra), as well as the eclipse of the Great Mother by the warrior sun gods.

874. Bradley, Marion Zimmer, ed. *Spells of Wonder.* New York: NAL/DAW, 1989. 288 p.
Feminist sword-and-sorcery stories, the majority by women.

875. Bradley, Marion Zimmer, ed. *Sword and Sorceress: an*

anthology of heroic fantasy. New York: DAW Books, 1984. 255 p.

Feminist tales of warrior women and enchantresses, by women and men, including well-known fantasy authors Phyllis Ann Karr, Charles R. Saunders (whose fine stories and books are inspired by African culture), Jennifer Roberson, and Pagan priestesses Anodea Judith and Diana L. Paxson.

876. Bradley, Marion Zimmer, ed. *Sword and Sorceress II.* New York: DAW Books, 1985. 287 p.

Stories by Diana L. Paxson, C. H. Cherryh, Charles Saunders, Rachel Pollack, and others.

877. Bradley, Marion Zimmer, ed. *Sword and Sorceress III.* New York: DAW Books, 1986. 284 p.

Authors include Paxson, Mercedes Lackey, Jennifer Roberson, Pagan priestess Morning Glory Zell, others.

878. Bradley, Marion Zimmer, ed. *Sword and Sorceress IV.* New York: DAW Books, 1987. 285 p.

Stories by eleven women and seven men.

879. Bradley, Marion Zimmer, ed. *Sword and Sorceress V.* New York: DAW Books, 1988. 284 p.

More stories by Paxson, Roberson, Lackey, Morning Glory Zell, and other women and men.

880. Bradley, Marion Zimmer, ed. *Sword and Sorceress VI.* New York: DAW Books, 1984. 255 p.

Authors includes Diana Paxson, Morning Glory Zell, Jennifer Roberson, Mercedes Lackey.

881. Bradley, Marion Zimmer, ed. *Sword and Sorceress VII.* New York: DAW Books, 1990. 288 p.

Twenty-five stories, most of them by women, including Diana Paxson, Mercedes Lackey.

882. Bradley, Marion Zimmer, ed. *Sword and Sorceress VIII.* New York: DAW Books, 1991. 285 p.

Twenty-two stories.

883. Bradley, Marion Zimmer, ed. *Sword and Sorceress IX.* New

York: DAW Books, 1992.

884. Bryan, Jessica. *Across a Wine-Dark Sea*. New York: Bantam Books, 1991. 355 p.

An Amazon travels to Atlantis and meets its king.

885. Burdekin, Katherine. *The End of This Day's Business*. Afterword by Daphne Patai. New York: Feminist Press at the City University of New York, 1989. 190 p.

A feminist utopian novel which was first published in 1935 yet is extraordinarily modern in its politics. In this story, set in a peaceful, prosperous, future Earth governed by women for 4,000 years, only women bear the knowledge of the past. One woman transgresses the law by relating our history to a young man who, like all males, has been kept ignorant of men's violent heritage. This is an ardently feminist novel, grounded in the anti-fascist movement of the 1930's, yet well aware of the tragic effects of patriarchal domination. Burdekin wrote many feminist and political novels, and spent most of her life with a woman companion.

886. Caldecott, Moyra. *Guardians of the Tall Stones: the sacred stones trilogy*. Berkeley: Celestial Arts, 1986. 521 p.

Three novels about the Stonehenge culture, first published separately in Britain: *The Tall Stones, The Temple of the Sun,* and *The Shadow on the Stones.*

887. Caldecott, Moyra. *Women in Celtic Myth: tales of extraordinary women from the ancient Celtic tradition.* London: Arrow, 1988; Rochester, VT: Destiny Books, 1992. 259 p.

The Stories of Welsh and Irish goddesses and heroines, including Rhiannon, Arianrhod, Etain, Emer, Macha, the Morrigan, Deirdre, Grania, and others.

888. Cameron, Anne. *Dzelarhons: myths of the Northwest coast.* Madeira Park, BC: Harbour Publishing, 1986. 160 p.

Stories inspired by those told to the author as a child by a Salish Indian woman: myths about Raven and Orca, Spider Woman, Dzelarhons the First Mother, and the powerful Bearded Woman.

889. Cameron, Anne. *Tales of the Cairds*. Madeira Park, B. C. :

Harbour Publishing, 1989. 191 p.

Traditional tales, reworked in Cameron's delightful feminist style, drawn from the nomadic Celtic Cairds (the Irish tinkers), who travelled throughout Britain, Scandinavia, and Spain and are said to have survived to the 19th century. The tales are of animals, clever women, and Celtic goddesses, especially Banba, the Mother Goddess of Ireland. Appended is a glossary of the various Celtic sprites, fairies, and other spirit-beings found in folklore.

890. Chernin, Kim. *The Flame Bearers*. New York: Random House, 1986. 275 p.

A novel about a hereditary sect of women healers which has kept alive the worship of the Goddess within Judaism from pre-Hebraic Canaanite times to the present. The story is less about the shadowy sect itself than about the struggle of Rae, the young protagonist, who for years has fought to distance herself from her family and heritage, only to find that she has been named the successor to the leader of the cult.

891. D'Ambrosio, Margaret. *Meggie's Journeys*. London: Polygon Books; dist. in the U.S. by Dufour Editions, 1987. 175 p.

A young Celtic girl journeys via dreams and imagination to the world of the Goddess and the fairy-folk (the Sidhe).

892. Duane, Diane. *The Door into Shadow*. New York: Bluejay Books, 1984. 298 p.

Fantasy fiction set on a world dedicated to a Goddess whose adversary is the Shadow. A sorceress/warrior is the protagonist. This novel is the sequel to *The Door into Fire*.

893. Fallingstar, Cerridwen. *The Heart of the Fire*. San Geronimo, CA: Cauldron Publications, 1990. 521 p.

Novel about a Celtic girl learning the Old Ways from her mother, the village coven's leader. She falls in love with women and men and is imperilled by the witch-hunts. This novel is based on the author's "far memory" of a past life.

894. Frye, Ellen. *The Other Sappho*. Ithaca, NY: Firebrand Books, 1989. 214 p.

A young Greek woman studies poetry with Sappho while struggling to know herself as a daughter of the pre-Olympian

Great Mother. In this version, Sappho is an egotistical woman who knows nothing of the Great Goddess.

895. Galford, Ellen. *The Fires of Bride*. Ithaca, NY: Firebrand Books, 1988 (first published: London: Women's Press, 1986). 229 p.

Humorous novel in which a contemporary Scottish woman goes to a remote island and encounters unexpected love and the remnants of goddess worship, by the author of *Moll Cutpurse*.

896. Garcia y Robertson, R. *The Spiral Dance*. New York: Morrow, 1991. 227 p.

No doubt with a nod to Starhawk, this is a historical novel of 16th-century Scotland featuring witchcraft and the English fairy faith, by a historian who adds an afterword on the witch-hunts. He estimates that in 16th- and 17th-century Scotland it was about as common for a woman to be executed for witchcraft as it is for a 20th-century woman to die in an automobile crash.

897. Gibson, Roberta. *Home Is the Heart*. Santa Fe: Bear & Co., 1989. 158 p.

A story about a woman's fight with cancer, inspired by a friend of the author. The protagonist works at healing both spirit and body via Native American wisdom. With an afterword by Brooke Medicine Eagle on conducting a women's moon-lodge and the importance of our moon-time.

898. Grahn, Judy. *Mundane's World*. Freedom, CA: The Crossing Press, 1988. 191 p.

The story of the daily life and coming of age of five girls in a mythical matriarchal society.

899. Grahn, Judy. *The Queen of Swords*. Boston: Beacon Press, 1987. 192 p.

A poetic drama which places the Sumerian goddess Inanna in the underworld of a lesbian bar.

900. Gregory, Roberta. *Winging It*. Solo Productions (Box 3335, Van Nuys, CA 91407), 1988. 156 p.

A feminist comic book about a woman seeking spirituality beyond conventional Christianity, written as a science fiction story featuring aliens, demons, and friendly dolphins.

901. Hambly, Barbara. *The Ladies of Mandrigyn.* New York: Ballantine Books, 1984. 311 p.
    Sword and sorcery novel featuring a woman warrior named Starhawk.

902. Jong, Erica. *Fanny: being the true history of the adventures of Fanny Hackabout-Jones.* New York: New American Library, 1980. 505 p.
    A pastiche *Fanny Hill,* written in pseudo-18th-century English, about a woman who, among other things, is initiated into a traditional witch coven, enters a London brothel, meets various historical figures of 18th-century England, and goes to sea. In the course of the novel she comments on witchcraft as a revolt by oppressed women and on the decline of female midwifery.

903. Joseph, Jenny. *Persephone.* Newcastle upon Tyne, Eng.: Bloodaxe Books, 1986; dist. by Dufour Editions, Chester Springs, PA. 294 p.
    The story of Demeter's search for Persephone is woven through grim vignettes of the life of a contemporary English woman, using poetry, prose, drama, and a photo essay.

904. Kaplický, Václav. *Witch Hammer.* Tucson: Harbinger House, 1990.
    An historical novel—the title comes from the notorious witchfinders' handbook, the *Malleus Maleficarum*—based on an actual witch-craze episode in 17th-century Moravia. This gripping and tragic story was first published in in 1963 Czechoslovakia, where it was filmed in 1969.

905. Kernaghan, Eileen. *The Sarsen Witch.* New York: Ace Books, 1987. 217 p.
    A novel about the building of Stonehenge, featuring conflict between a young woman seer of the Neolithic, Goddess-worshipping tribes and patriarchal Bronze Age warriors. Strong period detail.

906. Kim, Dong-Ni (Tongni). *The Shaman Sorceress.* New York:

KPI (Routledge), 1989. 156 p.

A translation of a Korean novel about a woman who practices traditional shamanism while her son tries to convert her to Christianity; not an uncommon phenomenon in modern South Korea, where Christianity is fervently embraced by the middle class, but women often find a modicum of empowerment through the practice of traditional shamanism and spirit mediumship.

907. Kinstler, Clysta. *The Moon Under Her Feet.* San Francisco: Harper and Row, 1989. 315 p.

Shades of *The Satanic Verses!* In a sacred marriage rite in the Jerusalem Temple, priestess Almah Mari becomes pregnant with the twins Seth (Judas) and Yeshua; as an adult, Yeshua conceives a daughter in a similar rite with the novel's narrator, Mari Anath, the Magdalene or High Priestess of the Goddess. Written by a philosophy professor, this novel includes a bibliography and references as evidence for the worship of the Great Goddess in the Holy Land.

908. Kurtz, Katherine. *Lammas Night.* New York: Ballantine Books, 1983. 438 p.

According to Doreen Valiente and Gerald Gardner, revivers of British witchcraft, in 1940 a witch coven raised a cone of power to prevent Hitler's invasion of England. (This was apparently the inspiration for the children's book and Disney film *Bedknobs and Broomsticks.*) The power raised by the witches was so intense that at least one coven member died. Fantasy author Kurtz has turned this story into a World War II thriller, in which the ritual takes place on Lammas (August 1), a European pagan holyday and rite of the corn god's sacrifice.

909. Lessing, Doris. *The Marriages Between Zones Three, Four, and Five (as narrated by the chroniclers of Zone Three).* New York: Knopf, 1980. 244 p.

Part of Lessing's science fiction series "Canopus in Argos," this novel features the queen of Zone Three, a peaceful, matrifocal society, who must marry a man from the militaristic Zone Four. They are both nonplussed when the man must also marry a warrior woman from the barbaric Zone Five.

910. Littlepage, Layne. *Wonkers.* New York: Dutton, 1990.

294 p.

A humorous novel in which a feminist woman experiences a "Hormonic Convergence" in a women's spirituality circle and is transformed into a man. The author mercilessly skewers feminism, gay men, "sensitive" men, Wicca, and the New Age.

911. Marchessault, Jovette. *Lesbian Triptych*. Toronto: Women's Press, 1985 (translation of *Triptyque lesbian*, Montreal: L'Éditions de la Pleine Lune, 1980). 100 p.

Contains an introductory essay by Barbara Godard, three stories by Marchessault, and a "Postface" by Gloria Feman Orenstein, who analyzes Marchessault's writing as an example of the lesbian imagination asserting itself under patriarchal Catholic domination, where it recreates the Mother Goddess culture of autonomous womanhood.

912. Marchessault, Jovette. *Mother of the Grass*. Vancouver: Talonbooks, 1989. (Translation of *La Mère des herbes*, Montreal: Quinze, 1980, which has an introduction by Gloria Orenstein). 173 p.

The second part of Marchessault's autobiographical trilogy, in which a child comes to see her grandmother (*grand-mère*) as an embodiment of the Great Mother (*la Grande-Mère*).

913. Mark, Teressa. *She Changes: a goddess myth for modern women*. Oak Park, Ill.: Delphi Press, 1991. 223 p.

A fictionalized story of a nun studying midwifery in the Appalachians who finds a new spirituality among the traditional healers and local witches, causing her to reject both male-defined medicine and the Catholic Church.

914. Mielke, Thomas R.P. *Inanna: Odyssee einer Göttin [Inanna: odyssey of a goddess]*. Munich: Schneekluth, 1990. 521 p.

Inanna's own story, from the fall of Atlantis ten thousand years ago.

915. Mitchison, Naomi. *The Corn King and the Spring Queen*. London: Virago, 1983; Overlook Press, 1990 (first published in 1933). 719 p.

Historical fiction about a third century B.C.E. Scythian

priestess/witch who is compelled to become Spring Queen to a tribal Corn King and also becomes involved with a ship-wrecked Spartan. This is such a long and complex story that the author adds genealogies and a summary of events after each section of the novel.

916. Monroe, Judith W. *Widdershins*. Durham, NC: Crone's Own Press, 1989. 227 p.
A whimsical story about a budding feminist coven in Maine whose members work to stop unscrupulous land developers.

917. Mushroom, Merril. *Daughters of Khaton*. Denver: Lace Publications, 1987. 132 p.
A science fiction story of a group of space explorers who land on a peaceful, paradisaical, all-female planet.

918. Orlock, Carol. *The Goddess Letters: the Demeter-Persephone myth retold*. New York: St. Martin's Press, 1987. 220 p.
A wry and wistful epistolary novel of Demeter and Persephone, which follows them from prehistoric times to the closing of the temple at Eleusis in the fourth century C.E.

919. Paxson, Diana L. *White Mare, Red Stallion*. New York: Berkeley Books, 1986. 242 p.
Historical fantasy set among the Pagan Gaels of Scotland; the protagonist is a chieftain's daughter who battles both Romans and enemy clans.

920. Rinser, Luise. *Mirjam*. Frankfurt am Main: Fischer, 1983. 331 p.
By a one-time Green Party candidate for the presidency of West Germany, this novel is about a feminist Mary Magdalene who follows a non-violent Jeschua (Jesus). To my knowledge it has not yet been translated into English.

921. Roessner, Michaela. *Walkabout Woman*. New York: Bantam Books, 1988. 276 p.
The friendship between a Welsh witch and an Australian Aboriginal woman who wants to pursue traditional shamanism.

922. Rominski, F. Zarod. *Seven Windows: stories of women.* Durham, NC: Crone's Own Press, 1985. 151 p.

Stories about women and witches.

923. Salterberg, B.J. *The Outlander: Captivity.* Tucson: Harbinger, 1989. 293 p.

"A defector from a militaristic patriarchal society falls into the hands of a matriarchal warrior woman" and thereby upsets the apple cart. Followed by *The Outlander: Quest* (1991).

924. Schuler, Laura Lay. *She Who Remembers.* New York: Arbor House, 1988. 400 p.

A novel about a woman of the Anasazi culture, which flourished in the American Southwest a thousand years ago. She becomes a priestess and encounters both Viking explorers and the Toltecs of Mexico.

925. Simpson, Elizabeth Léonie. *I, Lilith.* Brooklyn: The Smith, 1991. 176 p.

Sardonic autobiography of Lilith: how she left her domineering yet spineless husband Adam and set off on the path to perversity.

926. Stirling, S. M., and Shirley Meier. *The Sharpest Edge.* New York: Signet/NAL, 1986. 255 p.

Sword-and-sorcery novel featuring a lesbian couple.

927. Sunlight. *Womonseed: a vision.* Little River, CA: Tough Dove Books, 1986. 231 p.

A collection of linked stories, written with gentleness and love, of women coming together onto women's land in the late 1990's to create a truly woman-identified, multicultural society. Very characteristic of lesbian-feminist culture of the early 1980's.

928. Thomas, Elizabeth Marshall. *Reindeer Moon.* Boston: Houghton-Mifflin, 1987. 338 p.

Engrossing novel about a young woman in Paleolithic Siberia whose people are matrilineal and goddess-worshipping. The author is an anthropologist who worked for many years among the South African Bushmen. Her experience and research provide her with an intimate knowledge of the patterns of hunting-gathering life that makes *Reindeer Moon* far superior to most fiction of this genre. The story of some of the characters is continued in *The Animal Wife* (Houghton Mifflin, 1990), which is related by a young man who captures a woman from a strange tribe and tries to come to terms with their differences.

929. Warren, Patricia Nell. *One Is the Sun.* New York: Ballantine Books, 1991. 535 p.

A Native American medicine woman, a priestess from the remnants of the Mayan civilization, and a German woman whose grandmother wants her to learn the Old Ways, come together in the 19th-century American West.

930. Warrior, Marada [Ma Ra] Heart. *And the Truth Will Be Told by the Yearning of the Warrior Spirit.* Woman Warrior of the Heart (Box 551, Fairfax, CA 94978), 1991. 149 p.

Novel about a Black woman's struggle with her family as she studies with a woman teacher resembling the author, a spiritual teacher who believes she has attained Enlightenment in this incarnation.

931. Williams, Maureen. "Moon Time," *Broomstick* 11(3):3-10; May-June 1989.

Short story about a woman who learns from a friend of Native American/Welsh descent how to make her hobby of basket-weaving into an art that reflects women's ancient knowledge.

932. Wolf, Joan. *Daughter of the Red Deer.* New York: Dutton, 1991. 420 p.

A novel of the Ice Age in which a group of men, whose patriarchal tribe has lost all its female members, capture women from a matriarchal people, causing the transformation of both societies.

933. Woolley, Persia. *Child of the Northern Spring.* New York: Poseidon Press, 1987. 428 p.; *Queen of the Summer Stars.* New York: Poseidon Press, 1990. 415 p.

First two parts of an Arthurian trilogy, emphasizing the conflicts among Pagan and Christian, Briton, Saxon, and Pict.

The second novel is narrated by Guinevere, priestess and queen. In Woolley's retelling, Morgan Le Fey is a priestess of the Goddess but still the villain of the story.

934. Yolen, Jane. *Sister Light, Sister Dark*. New York: T. Doherty Associates, 1988. 244 p.

Sword and sorcery novel about a young girl who is raised in a clan of women warriors who regard her as an incarnation of the Goddess, set in a land where patriarchal tribes have overthrown the Goddess-worshipping people. Includes music and lyrics for several songs of the warrior women. The sequel is *White Jenna* (1989).

935. Zahava, Irene, ed. *Hear the Silence: stories by women of myth, magic & renewal*. Trumansburg, NY: The Crossing Press, 1986. 194 p.

An anthology encompassing several literary genres, including science fiction by Merlin Stone, mythic tales by Anne Cameron, Kitty Tsui, and Deena Metzger, Ursula LeGuin's anti-Genesis "She Unnames Them," and early sections from Judy Grahn's *Mundane's World*.

936. Zipes, Jack, ed. *Don't Bet on the Prince: contemporary feminist fairy tales in North America and England*. New York: Methuen, 1986. 270 p.

Literary criticism and modern feminist fairy tales—one section for children and one for adults—with contributions by Margaret Atwood, Tanith Lee, Anne Sexton, Jane Yolen, Olga Broumas, Joanna Russ, Angela Carter, others.

Children's Literature

The following titles represent a selection of the many children's books that have arisen from the Goddess, Wiccan, and New Age communities, in particular those works most relevant to feminist spirituality. Each book is identified according to age group, which of course are only suggestions, as people read at varying levels. Many of the Young Adult novels, for instance, can be enjoyed by us older adults as well, and teenagers often read adult fantasy fiction.

Books and Tapes

937. Adler, David A. *I Know I'm a Witch.* Illus. by Suçie Stevenson. New York: Henry Holt, 1988. [30] p.
    A gently humorous story of a little girl who *knows* she's a witch and tries to use magic to make her aunt less annoying. Ages 4-7.

938. Amber K. *Pagan Kids' Activity Book.* Moonstone Publications (Box 176, Blue Mounds, WI 53517), 1985. 32 p.
    A coloring book of pictures and activities for children growing up in Pagan families. Images of the Goddess and God, Sabbats, "Put the Moon Phases in Order," maze games, Pagan vocabulary. Ages 5-10.

939. Amber K, and Muriel Mizach Shemesh. *The Picture Book of Goddesses.* Nine Candles Publications (Box 93, Mt. Horeb, WI 53572), 1988. 32 p.
    A simple but elegant coloring book by two Wiccan priestesses showing goddesses from many cultures, with a brief

description of each. Suitable for instruction. Ages 6-10.

940. Anderson, Margaret J. *The Druid's Gift*. New York: Knopf, 1989. 211 p.

Novel about a girl who lives on a Scottish island in Druidic times, is able to time-travel, and mediates between Druids and non-Druids. Ages 10-14.

941. Beechsquirrel, Nicola. *Mother Earth's Colouring and Story Book*. Available from Pagan Parenting Network, Blaenberem, Mynyddcerrig, near Llanelli, Dyfed, Wales. 16 p.

Eleven illustrations of Pagan folk and two Pagan-themed pieces: "Song of the Rainspirits" and "Jack Frost and Jack-in-the-Green." Ages 5-10.

942. Bennett, Anna Elizabeth. *Little Witch*. Philadelphia: Lippincott, 1953; New York: Scholastic Book Services, 1961. 116 p.

A story about a girl raised by an ill-natured witch—a resourceful girl who knows some magic herself. (Perhaps my earliest foray into witchcraft occurred when I was ten and tried to imitate little Minx by tossing kitchen herbs into a pot on the stove.) Ages 8-12.

943. Birrer, Cynthia and William. *Song to Demeter*. New York: Lathrop, Lee & Shepard Books, 1987. 32 p.

A very abbreviated version of the Demeter-Persephone story, concentrating on the seasonal aspect and illustrated with needlework illuminations. Ages 3-7.

944. Bourdillon, Hilary. *Women as Healers: a history of women and medicine*. Cambridge, Eng.; New York: Cambridge University Press, 1988. 48 p.

A history of women in Western medicine, from the healing goddesses of the ancient Near East to modern surgeons, with a distinctly feminist perspective. Chapters on the traditional healer in the Middle Ages, the decline of midwifery, and witchcraft and the Burning Times as misogynistic suppression of the wise-woman healers. Designed for use as a textbook for junior high or high school.

945. Bridwell, Norman. *The Witch Next Door*. New York: Scho-

lastic, Inc. 1986 (first published 1965). 30 p.

Delightful picture book about a cheerful neighborhood witch and her friendship with two children. The message, possibly inspired by the civil rights movement, is that how someone treats others is more important than what they are. Highly recommended. Other witch books by Bridwell are: *The Witch Grows Up* (New York: Scholastic, 1979); *The Witch's Catalog* (Scholastic, 1976); *The Witch's Christmas* (Scholastic, 1970); and *The Witches' Vacation* (Scholastic, 1973).

946. Budapest, Zsuzsanna (Z). *Selene, the most famous bull-leaper on earth.* Illus. by Carol Clement; edited by Helen Beardwoman. Oakland, CA: Diana Press, 1976. 52 p.

A charming story of a young girl who travels from Greece to her mother's native land of Crete, where she learns the sacred rite of bull-leaping. This book is out of print but should be available through libraries. My daughter has loved it from age three.

947. Cameron, Anne. *Spider Woman.* Madeira Park, BC: Harbour Pub. Co., 1988. 27 p.

The story of the Native American goddess's creation of the world, alternating text and illustrations. Ages 4-8.

948. Cazet, Denys. *Mother Night.* New York: Orchard Books, 1989. 32 p.

Dreams and the beauty of the night. Ages 3-6.

949. Collins, Meghan. *The Willow Maiden.* Illus. by Laszlo Gal. New York: Dial Books for Young Readers, 1985. 40 p.

A young man meets the Willow Folk and marries one of their number; a variation on the folktale theme of the fairy-wife. Ages 5-8.

950. Cope, Wendy. *The River Girl.* Illus. by Nicholas Garland. Boston: Faber and Faber, 1991. 52 p.

Isis, the daughter of the British river god Father Thames, falls in love with a human man. (Isis is the name of a tributary of the Thames River.) Age 12 and up.

951. *The Daughter of the Moon and the Son of the Sun.* Translated

from the Russian by Eve Manning; illus. by G. Yurdin. Moscow: Progress Publishers, 1976; available from Imported Publications, 320 W. Ohio St., Chicago, Ill. 60610. 16 p.

Brilliantly colored folk designs tell the story of the Moon's daughter, who is wooed by Sunbeam but loves only the eldest of the Northern Lights. Ages 4-8.

952. De Paola, Tomie. *The Legend of the Bluebonnet: an old tale of Texas*. New York: Putnam, 1983. 30 p.

A retelling of the Comanche legend of a girl who sacrifices her doll to the gods in order to end a drought and save her tribe. Ages 5-8.

953. De Paola, Tomie. *Strega Nona: an old tale*. Englewood Cliffs, N.J.: Prentice-Hall, 1975. 32 p.

A traditional Italian tale about kindly Strega Nona ("Grandma Witch") and her magic cauldron which produces an endless supply of spaghetti. Winner of the Caldecott medal. Also available as an audiocassette and on video. Ages 3-7.

954. De Paola, Tomie. *Strega Nona's Magic Lessons*. New York: Harcourt Brace Jovanovich, 1982. 32 p.

Strega Nona takes on two apprentices, a girl who pays attention, and Big Anthony, who disguises himself as a girl ("Who ever heard of a man being a *strega*?") but can't get any of the magic right. Ages 3-7.

955. Dillon, Mary, with Shinan Barclay. *Flowering Woman: moontime for Kory: a story of a girl's rites of passage into womanhood*. Illus. by Elizabeth Manley; foreword by Vicki Noble. Sunlight Productions (Box 1300, Sedona, AZ 86336), 1988. 45 p.

A girl named Kory, who lives in a goddess- and woman-loving society of long ago, is assisted at her menarche by friends, relatives, and a wise dolphin. Includes a glossary of menstruation terms and a bibliography. Ages 10-13.

956. Douglas, Marjie. *Matrix Witch*. Minneapolis: Dillon Press, 1988. 285 p.

A teenage white witch is threatened by an evil witch. Age 12 and up.

957. *The Enchanted Forest: a mystical roadmap for children.* New York: New Moon Entertainment, 1987. 9 v.

Each issue contains an episode of an interactive fantasy story, which instructs the reader in psychic development, the principles of Wiccan magic, and personal growth. Also available is the Enchanted Forest Magickal Tools Kit, to be used in conjunction with the story, containing a Book of Shadows, a crystal, a wand, and a pentacle ring.

958. Esbensen, Barbara Juster. *The Star Maiden: an Ojibway tale.* Illus. by Helen K. Davie. Boston: Little, Brown, 1988. 32 p.

A picture book version of a Native American story. The Star Maiden comes down from the spirit world to live among the Ojibway, taking the form of the water lily. Ages 4-8.

959. Fast, Suellen M. *Celebrations of Daughterhood: poetry for young girls.* Ed. Gina L. Sherman. Rev. 2nd. ed. Capitola, CA: Daughter Culture Publications, 1988. 73 p.

Poems about the Goddess and women's strength, to remind girls of the feminine divine.

960. Furlong, Monica. *Wise Child.* New York: Knopf, 1987. 228 p.

A British novel set in mediaeval Scotland about an abandoned girl, Wise Child, who is raised and trained by a wise-woman herbalist. The author, who has written many books about the Anglican Church, presents a very positive view of paganism. Age 9 and up.

961. Goble, Paul. *Buffalo Woman.* Scarsdale: Bradbury Press, 1984. 32 p.

The Plains Indian legend of a hunter who marries a buffalo cow. When she transforms herself into a woman, he asks to be changed into a buffalo himself in order to be with her forever. Ages 5-8.

962. Goldblatt, Eli. *Lissa and the Moon's Sheep.* Illus. by Laura Marshall. Tucson: Harbinger House, 1990. 48 p.

Fairy tale of "a girl who journeys to shear the Moon's sheep to renew the Earth and her village."

963. Griffin, Sarah Ure. *Earth Circles.* New York: Walker, 1989.

28 p.

Together a mother and daughter discover the cycles of nature. Ages 4-8.

964. Harrison, Michael. *Scolding Tongues: the persecution of "witches."* Cheltenham, Eng.: Stanley Thornes Ltd., 1986. 52 p.

A textbook for middle-school/junior-high students, emphasising critical thinking skills to evaluate the evidence for witchcraft used in the trials of the Burning Times. Harrison relates the story of an actual witchcraft case, using photographs of the English town in which the proceedings took place. A very thorough treatment of the witch-hunts, useful for any course on the history of European witchcraft.

965. Hawthorne, Teri Berthiaume, and Diane Berthiaume Brown. *Many Faces of the Great Mother: a Goddess coloring book for all ages.* St Paul: Tara Educational Services, 1987. 44 p.

Two sisters, both mothers, have put together re-creations of famous goddess images, as well as some original ones, from the ancient world, the Americas, Asia, and Africa. Illustrations by Brown with text on facing pages. For older readers.

966. Heslewood, Juliet. *Earth, Air, Fire and Water.* Oxford, Eng.; New York: Oxford University Press, 1985. 181 p.

International myths and folktales on the primordial elements (e.g. Persephone as symbol of Earth). Ages 9-12.

967. Hollander, Scott. *My First A-B-C: a primer for Wiccan children.* Green Egg, Box 1542, Ukiah, CA 95482. 32 p.

A coloring book for Pagan children, utilizing the lore and symbols of Wicca.

968. Hoover, H. M. (Helen) *The Dawn Palace: the story of Medea.* New York: Dutton, 1988. 244 p.

A retelling of Medea's story from a feminist, matriarchal perspective. In this version, set ca. 1300 B.C.E., Medea learned in her girlhood to be a priestess of the Goddess, under the direction of the great magician Circe. In an afterword Hoover points out that there were many ancient writings about Medea, but until Euripides in the 5th century B.C.E. none portrayed her as a murderess. Recommended as a prelude to the works of Mary Renault. Young adults.

969. Joyce, Susan. *Naro, the Ancient Spider: the creation of the universe.* Illus. by D.C. DuBosque. Molalla, OR: Peel Productions, 1991. 29 p.
A Polynesian myth of the spider goddess who created the world.

970. Kane, Herb Kawainui. *Pele: goddess of Hawaii's volcanoes.* Captain Cook, Hawaii: Kawainui Press, 1987. 63 p.

971. Kehret, Peg. *Sisters, Long Ago.* New York: Cobblehill Books, 1990. 149 p.
While her sister is dying of leukemia, thirteen-year-old Willow has flashbacks to a past life in Egypt. She investigates reincarnation and past-life regression, has a falling-out with her Christian best friend, but ultimately is able to come to terms with death. Age 10 and up.

972. Kolkmeyer, Alexandra. *The Clear Red Stone: a myth and the meaning of menstruation.* In Sight Press (535 Cordova Rd., Suite 228, Santa Fe, NM 87501), 1982. 64 p.
A story about 13-year-old Cayenne who goes on a quest to learn why she bleeds, meeting Mother Earth and animal helpers on the way. The second half of the book explains the physiology of menstruation.

973. Lattimore, Deborah Nourse. *The Prince and the Golden Ax: a Minoan tale.* New York: Harper and Row, 1988. 40 p.
An arrogant prince on the Minoan island of Thera (Santorini) comes up against the goddess Diktynna. Ages 5-8.

974. Lobby, Theodore. *Jessica and the Wolf: a story for children who have bad dreams.* New York: Magination Press, 1990. 32 p.
A little girl fights her nightmares. Ages 4-10.

975. Mariechild, Diane, with Shuli Goodman. *Motherwit for Children.* [audiocassette] Aquila C-6. Available from Ladyslipper, Box 3124-R, Durham, NC 27715.
Meditations for children from Diane's adult book

Motherwit: a feminist guide to psychic development (The Crossing Press, 1981), with music by Kay Gardner.

976. Mayer, Marianna. *Iduna and the Magic Apples.* Illus. by Laszlo Gal. New York: Macmillan, 1988. 40 p.

Beautiful drawings tell the story of the Norse goddess whose apples give immortality to the gods.

977. McCaffrey, Kevin. *Deirdre and Other Heroines of Celtic Folklore.* Dublin: Fitzwilliam, 1989. 41 p.

978. McClain, Gary. *The Indian Way: learning to communicate with Mother Earth.* Santa Fe: John Muir; dist. by Norton, 1990. 103 p.

Each full moon two Arapaho children listen to their grandfather tell a story with an ecological theme. With appendix of seasonal activities to do with children, based on the stories. Ages 6-12.

979. McDermott, Beverly Brodsky. *Sedna: an Eskimo myth.* New York: Viking Press, 1975. 30 p.

The story of Sedna, mistress of animals who live in the sea. Ages 4-8.

980. Minard, Rosemary, ed. *Womenfolk and Fairy Tales.* Boston: Houghton Mifflin, 1975. 163 p.

Tales of heroic women and girls from Europe and Asia, including favorites like "East of the Sun, West of the Moon," and many lesser-known stories. Ages 6-10.

981. Moulton, Charles. *Wonder Woman.* Introd. by Gloria Steinem; interpretive essay by Phyllis Chesler. New York: Holt, Rinehart and Winston, and Warner Books, 1972.

The classic comic book, with a contemporary feminist analysis.

982. Phelps, Ethel Johnston. *The Maid of the North: feminist folk tales from around the world.* New York: Holt, Rinehart and Winston, 1981. 176 p.

Wise women, brave queens, and resourceful heroines in fairy and folk tales from the British Isles, Africa, Japan, India, Native America, Scandinavia, Russia, and Persia.

983. Phelps, Ethel Johnston, ed. *Tatterhood and Other Tales: stories of magic and adventure.* Illus. by Pamela Baldwin-Ford. Old Westbury, NY: Feminist Press, 1978. 165 p.

Strong heroines in traditional folk and fairy tales from many cultures: Celtic, Norse, African, Chinese, Incan, Native American, Indian. With an introduction and background notes for adults. Age 6 and up.

984. Pierce, Meredith Ann. *The Woman Who Loved Reindeer.* Boston: Joy Street Books/Little Brown and Co., 1985. 242 p.

An unusual fantasy novel of a Lapp-like culture, centered on a young wise woman whose destiny is entwined with that of a spirit-being who can take both human and reindeer form. Recommended. Young adult.

985. Pierce, Tamora. *The Woman Who Rides Like a Man.* New York: Atheneum, 1986 (her *Song of the Lioness*, book 3). 253 p.; *Lioness Rampant.* New York: Atheneum, 1988 (*Song of the Lioness,* book 4). 320 p.

Sword-and-sorcery novels set in a quasi-mediaeval world. The first two novels, *Alanna: the first adventure,* and *In the Hands of the Goddess,* were described in *Feminist Spirituality and the Feminine Divine.* In Book 3, young Alanna, now a knight-errant, encounters a desert society in which women are kept veiled and oppressed. She becomes the tribe's shaman and is able to help the women before riding off to her next adventure. Young Adult.

986. Plume, Ilse. *The Story of Befana: an Italian Christmas tale.* Boston: D.R. Godine, 1981; also published as *The Christmas Witch* (New York: Hyperion, 1991). 27 p.

Befana is the Italian good fairy who brings gifts at Epiphany. Ages 5-8.

987. Robbins, Trina. *Catswalk: the growing of Girl.* Berkeley: Celestial Arts, 1990. 64 p.

Her name is Girl, and she is raised by a grey Great Cat named Mother, as they follow a mysterious map through ancient Mesopotamia. Ages 5-8.

988. Rohmer, Harriet, and Mary Anchondo. *Skyworld Woman/La Mujer del Mundo-Cielo.* San Francisco: Children's Book

Press, 1975. 21 p.

A myth of a native Philippine creatrix, in a bilingual edition.

989. Russ, Joanna. *Kittatinny: a tale of magic*. New York: Daughters Publishing Co., 1978. 92 p.

A young girl learns lessons of womanhood from a woman warrior, a mermaid, a sleeping beauty, and a satyr.

990. San Souci, Robert D. *Song of Sedna*. Illus. by Daniel San Souci. Garden City, NY: Doubleday, 1981. 32 p.

Picture book about the Inuit goddess who guards the sea animals. Ages 5-10.

991. Shahastra. *The Crystal Goddess*. Magical Rainbow Publications (Box 717, Ojai, CA 93023), 1983. 61 p.

Illustrated story in which the Magical Rainbow Man rescues the Crystal Goddess from a cloud of bad thought. She then teaches children about the power of crystals. Ages 5-8.

992. Sherman, Josepha. *Swept Away*. New York: Fawcett/Columbine, 1988. (Part 1 of *The Secret of the Unicorn Queen*).

An ordinary teenage girl is magically transported to a world where women warriors battle to save the unicorns from demons and giants. Age 11 and up.

993. Shyer, Marlene Fanta. *Ruby, the Red-Hot Witch at Bloomingdale's*. New York: Viking, 1991. 160 p.

A sister and brother whose parents have separated are befriended by a kindly witch they meet at Bloomingdale's department store in New York City. Ages 9-12.

994. Singer, Marcia. *Crystal Kids P.L.A.Y.book: healing arts, metaphysics, meditations, crystals*. Illus. by Camille Randal. Pacific Palisades, Calif.: P.L.A.Y. Books; available from P.L.A.Y.house, attn. Marcia Singer, 4376 Stewart Ave., Los Angeles, CA 90066-6134; distributed by New Leaf, Bookpeople, etc.

Crystal activities, meditations, songs.

995. Spretnak, Charlene. *Lost Goddesses of Early Greece: a collection of pre-Hellenic myths*. New ed. Boston: Beacon

Press, 1984. 132 p.

Favorite myths of the Greek goddesses, reconstructed from pre-patriarchal evidence to show the deities as powerful, loving and whole (e.g. Pandora is not the origin of evil but lives up to her name of "All Gifts," Persephone goes down into the Underworld of her own accord, etc.). Spretnak describes each goddess as she appears in Olympian mythology, then retells her story. The myths themselves can be read aloud to children. Age 6 and up.

996. Strichartz, Naomi. *The Wisewoman.* Pictures by Ella Miller Moore. Cranehill Press (708 Comfort Rd., Spencer, NY 14883), 1986. 43 p.

Two children who have moved to the country become friends with a wise old woman who shares her knowledge of herbs, Tarot, and celebrating the seasons. Ages 7-10.

997. Strichartz, Naomi. *The Wisewoman's Sacred Wheel of the Year.* Pictures by Ella Moore. Cranehill Press (708 Comfort Rd., Spencer, NY 14883), 1988. 48 p.

Young Amber amd Jesse celebrate May Day, Bridget's Day, and Spring Equinox with their wise-woman friend, who tells them stories of nature and of powerful women and girls from long ago.

998. Walker, Mary Alexander. *The Scathach and Maeve's Daughters.* New York: Atheneum, 1990. 119 p.

In 8th-century Scotland, 12th-century England, 18th-century Canada, and present-day New York City, four girls named Maeve are aided by the Scathach (literally, "Shadow"), an Amazon who appears in ancient Irish literature. These are stories of female courage and survival. Young Adults.

999. Watson, Clyde. *Midnight Moon.* Cleveland: Collins, 1979. 24 p.

Poetry about the Man in the Moon and Mother Sun. Age 3 and up.

1000. Weber, Andy, and Nigel Wellings; text by Jon Landaw. *Tara's Colouring Book.* Boston: Wisdom Publications, 1979.

Twelve detailed outline drawings of Tara, the Buddha,

and other sacred beings, adapted from Tibetan art. For children who color well.

Periodicals

1001. *HAM: How About Magic: a magazine for Pagan youth.* Quarterly, 1990—. c/o Green Egg, Box 1542, Ukiah, CA 95482. $6/year; back issues $2 each.

   The first issue of *HAM* appeared as a supplement to the popular Pagan periodical *Green Egg* (no. 86). This is a lively, attractively produced magazine for, and largely by, Pagan children and teenagers. Each 12-page issue contains articles, instruction in Wicca, artwork, stories, poetry, book reviews, and comic strips.

1002. *The Littlest Unicorn.* 8 times/year, 1984—. The Rowan Tree Church, Box 8814, Minneapolis, MN 55408. $7/year.

   Fairy stories, poetry, and artwork for young children.

Audio-Visual Materials

Included here are lectures and interviews on tape, as well as films and videos. Most of these items and hundreds of other recordings of women's spiritual music are available from Ladyslipper, Box 3124-R, Durham, NC 27715.

Audio Cassettes

1003. Adler, Margot. *From Witch to Witch Doctor: healers, therapists and shamans.* 60 min. Association for Consciousness Exploration (1643 Lee Rd. #9, Cleveland Heights, Ohio 44118), 1987.
   A lecture on the interrelation between psychic healing and psychological and medical therapy. Side 2 includes questions from the audience and an excerpt from a talk by R. D. Laing at an American Psychological Association convention.

1004. Antiga (Mary Lee George). *I Dance to Be the Woman I Can Be.* St. Paul: Llewellyn Publications.
   The Minneapolis-based feminist witch sings chants and circle songs, and adds commentary.

1005. Barr, Judith. *The Call of My Blood Mysteries.* Mysteries (Box 552, Pound Ridge, NY 10576), 1990.
   Poetry on menstruation: the voice within, the fears, terrors, anguish and anger of the young girl; the power hidden within. A skilled performer, Barr reads slowly and clearly.

1006. Bolen, Jean Shinoda. *Goddesses as Inner Images.* San Francisco: New Dimensions Foundation, 1989.
   An interview from the radio program "New Dimensions,"

in which Bolen discusses her popular book *Goddesses in Everywoman.*

1007. Bolen, Jean Shinoda. *Wise-Woman Archetype: menopause as initiation.* 60 min. Sounds True, 1825 Pearl St., Dept. CB11, Boulder, CO 80302.

A lecture on the Old Wise Woman: the Crone aspect of the Triple Goddess, the post-menopausal woman whose wisdom resides in her retained blood.

1008. *Buddhist Mantra: Om Tara Tuttare.* Timeless Books, Box 160, Porthill, Idaho 83853.

Mantra invoking Tara, "She who eliminates all fear and She who grants all success."

1009. Carney, Janet. *Our Mother Who Is in Heaven; The Touch of Mary Magdalene*, and *Our Mother Who Is in Heaven; The Wise Woman Within.* Credence Cassettes, Box 419491, 115 E. Armour Blvd, Kansas City, MO.

Each side of these tapes contains a 15-minute guided meditation.

1010. *Dianic-to-Amazon Wicce Pagan Primer.* 90 min. Bastet, Box 134, Mentone, CA 92359. Transcript also available.

1011. Estés, Clarissa Pinkola. *Women Who Run With the Wolves: myths and stories about the Wild Woman archetype.* 2 cassettes, 160 min. Boulder, CO: Sounds True, 1989.

A Jungian analyst tells stories and myths of the Wild Woman archetype, a species as endangered as the wolf. Expanded into a book to be published by Ballantine in 1992.

1012. Faiella, Ida, and John McDonough. *Dishpan Fantasy: a real soap opera.* 75 min. Available from Ladyslipper.

A satirical radio comedy in which a housewife finds the Goddess and leaves her husband for metaphysical adventures.

1013. *The Feminine Side of Spirituality.* 60 min. Theosophical Publishing House (Box 270, Dept. AV, Wheaton, Ill. 60189-0270), 1990.

An adaptation of the nationally syndicated radio series,

"The Eternal Quest."

1014. Flowers, Felicity Artemis, and Ruth Barrett. *An Invocation to Free Women.* Circle of Aradia Publications (4111 Lincoln Blvd. #211, Marina Del Rey, CA 90292), 1987.

A popular tape of poetry, songs, and stories of matriarchal herstory and the return of the Goddess, narrated by Felicity, sung by Ruth.

1015. *Gaia's Children.* 60 min. Theosophical Publishing House, Box 270, Dept. AV, Wheaton, Ill. 60189-0270.

From the "Eternal Quest" radio program: feminism and myths of the Goddess.

1016. Goldspinner, Jay. *Rootwomen Stories.* 60 min. Ashfield, MA: Jay Goldspinner, 1987 (available from Ladyslipper).

Stories of Lilith, Hippolyta the Amazon, and other strong women, from Africa, ancient civilizations, and the present.

1017. Jong, Erica. *The Matriarchal Vision of the Witch.* 60 min. Available from Ann Forfreedom, 2441 Cordova St., Oakland, CA 94602.

A lecture given at the Goddess Rising Conference in Oakland, California, March 1982.

1018. Meador, Betty. *Uncursing the Dark: the representation of the Goddess and the recovery of the feminine in our times.* 60 min. Wilmette, Ill.: Chiron Publications, 1987.

1019. Medicine Eagle, Brooke. *The Earth Is Our Mother.* San Francisco: New Dimensions Foundation, 1990.

A Native American medicine woman speaks about our relationships to the earth and to each other.

1020. Medicine Eagle, Brooke. *Moon Time.* c/o Linda Waite, 823 Oeste Drive, Davis, CA 95616.

Beginning and ending with a song, Brooke brings us to the Native American moon lodge, where menstruating women ask the Grandmothers for a vision for the people. She speculates that women who attain premature menopause due to the loss of reproductive organs are being called to share the wisdom of the crone.

1021. Meyer, Carol. *Our Mother Who Is in Heaven: Mother Eagle*. 30 min. Credence Cassettes, Box 419491, 155 E. Armour Blvd., Kansas City, MO.

Two 15-minute meditations using feminine imagery of God.

1022. Miles, Midge. *Stories in Our Souls: women's spirituality*. 6 cassettes, totaling 5 hours, and a leader's guide. Available from Credence Cassettes (see above), 1984.

Each cassette has on one side stories of women in the gospels (the Blessed Virgin, Mary and Martha of Bethany, St. Elizabeth, others), and on the other, a guide to reflection.

1023. Mosich, S. Kathena. *The Aphrodite Meditations*. San Diego: Shapes of Spirit, Inc. Available from Magickal Childe, 35 W. 19th St., New York, NY 10011.

1024. Mountainwater, Shekhinah. *A Winter Solstice Legend*. Available from Ladyslipper.

An original Yuletide myth, with musical accompaniment, of the birth of the Star Child, who is the Maiden Goddess. Suitable for children's entertainment and enlightenment.

1025. *Return of the Goddess*. 4 cassettes, each approx. 1 hour. CBA Audio Products (Box 500, Station A, Toronto, Ont. Canada M5W 1E6), 1986.

Outstanding series of radio programs on the contemporary feminist spirituality movement, produced by Merlin Stone. Interviews, readings, and music by virtually every important figure in the movement, from Z Budapest and Starhawk to Luisah Teish and Shekhinah Mountainwater. It is thrilling to actually hear the voices of the women whose works we have admired. Each program has a theme: women's music and art; literature, performance and psychology; history, thealogy and religion; and politics. This is a major resource that should be in every women's studies collection.

1026. Simms, Laura. *Moon on Fire! calling forth the power of the feminine*. 48 min. Yellow Moon Press (Box 1316, Cambridge, MA 02138), 1987.

Folktales of strong women, told from a feminist Jungian

perspective, from Africa, Hawaii, Persia, Siberia.

1027. Spretnak, Charlene. *Mother Goddess and Female Spirituality*. San Francisco: New Dimensions, 1983.
   A discussion of the role of feminist spirituality in New Paradigm politics. From an interview on the "New Dimensions" radio program.

1028. Starhawk. *Rebirth of the Goddess*. Madison, WI: Circle, 1981.
   A lecture on witchcraft and feminism given at the University of Wisconsin, directed towards an unsophisticated audience.

1029. Stein, Diane. *Crystal Healing Workshop*. St. Paul: Llewellyn Publications.

1030. Stein, Diane. *Meditation on the Goddess Within; Meditation on the Chakras*. St. Paul: Llewellyn Publications.

1031. Stein, Diane. *Rachida Finds Magick*. St. Paul: Llewellyn Publications.
   A young girl searching for magic meets the Goddess in several forms, ultimately finding magic within herself.

1032. Stein, Diane. *Kwan Yin Workshop*. St. Paul: Llewellyn Publications.
   A taped workshop on the feminist interpretation of the I Ching, based on her book *The Kwan Yin Book of Changes* (Llewellyn Publications, 1985).

1033. Strauss, Susan. *Witches, Queens, Goddesses*. Available from Ladyslipper.
   Stories of Persephone, Venus and Adonis, a Russian tale, and an original story.

1034. Sutphen, Tara. *Goddess of the Temple*. 60 min. Valley of the Sun, Box 38, Malibu, CA 90265.
   A guided meditation with music.

1035. Urashan. *Tropos: the sacred wheel*. 60 min. New Woman Press, Sunny Valley, OR 94797-9799.

Selections from a feminist opera based on the Eurydice/ Orpheus myth. Includes libretto.

1036. Weaver, Ariadne. *Menstrual Myths and Mysteries.* Welcome Home (484 Lake Park, Suite 260, Oakland, CA 94610), 1984.

A scholar and priestess of Wicca talks about the sacredness of menstruation and how to create a ritual for menarche or any bleeding woman. Includes songs and a reading by poet Ellen Bass.

1037. Wiedemann, Florence. *Looking Good/Feeling Bad: Pandora and Hera as representations of the second stage of animus.* Willmette, Ill.: Chiron Publications.

A lecture by a Jungian analyst.

1038. Wolfe, Amber. *Moon Dancing.* Music by Kay Gardner. St. Paul: Llewellyn Publications.

Meditations on the Moon Goddess as symbol of a woman's life cycles.

1039. Wolfe, Amber. *Rainflowers.* St. Paul: Llewellyn Publications.

Meditations on accepting oneself and on the element of water.

1040. Wolfe, Amber. *Shamana.* St. Paul: Llewellyn Publications.

A shamanic journey leading the listener to experience the energy of Mother Earth.

1041. *Women and Spirituality.* Learning Alliance, 494 Broadway, New York, NY 10012.

An evening program featuring Starhawk, Tsultrim Allione, Mary Thunder, and Betty Jacobs.

Films, Videos and Slideshows

1042. *Ancient Women's Spirituality.* By Barbara Des Marias. Video, 56 min. Available from Ladyslipper.

Ancient women's spirituality, contemporary feminist rituals, and witchcraft as folk religion.

1043. *Between the Worlds: Paganism in Northern California.*
Produced by Greg Harder; computer graphics by Owen
Rowley. VHS video, 83 min. Available from Magickal Childe,
35 W. 19th St., New York, NY 10011.

Features Z Budapest's cable television series, Starhawk,
Pagan musician Charlie Murphy, rituals, and Morris dancing.

1044. *The Burning Times.* Directed by Donna Read; produced by
Mary Armstrong and Margaret Pettigrew. VHS video, 58
min. National Film Board of Canada, 1990.

Outstanding documentary and excellent instructional resource on the European witch-hunts from a feminist, Goddess-centered point of view, with commentary on the persecution of women and the philosophy of witchcraft by Margot
Adler, Starhawk, Matthew Fox, and several historians. Available to individuals for $29.95 and to groups and institutions
for $79.39 from the National Film Board of Canada, Studio
D, Box 6100, D-10, Montreal, Que., Canada H3C 3H5, or
from Ladyslipper.

1045. *The Goddess in Contemporary Women's Music and Arts.* A
slideshow conceived by Merlin Stone; organized by Mary
Kelly. 61 col. slides and 40 min. audiotape. Dryden, NY:
Tompkins-Cortland Community College, 1989.

On the tape are interviews with feminist artists, edited
from Merlin Stone's radio series *Return of the Goddess*.

1046. *Goddess Remembered.* Directed by Donna Read; produced
by Margaret Pettigrew. VHS video, 54 min. National Film
Board of Canada, 1989.

Excellent documentary on ancient and contemporary
Goddess religion, filmed at ancient goddess sites in Greece,
Crete, Malta, Britain, Mexico, France, and with footage of
contemporary femnist rituals. Comments by Starhawk, Su-
san Griffin, Jean Shinoda Bolen, Charlene Spretnak, Shekhinah
Mountainwater, Luisah Teish, Merlin Stone, others.

1047. *The Great Goddess.* Barbara Hammer, director. 16mm film,
25 min.; *Moon Goddess.* 16mm, 15 min.

Hammer is a successful filmmaker who has produced

---

many works with feminist, lesbian, and Goddess themes.

1048. *Honored by the Moon.* Produced by Mona Smith for Minnesota American Indians AIDS Task Force. VHS, 15 min., 1990. Dist. by Women Make Movies, 225 Lafayette St., Suite 212, New York, NY 10012.

Historical images of gay Native Americans and the spiritual role gay people have played in traditional culture; interviews with men and women from a variety of tribes on the place of gay people in Native American life.

1049. *Inanna.* Performed by Diane Wolkstein; directed and produced by Bob Sykes. VHS, 49 min., 1988. Cloudstone, 40 S. Middletown, Montvale, NJ 07645.

Interviews with Wolkstein and excerpts of her performance of the myth of the Babylonian goddess Inanna.

1050. *The Living Goddess.* B Frank and Josette Heimans, Cinetel Productions (Australia), 1976. 30 min. video plus teacher's guide; also available on 16mm film. Available from Wombat Productions, Ossining, NY.

On the Kumaris—girls worshipped as incarnations of the Goddess among the Newar people of Nepal.

1051. *The Mystery of the Full Moon.* University of Illinois Film Center. VHS video, 51 min.

On the influence of the moon on nature and culture, in fertility and agriculture.

1052. *Mystery Religions Lecture Series: The Eleusinian Mysteries; The Isis-Sarapis Cult; Cybele and Attis; The Syrian Goddess.* Slide programs, with colored slides and script with bibliography. Produced by the Religion and Ethics Institute, Evanston, Ill.; available from Bolchazy-Carducci Publishers, Unit 1, 1000 Brown St., Wauconda, Ill. 60084.

1053. *The Presence of the Goddess: a vision whose time has returned.* Produced and directed by Christy Baldwin; screenplay by Baldwin and Christine Andreae-Ashton; narrated by Cleste DeBlasis. VHS, 68 min., 1986. Balcorma Films, 202 Meda Lane, Mill Valley, CA 94941.

On the goddess-centered civilizations of Crete, Mycenae,

and Greece, and the transition from matriarchal to patriarchal religion.

1054. *Remember the Witches.* Directed, written and edited by Laurie Meeker. 16mm film, 22 min., 1985. Women in Focus, 456 W. Broadway, Vancouver, BC.

On the witch-hunts as gynocide of wise women and midwives, intercut with scenes of modern feminist witches at rituals. Also available as a videocassette from the University of British Columbia, where it was created as Meeker's M.F.A thesis.

1055. *Return of the Goddess for the New Millenium: an initiation into the feminine.* VHS video, 32 min. U-Music, 389 Marin Ave., Mill Valley, CA 94941.

A dance to the Goddess performed by Jamie Miller, with music by Paul Silbey.

1056. *Singing the Sacred.* Produced, directed, and edited by David A. Karp. Ketchum, ID: Planetwork, Inc.; dist. by Access Audio/Visual Productions, Berkeley, 1988. 69 min.

A presentation by Brooke Medicine Eagle at the San Francisco symposium "Dreaming the New Dream 1988: choices for a positive future," on living in harmony with our bodies and the world around us. Concludes with a traditional Native American circle dance.

1057. *Snake Talk: urgent messages from the Mother.* Produced by the Travelling Jewish Theatre; performed by Naomi Newman. Video; also available on audiocassette. Available from Ladyslipper.

Newman portrays three women representing the Maiden, Mother, and Crone, whose ally in matriarchal times was the serpent.

1058. *Sorceress (La Sorcière et le Moine).* Directed by Suzanne Schiffman; produced by Pamela Berger, Annie Leibovici, and George Reinhart; script by Berger and Schiffman. VHS video, 98 min. New York: Mystic Fire Video, 1988.

A quiet, beautifully filmed story of a peasant healer in medieval France who is persecuted as a witch by a wandering monk (fighting demons of his own in addition to rural pagan superstition and heresy). That the film was made at all is amazing, for it was conceived by Pamela Berger, who is not a filmmaker but a professor of art history. She was inspired by a mediaeval French account of a dog transformed into a saint, and by other historical references to wise women healers in the region of this peculiar cult.

1059. *Vali: the witch of Positano.* Directed by Sheldon Rochlin. Video, 65 min. New York: Mystic Fire Video.

A film about Vali Myers, an artist, shaman, and mystic living in the mountains in Italy.

1060. *Witchcraft.* Video, 28 min. Available for purchase or rental from Films for the Humanities and Sciences, Box 2053, Princeton, NJ 08543-2053.

Describes witchcraft, relating it to magic and mysticism, and includes an interview with a woman who practices the Craft.

1061. *Woman and Her Symbols.* Produced by Claire Simon; written and narrated by Mary R. Hopkins. 3 videotapes, available from Ladyslipper (QV2VC, QV2VC, QV4VC): I. *The Great Mother Earth.* II. *From Earth Mother to Love Goddess.* III. *Women Revisioning Ourselves.* With an emphasis on the Goddess and the feminine principle as expressed in art.

1062. *Women and Spirituality.* Video, 75 min. Mankato, MN: Mankato State University, 1986.

A lecture by Starhawk at the 1986 Women and Spirituality conference held at Mankato State. Also available are videos of the keynote addresses by Charlotte Black Elk, an Oglala Sioux, at the 1987 conference, Christian theologian Valerie Russell at the 1988 conference, and Judith Plaskow at the 1989 conference.

1063. *The World of the Goddess.* Directed by Alan Babbitt; produced by Richard Sydel. VHS video, 103 min. El Verano, CA: Green Earth Foundation, 1990.

Marija Gimbutas describes the Goddess-centered civilization of Old Europe whose deity controlled life, death, and rebirth. With over a hundred images of the Goddess.

Periodicals

The periodicals listed below fall into three categories: those which are dedicated to feminist spirituality or Goddess religion, feminist or Pagan publications which regularly devote a significant amount of space to the Goddess and Her rituals, and special issues of other feminist and spiritual publications. Additional listings of Pagan and Goddess-friendly periodicals can be found in an appendix to the second edition of Margot Adler's *Drawing Down the Moon* (see the section on Witchcraft in this book) and in most issues of the feminist Wiccan newspaper *Of A Like Mind* (listed below). A basic academic collection ought to include *Anima, Circle Network News, Daughters of Sarah, Green Egg, Journal of Feminist Studies in Religion, Lilith, Of a Like Mind, SageWoman, Shaman's Drum,* and *Woman of Power*; however, everyone has her own favorites.

Some publications use the matriarchal-feminist A.D.A (After the Development of Agriculture) system of reckoning years (e.g. "1991 A.D." becomes "9991 A.D.A.") Here, however, to facilitate the verification of library holdings, I have taken the liberty of converting all years into the Common Era system.

By the time you read this, some of these publications will have moved and others may no longer exist; new titles appear constantly. I have given the latest addresses and subscription rates found, but bear in mind that these often change. Current addresses and prices for some of the larger periodicals may be found in the most recent edition of *Ulrich's Guide to Periodicals*, located in most libraries.

1064. *The Ancient Arts.* Quarterly. c/o The Witching Well, Box 1490, Idaho Springs, CO 80452.

Newsletter on Goddess religion and Paganism, with rituals, recipes, etc.

1065. *Anima: an experiential journal.* Quarterly, 1974—. 1053 Wilson Ave., Chamberburg, PA 17201. $18.95/year.

A journal devoted to the feminine presence in religion, psychology, and art, filled with thoughtful essays, poetry, and artwork.

1066. *Aporia.* 14 Condict St., New Brunswick, NJ 08901. $5/year.

Essays, fiction, poetry, reviews on women's spirituality.

1067. *Arachne: a journal of matriarchal studies.* Semi-annual, 1983—. Matriarchy Research and Reclaim Network, 14 Hill Crest, Sevenoaks, Kent, UK, TN13 3HH. £4.70 airmail (may send international money order).

Articles, reviews, poetry, and artwork on the Goddess and ancient matriarchy.

1068. *Artemis.* Monthly, 1983—. B.M. Perfect, London, UK, WC1N 3XX.

Lesbian-feminist periodical.

1069. *Asynjur.* Quarterly. c/o Cheryl Newton, Box 567, Granville, Ohio 43023. $8/year; $2.50 sample.

Periodical devoted to Germanic religion and the Norse goddesses.

1070. *Bay Area Pagan Assemblies Newsletter.* Bi-monthly, 1990— Box 850, Fremont, CA 94537. $23/year; $3.95 sample.

News of events in the Bay Area, Wicca and the Craft in the news and media, interviews, Pagan parenting articles, book and film reviews. Visitors to the Bay Area are encouraged to check out the latest issue for news of upcoming events and classes.

1071. *Bay Area Women's News.* Bimonthly. Box 557, 5251 Broadway, Oakland, CA 94618. $9/year; $1.50 sample.

This newspaper of women's culture contains many articles on the spiritual movement.

1072. *La Bella Figura.* Quarterly. Box 411223, San Francisco,

CA 94141-1223. $3.

A literary magazine for Italian-American women; in 1989 there was a special issue on spirituality.

1073. *The Beltane Papers: a journal of women's spirituality and thealogy.* 8 times a year. Box 8, Clear Lake, WA 98235.

Pagan- and Goddess-oriented but also includes contributions from other spiritual traditions.

1074. *Bentwood.* Quarterly. Box 021926, Juneau, AK 99802-1926. $8/year; $2.25 sample.

Goddess-centered Paganism, whole-earth living.

1075. *Broomstick: by, for, and about women over 40.* Bimonthly, 1978—. 3543 18th St. #3, San Francisco, CA 94110. $15/year; $3.50 sample.

Includes occasional articles on witchcraft and spirituality; special issues on the subject for May/June 1983, July/Aug. 1988, and Winter 1991.

1076. *Children of the Earth.* Box 116, Berkeley Springs, WV 25411-0116.

Dedicated to Pagan parenting and "the joys and hassles of raising (or being) Pagan children."

1077. *Chrysalis: journal of the Swedenborg Foundation.* 3 times a year, 1986—. Swedenborg Foundation, 139 E. 23rd. St., New York, NY 10010. $20/year.

Special issue in 1987 on "The Wise Woman: a human process." This journal of spirituality, esoteric philosophy and consciousness is thoughtful, attractively produced, and similar in tone to *Parabola* or *Anima.*

1078. *Circle Network News.* Quarterly, 1980—. Box 219, Mt. Horeb, WI 53572. $9/year; $3 sample.

One of the most important resources for information about the Neo-Pagan, Wiccan, and Goddess community, published by Wiccan priestess Selena Fox. If you want to contact Pagan or Wiccan groups, this is one place to start.

1079. *The Coming Age.* Quarterly, 1976—. Lux Madriana, An Droichead Beo, Burtonport, Co. Donegal, Ireland.

Published by Lux Madriana, an ancient sisterhood based in England and Ireland dedicated to the return of matriarchy. They have an intentional community in Burtonport (see *WomanSpirit*, Fall 1983, p. 17 for a report by a visitor).

1080. *Connexions: an international women's quarterly.* 1981—. 4228 Telegraph Ave., Oakland, CA 94609. $15/year; $4 back issues.

Special issue, no. 28 (1988-89) on "Feminism and Religion," with articles on women in the Arab world, fundamentalism in Islam and Hinduism, Italian feminists, lesbians in East Germany, the 17th-century Mexican poet Sor Juana de la Cruz, female gurus in India, women in Buddhism, the Afro-Brazilian goddess Iemanjá, and contemporary Swedish witches (see entry 658).

1081. *Converging Paths.* Quarterly, 1986—. Box 63, Mt. Horeb, WI 53572. $13/year; $3 sample.

Wiccan periodical.

1082. *Cosmic Awareness Cauldron.* Quarterly. Box 1144, Aurora, CO 80040. $18/year; $4.50 sample.

Goddess-oriented; articles on magic, herbs.

1083. *Covenant of the Goddess Newsletter.* 8 times a year. Box 1226, Berkeley, CA 94704. $15/year; free to members.

The newsletter of the Covenant of the Goddess, a federation of Pagan and Goddess groups and one of the first Pagan organizations to become a legally recognized church. Starhawk was one of its founding members.

1084. *Creation: earthy spirituality for an evolving planet.* Bimonthly, 1985—. Oakland, CA.

Published by Matthew Fox, a Catholic priest who has developed a theology of creation-centered spirituality, inspired by the writings of Christian mystics such as Hildegard of Bingen and Meister Eckhart. He has been roundly criticized within the Church for working with Starhawk and for his New Age leanings, and in 1989 was officially forbidden to publish or speak publicly for one year. The Nov./Dec. 1990 issue of *Creation* is dedicated to women's spirituality, with articles on the feminine perspective on science, Pele as spirit of the Earth, the Goddess in the work of Canadian artist Elaine Carr, and an assessment and criticism of creation spirituality by Rosemary Ruether, with a response from Fox.

1085. *The Crone Papers.* 8 times a year. c/o Grey Cat, Box 181, Crossville, TN 38555. $7/year; free sample for 2 first-class stamps.

On the Crone (and the Crone in older men), magic, issues in the Pagan community.

1086. *Crone's Nest Newsletter.* 207 Coastal Highway, St. Augustine, FL 32084.

Crone's Nest is an intentional community for older lesbians, under the auspices of the Pagoda, a feminist spiritual community.

1087. *Daughters of Inanna.* 8 times a year. 1707 Red Fox Drive, Fairbanks, AK 99709. $5-10/year (sliding scale).

Newsletter of the Fairbanks Women's Circle.

1088. *Daughters of Sarah.* Bimonthly, 1974—. Box 411179, Chicago, Ill. 60641. $18/year.

The foremost journal of Christian feminism. Issues often focus on a special topic, e.g. work, mothering, lesbian-straight dialogue, containing essays, poetry, fiction, history, book reviews.

1089. *Demeter's Emerald.* 8 times a year. Box 612603, S. Lake Tahoe, CA 95761. $13/year; $2 sample.

Promotes birthing the natural, Pagan way; published by Pagans for Peaceful Parturition.

1090. *Diana's Arrow: a newsletter of feminist witchcraft.* 8 times a year. Circle of Aradia Publications, 4111 Lincoln Blvd. #211, Marina Del Rey, CA 90292. $20/year; $2.50 sample.

1091. *Earth's Daughters: a feminist arts periodical.* 1971—. Box 622, Station C, Buffalo, NY 14209.

Special issue, "Mother Comforter," no. 25/26, 1985. In the Bell and Howell "Herstory" microfilm collection.

1092. *EarthSong: a journal of earth awareness and magickal spirituality.* Quarterly. EarthSong Publications, Box 5628, Baltimore, MD 21210. $10/year; $4 sample.

Earth religion, tribal cultures, Pagan parenting, rituals.

1093. *Feminist Connection: the New Age women's newsletter.* Monthly, 1984—. Suite 646, Box 15068, San Francisco, CA 94115-0068. $10/year; $1 sample.

Articles, fiction, art, reviews, interviews, announcements.

1094. *The Flame: the quarterly of the Coalition on Women and Religion.* 1975—. 4759 15th Ave. NE, Seattle, WA 98105. $12/year; free sample.

An interfaith coalition supporting many aspects of spiritual feminism. Articles, poetry, reviews, calendar.

1095. *Frontiers: a journal of women studies.* Mesa Vista Hall 2142, University of New Mexico, Albuquerque, NM 87131.

Special issue on "Spirituality, Values, and Ethics," v. 11, no. 2-3, 1990. Articles on the sun goddess, women and ritual.

1096. *Gnosis: a journal of the Western inner traditions.* Quarterly, 1986—. Box 14217, San Francisco, CA 94114. $20/year; $5 sample.

Articles on Western esoteric spirituality, Hermetic philosophy, the Feminine, depth psychology. The Fall 1989 issue, whose theme is the Goddess, has articles by Caitlín Matthews on Sophia, De-Anna Alba on the rise of the Goddess movement, and other pieces by women and men on the image of the Goddess, the value of polytheism, the Lady of the Animals, apparitions of the Virgin, and a hymn to Shekhinah by Rabbi Leah Novick. This is an outstanding resource on the wonderful variety of the Goddess. The Fall 1990 issue, "Sex and Spirituality," contains articles on Aphrodite (by a Pagan priestess), sex magic, and sexuality in the Biblical religions.

1097. *Goddess Rising: a journal of womyns spirituality.* Quarterly, 1983—. 4006 First Ave. NE, Seattle, WA 98105. $6/year; $1.50 sample.

Articles, reviews, and networking in Dianic Wicca, with a lesbian-feminist orientation.

1098. *Green Egg: a magazine of Goddess and nature religion.* Quarterly, 1988—. Box 1542, Ukiah, CA 95482. $12/year; $3.50 sample.

Published by the Church of All Worlds, this was *the* source for Neo-Pagan opinion from 1968 to 1976, when publication was suspended. It has been revived as a well-produced magazine, filled with articles, interviews, news about the Pagan community, reviews, rituals, and many pages of letters. *Green Egg* also publishes *HAM: How About Magic*, a children's magazine (see the Children's section in this bibliography), and *Amargi: interdisciplinary journal of the Ecosophical Research Association* (Box 982, Ukiah, CA 95482), which is devoted to sacred sites and earth magic and is printed as an insert to *Green Egg*. An indispensible resource on the Pagan community.

1099. *Green Witch Network Newsletter.* Quarterly. Pan's Forest Herb Co., 60780 River Bend Drive, Bend, OR 97702. $4/year.

Single-sheet newsletter for women herbalists.

1100. *Hag Rag: intergalactic lesbian feminist press.* Bimonthly, 1986—. Box 93243, Milwaukee, WI 53203. $10/year, $2 sample.

Special issue on "Lesbian Ritual," May/June 1990. Articles on the nature of ritual, "Lesbian Rites of Passage, "Matriarchs and Amazons." Other issues often have articles on radical lesbian spirituality.

1101. *Harvest.* 8 times a year, 1980—. Box 228, S. Framingham, MA 01701. $10/year; $2 sample.

Nature religion, Neo-Paganism, Goddess religion. Margot Adler considers this the best Pagan journal of the Northeast.

1102. *Heartsong Review.* Semi-annual. Box 1084-SW, Cottage Grove, OR 97424. $8/year; cassette tape for each issue, $4 additional.

Edited by Wahaba Heartsun, artist and contributor to *SageWoman*, this periodical reviews music from the Pagan, Goddess, Native American, and New Age spirituality communities, much of which is self-produced and not widely reviewed elsewhere. Chants, songs of the peace and ecology movements, and children's tapes are covered.

1103. *Images*. Quarterly, 1983—. Box 436, Planetarium Station, New York, NY 10029. $15/year.

Published by the Conference for Catholic Lesbians.

1104. *In Context*. Quarterly, 1983—. Box 11470, Bainbridge Island, WA 98110. $18/year.

Special issue, Spring 1987, on "Gender: fresh visions and ancient roots," with an interview with Jean Shinoda Bolen, articles on contemporary male and female initiation rites, Native American views of gender, several articles on masculinity and wholeness, the Queen as archetype of women's power. This issue is illustrated by photos of powerful sculptures by Sandra Orgel and Gustav Vigeland.

1105. *Inner Woman* (continues *Spiritual Woman Times*). Quarterly, 1990—. Box 5186, Seattle, WA 98115-1186. $7.50/year; $1 sample (free in some bookstores).

Articles and interviews on healing, Native American women, New Age spirituality.

1106. *Interfaith Women's News and Network*. Quarterly, 1980—. 790 11th Ave., 32H, New York, NY 10019. $4/year; .50 sample.

Women's spirituality of East and West.

1107. *Isian News*. Quarterly. Fellowship of the Goddess, Cesara Publications, Clonegal Castle, Enniscorthy, Ireland.

The newsletter of the Fellowship of the Goddess, available to members only (send three International Reply coupons or $2 postage to enquire about membership).

1108. *Journal of Feminist Studies in Religion*. Semi-annual, 1985— Atlanta, GA: Scholars Press. $18/year; back issues $15.50 each, available from Scholars Press Customer Services, Box 6525, Ithaca, NY 14851.

Important journal of feminist theology, women's studies, and Goddess research, with scholarly articles, roundtable discussions, and reviews on all aspects of women and religion. Essential for academic libraries.

1109. *Journal of Women and Religion.* Semi-annual, 1981-1986; annual, 1987—. Berkeley, CA: Center for Women and Religion, Graduate Theological Union, 2400 Ridge Road, Berkeley, CA 94709. $30/year; $20 for students, $3.50 sample.

Subscription includes membership, monthly mailings and bibliography on women and religion. Each issue has a special theme.

1110. *Labyrynth Notes* (also published as *Sisters of the Winds*). Bimonthly, 1986—. Labyrynth Institute, Box 712, Wabash, IN 46922. $10/year.

New Age feminism, with articles on matriarchy, Native Americans, etc.

1111. *Lady-Unique-Inclination-of-the-Night.* 6 issues, published 1976-1983. Some back issues available c/o Kay Turner, Folklore Center, SSB 3.106, University of Texas, Austin, TX 78712.

Named after one of the Mayan goddesses, this beautiful little journal was one of the earliest to document the rebirth of women's spirituality. The articles ranged from personal to scholarly, with an emphasis on literature and art. Dreams, poetry, altar-making, mythology of the Americas, all produced with a loving touch.

1112. *Lavender Pagan Newsletter.* Quarterly, Beltaine 1991— LPN, Box 20673, Oakland, CA 94620. $2-10/year, sliding scale.

Newsletter for lesbian, gay, and bisexual Pagans, providing news about lesbian/gay Pagan events, classes, and circles open to new members. Most articles in the issue examined were by gay men.

1113. *Lesbian Contradiction: a journal of irreverent feminism.* Quarterly, 1982—. 584 Castro St., Suite 263, San Francisco, CA 94114. $6/year, back issues $1.

Special issue on "Womon, Spirituality, and Religion," no. 16, Fall 1986.

1114. *Lilith.* Quarterly, 1976—. Lilith Publications, 250 W. 57th St., New York, NY 10107. $14/year, $4.50 sample.

Magazine of Jewish feminism, with articles on Jewish

law, ritual practice, history, anti-Semitism, re-visionings of Judaism.

1115. *Luna-See.* Quarterly. Goddess Womyn Network, Box 17312, Phoenix, AZ 85011. $13/$25/$50 membership (sliding scale).

1116. *Magical Blend.* Quarterly, 1980—. Box 11303, San Francisco, CA 94101-7303. $14/year.

A magazine of the mystical traditions that frequently publishes articles on women and spirituality, e.g. on women and magic (no. 13), the Tarot High Priestess (no. 16), the asteroid goddesses in astrology (no. 26), the work of Riane Eisler, Aboriginal women shamans (both in no. 21).

1117. *Maize: a lesbian country magazine.* 3 times a year, 1983— Word Weavers, Box 8742, Minneapolis, MN 55408-0742. $6 year; $3 sample.

Since the early 1970's many women seeking to live out a woman-centered vision have been moving to the country in order to create women's space and to free themselves as much as possible from the culture of patriarchal capitalism. While much of the theorizing and development of feminist spirituality has taken place in cities, notably in Boston and the California Bay Area, country women have also contributed to its grass-roots development. *WomanSpirit*, the first periodical of the feminist spirituality movement, came out of the country lesbian community. *Maize* focuses on the practicalities of country living, with frequent articles on healing and spirituality.

1118. *Mamaroots: an Afracentric spiritual & cultural forum.* Quarterly, 1990—. Asungi Productions, 3661 N. Campbell Ave., Suite 108, Tucson, AZ 85719-1524. $18-25/year; subscription included with membership in the Afragoddess Spiritual and Cultural Network.

A lively periodical for African American women who love the Goddess. Articles, poetry, health care, networking, peppered with African proverbs.

1119. *Manushi* (New Delhi, India). Bimonthly, 1978—. Dist. in the U.S. c/o Esther Jantzen, 5008 Erringer Place, Philadelphia, PA 19144. $19/year, $3 sample.

Special issue on women Bhakta poets, Jan.-June 1989 (nos. 50-52). Bhaktism is a mystical sect of Hinduism, often centered on a particular deity, which for centuries has produced women poets and spiritual teachers.

1120. *Many Smokes.* Box 9167, Spokane, WA 99209.

Fall 1981 issue, "Native American Women Speak," is on female energy.

1121. *Mara: tijdschrift voor feminisme en theologie [Mara: journal of feminism and theology].* 1987—.

Dutch journal of feminist theology; the premier issue contains interviews with Rosemary Reuther and Mary Daly.

1122. *Matriarchy News: quarterly newsletter of the Matriarchy Study Group.* London, Oct. 1981-July 1982.

1123. *Matriarchy Research and Reclaim Network Newsletter.* 8/year, 1981—.14 Hill Crest, Sevenoaks, Kent, UK. Newsletter for Goddess groups in Great Britain.

1124. *Medusan Update.* Semiannual, 1991—. c/o Oriethyia, Box 7184, Capitol Station, Albany, NY 12224.

Edited by Oriethyia and well-known herbalist Billie Potts, this new periodical "celebrates Amazon magic." Available for "a few dollars and a SASE."

1125. *Moccasin Line.* Quarterly, 1984—. Northwest Indian Women's Circle, Box 8279, Tacoma, WA 98408. $15/year.

Native American women's spirituality and concerns. Subscription includes a monthly calendar, *Moccasin Line Bulletin.*

1126. *Moonbreath.* Quarterly. Caney Indian Spiritual Circle, Box 6874, Pittsburgh, PA 15212. $6/year.

Rooted in the religion of a Central American Indian culture where women are equal in spiritual leadership, this periodical contains pieces on nature awareness, myth, and ritual.

1127. *Mooncircles.* Monthly, 1985—. Circles of Exchange, Box

021703, Juneau, AK 99802-1703.

When *WomanSpirit* ceased publication in 1984 and many of its readers felt bereft of the community the magazine had formed, Nan Hawthorne started the Circles of Exchange, a round-robin network of small groups of women interested in sharing ideas and knowledge about women's spirituality. Circle members receive packets of letters on any topic that interests them, add a letter of their own, and send the packet along to another member. *Mooncircles* is the newsletter for the entire network and is free to its members; *Asynjur* and *Bentwood* were founded by Circle members.

1128. *North Wind Network.* 8 times a year. Box 14902, Columbus, Ohio 43214. $9/year; $1 sample.
Goddess and Pagan rituals and networking.

1129. *Nuit-Isis: a journal of the nu* [sic] *equinox.* Semi-annual, 1986——. Box 250, Oxford, England OX1 1AP. £4/year.

1130. *Octava: a news-journal of women's spirituality and thealogy.* 8 times a year, 1984——. Box 8, Clear Lake, WA 98235. $10/year, $1.25 sample.
Newsletter for subscribers to *The Beltane Papers* (see above). Pieces are written by the subscribers.

1131. *Of a Like Mind: a quarterly newspaper for spiritual women.* 1984——. Box 6021, Madison, WI 53716. $13/$21/$33 sliding scale.
A publication of feminist Wicca and Goddess religion, with articles, regular columns on healing and 12-step programs, correspondence, reviews, and networking among Pagan, Wiccan, and like-minded women. Publishes a directory of groups, covens, healers, craftswomen.

1132. *On Wings.* Monthly. Women in Constant Creative Action (WICCA), Box 201, Monmouth, OR 97361. $16/year.
A networking organization for spiritual women.

1133. *Panakeia: a journal of feminist psychics and alternative healing.* Semi-annual, 1982——. Great Britain.
Women's spirituality, astrology, matriarchy, healing.

1134. *Panegyria Journal.* 8 times a year. Box 85507, Seattle, WA 98145. $8/year; free sample (send 3 stamps).

The newsletter of the Aquarian Tabernacle Church, with spirited debates and current news about the Seattle Pagan community.

1135. *Priest/ess.* Quarterly. Our Lady of the Woods, Box 176, Blue Mounds, WI 53517. $13/year.

Newsletter of the Ardantane/Singing Willow project, which is working towards constructing a residential Wiccan seminary and retreat center (no Crystal Cathedrals in the Pagan community!). Subscription is paid to the Our Lady of the Woods Land and Building Fund.

1136. *Project Summer Solstice.* Annual, 1984—. Womanswork Connection, Box 3083, Darien, CT 06820.

Periodical of women's spirituality.

1137. *PWSA Journal: Journal of the Progressive Women's Spiritual Association.* 3 times a year, 1990—. 94-38 212th St., Queens Village, NY 11428. $5/year.

The Association is a network of spiritual women who work to improve women's socio-political situation. The 14-page journal contains articles, reviews, and rituals, and is oriented towards Tantric Yoga but includes other spiritual traditions.

1138. *Rainbow City Express.* Quarterly, 1988—. Rainbow City, 414 Colusa, El Cerrito, CA 94530. $22/year; $5.50 sample.

Spiritually eclectic, with articles on the Great Mother and Kundalini, and contributors like Amber K and Shekhinah Mountainwater.

1139. *Reclaiming Newsletter.* Quarterly, 1981—. Reclaiming Center, Box 14404, San Francisco, CA 94114. $4-15 sliding scale/year; $1 sample.

Founded by Starhawk, the Reclaiming Center is a collective of Bay Area feminist witches and activists which sponsors classes and workshops. The newsletter contains articles, poetry, rituals, reviews, and Starhawk's itinerary, and does not take itself too seriously.

1140. *Sacred Cycles.* Monthly. Golden Dolphin Publications, 29636 Orinda St., San Juan Capistrano, CA 92675. $26/$3 sample.

"Dedicated to honoring the Divine Feminine in our lives." Astrology, meditations, rituals.

1141. *SageWoman: a quarterly magazine of women's spirituality.* 1986—. Box 641, Point Arena, CA 95418. $18/year; $6 sample.

Founded as a forum for grass-roots feminist spirituality after *WomanSpirit* ceased publication in 1984, *SageWoman* emphasizes Goddess and Pagan religion. Not as lesbian-oriented as *WomanSpirit*, but still by and for women only, each issue focuses on a theme such as Home, Moon, or Earth Magic, with articles, interviews, artwork, poetry, and a reader's forum.

1142. *Sappho's Understudies: a newsletter of Goddess and Wiccan lore.* Quarterly, 1980-1982. Cabalistic Wicca Church, Box 28633, Sacramento, CA 95828.

1143. *Scarlet Moon: a journal of the feminine.* Box 3248, Menstrual Health Foundation, Santa Rosa, CA 95402.

A newsletter published by a group that sponsors workshops on empowering women during menstruation.

1144. *Schlangenbrut: Streitschrift für feministisch und religiös interessierte Frauen [Serpent Brood: forum for feminists and women interested in religion].* Quarterly, 1983—. c/o Gabrielle Gummel, Giselbertstrasse 24, 5060 Ber-Gladsall, Germany.

1145. *Shadowplay: a quarterly journal of Wicca, Neo-Paganism, magic, art and celebration.* Box 343, Petersham, NSW 2049, Australia. $A15/year; $A3.50 sample.

1146. *Shaman's Drum: a journal of experiential shamanism.* Quarterly, 1985—. Box 2636, Berkeley, CA 94702. $15/year.

This publication deftly combines articles by anthropologists studying indigenous shamanism with pieces on contemporary neo-shamanism. See especially issue no. 4, Spring 1986, devoted to women in shamanism, for interviews with

Luisah Teish and a Huichol medicine woman, and articles by Vicki Noble and Brooke Medicine Eagle.

1147. *Shekhinah Magazine.* Quarterly, 1980—. Box 4098, Waco TX 76705.

Seeks to explore the femininity of the Holy Spirit, with contributions by Christians and Jews.

1148. *SheTotem.* Quarterly. Box 27465, San Antonio, TX 78227-0465. $8/year; 1 stamp for free sample.

Women's newsletter of magic. The publishers also run a mail-order lending library of occult and esoteric books.

1149. *Sing Heavenly Muse!: women's poetry and prose.* Box 13299, Minneapolis, MN 55414.

Special Lunar Issue, no. 14, 1986, with poetry, stories, and art all relating to the Moon. Nancy Passmore, publisher of the annual *Lunar Calendar*, adds notes on the Celtic lunar tree calendar.

1150. *Sisters United II.* Quarterly, 1979—. Woman Print Enterprises, 118 West Sparks St., Galena KS 66739. $7/year.

The editor writes that lesbianism is "a necessary step in our spiritual development that has resulted from our soul having advanced to a higher spiritual state in a past life." Promotes the Holy Spirit, rather than witchcraft or Goddess religion.

1151. *Snake Power: a journal of contemporary female shamanism.* 1989—. 5856 College Ave., #138, Oakland, CA 94618. $23/year; $7.50 sample.

Published by Vicki Noble, as of this writing (1991) only two issues have appeared of this colorful, spirited, glossy magazine. Articles, interviews, columns, reviews, artwork on many aspects of women's spirituality, with features by and about Marija Gimbutas, Elinor Gadon, Gabrielle Roth, Tsultrim Allione, astrology, Tarot, herbs. Magazines are an expensive proposition, but I for one would like to see this one survive.

1152. *Sphaera Imaginatio.* Semi-annual. Box 7293, Lincon Acres, CA 92047. $6/3 issues.

The Goddess, magic, and Wicca.

1153. *The Sphinx*. Quarterly. Temple of OISA, Winnisquam, NH 03289. $6/year; $2 sample.
   Published by the Coven of Isis.

1154. *Spiritual Mothering Journal*. Quarterly, 1980—. Box 213, Lyle, WA 98635. $10/ year.
   Articles, advice, and book reviews on the subject of spiritual parenting; Baha'i-oriented, but open to all religious persuasions.

1155. *Starlight*. Quarterly. Center of the Star Goddess, c/o Sirius, Box 452, Helsinki, Finland 00101. $4 ($5 airmail)/year.
   Newsletter of Sirius, a Finnish group dedicated to Isis. Also publishes a Finnish language edition, entitled *Sirius*.

1156. *Thesmorphoria's New Moon*. 8 times a year. Box 213, Oakland, CA 94618. $9-$13 sliding scale. Ed. Z Budapest.
   A newsletter for the Goddess community, with a calendar of events in the Bay Area, rituals, Goddess history.

1157. *The Voodoo Woman's Wisdom*. Quarterly. OCOT, Box 27152, Detroit, MI 48227. $13/year; $3.50 sample.
   The first known woman-centered magazine of Voodoo.

1158. *Waterwheel: a quarterly newsletter of the Women's Alliance for Theology, Ethics, and Ritual*. 1988—. WATER, 8035 13th St., Silver Spring, MD 20910. Available for a donation; back issues $2.
   WATER is a feminist educational and spiritual center working for peace and justice. Their periodical, edited by feminist theologians Mary E. Hunt and Diann Neu, includes articles, rituals, international news, and brief reviews.

1159. *The Waxing Moon*. Temple of the Elder Gods, Box 4172, Sunland, CA 91040.
   Members' newsletter of the Temple, a Goddess-oriented earth religion.

1160. *The Web*. Monthly. NWSNN, Box 2885, Portland, OR 97207. $8/year.

Newsletter for the Portland women's spirituality network.

1161. *A Web of Crones.* Quarterly, 1985——. Courageous Crones, Box 6, Hornby Island, BC, Canada V0R 1ZO. $6/year; $1.50 sample.
Newsletter for "far out older lesbians and courageous crones."

1162. *Wheel of Hekate.* Quarterly. Box 190, Lockport, Ill. 60441. $16/year; $4 sample.
Substantial journal of Pagan writing, art, poetry, myth, ritual.

1163. *Wiccan Exploration.* 8 times a year. WE, Box 807, Merrifield, VA 22116.
Goddess religion and Dianic Wicca.

1164. *The Winged Chariot.* 8 times a year. c/o Moonstar Enterprises, 864 20th St., San Diego, CA 92101. $10/ year; $2 sample.
Newsletter for practitioners of feminist Tarot.

1165. *Wisdom's Herald.* Quarterly. Sophia's House, 513 S. 48th St., Philadelphia, PA 19143.
Sophia's House is an organization dedicated to the study of Biblical Wisdom/Sophia (see the works by Susan Cady, et al., in the Christian-Jewish section above).

1166. *The WISE: Women In Search of Everything: a newsletter celebrating wimmin's spirituality.* 1986——. Box 6513, Minneapolis, MN 55406. $7-13/year (sliding scale); $3 sample.

1167. *The Wise Woman.* Quarterly, 1970——. 2441 Cordova St., Oakland, CA 94602. $15/year; $4 sample; complete set of back issues $100.
Published by Ann Forfreedom, one of the early leaders in feminist witchcraft, this magazine contains feminist Wicce and Goddess lore, news about women worldwide, cartoons, poetry.

1168. *Woman of Power: a magazine of feminism, spirituality, and politics.* 1984—. Box 2785, Orleans, MA 02653. $26/year; some back issues available for $7.

An important magazine documenting many aspects of women's spirituality and activism. Each issue has a theme, such as Women of Color, Art, Nature, Science, Healing, Revisioning the Dark, or International Feminism, with articles, interviews, poetry, art and photography, announcements. Many contributions are by women of color or from outside the United States. The emphasis is often less on spirituality than on political activism and women's lives, but this is certainly one of the essential periodicals of the women's spirituality movement.

1169. *WomanSpirit.* Quarterly, 1974-1984. Wolf Creek, OR 97497-9799. Some back issues still available. Separate index for all ten years available.

The first periodical of women's spirituality, published by Jean and Ruth Mountaingrove from their isolated home on women's land, it is gone but not forgotten. Jean, Ruth and a host of women around the country, many of whom had never published before, documented the development of feminism and women's spirituality in the late seventies and early eighties. Articles, fiction, poetry, art, correspondence, reviews, and announcements, provided information on virtually every aspect of women's spirituality and feminist politics for hundreds of women who had little or no other contact with the feminist spirituality community.

1170. *Women of Interest/Women's Spirituality.* Annual? 1984—. Womanswork Connection, Box 2282, Darien, CT 06820.

Classified directory published in association with *Project Summer Solstice* (see above). "Subscribers may appear in the book by submitting anonymous personal stories or connecting information."

1171. *Women's Spirituality Book Review.* Quarterly. Box 14658, Cleveland, Ohio 44114. $8/year, $2 sample.

Reviews fiction, non-fiction, music, periodicals from all spiritual traditions.

1172. *Wonder Woman.* Monthly, 1987—. New York: DC Comics.

She's back! This is a new series with a more explicitly

feminist and Goddess orientation. Also available is the *Wonder Woman Annual* (New York: DC Comics, 1988—.)

1173. *Wood and Water: a Goddess inclined Eco-Pagan magazine.* Quarterly. 4 High Tor Close, Babbacombe Rd., Bromley, Kent, UK, BR1 3LQ. £3.50/year; sample 85p (will accept U.S. equivalent in cash).

Articles on mythology, folklore, and the preservation of sacred spaces.

1174. *Word and World.* Quarterly, 1981—. Luther-Northwestern Theological Seminaries, St. Paul, MN.

Special issue on feminism, Fall 1988: new directions in feminism and feminist theology, the female Self and God.

1175. *Yoga Journal.* Bi-monthly, 1983—. Box 3755, Escondido, CA 92033-3755. $18/ year.

Special issues on women's spirituality: no. 44, May/June 1982; no. 68, May/June 1986 (profiles of Starhawk, Buddhist Tsultrim Allione, Sufi Irina Tweedie); no. 78, Jan./Feb. 1988.

Bibliographies and
Additional Resources

1176. Bass, Dorothy C. and Sandra Hughes Boyd. *Women in American Religious History: an annotated bibliography and guide to sources*. Boston: G.K. Hall, 1986. 155 p.

Lists books, articles, and primary sources, chiefly of historical materials. The great majority of the entries cover Protestant Christianity; there are additional sections on Catholicism, Judaism, Native American religion, and a few entries on other religious movements. Feminist spirituality is not included as a distinct category.

1177. Carson, Anne. *Feminist Spirituality and the Feminine Divine: an annotated bibliography*. Trumansburg, NY: The Crossing Press, 1986. 139 p.

Books, articles, dissertations, periodicals, and audiocassettes from the women's spirituality movement of the 1970's and 1980's, and pre-feminist and scholarly material on the Goddess, witchcraft, paganism, and the feminine face of God. With an introduction on the background of the feminist spirituality movement.

1178. *Feminist Collections: a quarterly of women's studies resources*. 1978—. Madison, WI: Office of the Women's Studies Librarian, University of Wisconsin.

Contains articles, book reviews, notices of new reference works and new periodicals (and the cessation of publication of others), and notes on new trends and ventures in feminist publishing. An essential resource for all women's studies collections.

1179. Finson, Shelley Davis. *Women and Religion: a bibliographic guide to Christian feminist liberation theology*. Toronto: University of Toronto Press, 1991. 207 p.

At long last, a comprehensive bibliography of feminist thought in Christianity and religious studies in general. Contains unannotated entries for books, articles, dissertations, and Christian periodicals, divided by topic: the Bible, history, inclusive language, Mariology, ministry, women in the church, women's spirituality, theology, and worship. The emphasis is on Christian writings, but there is also a section on Judaism and a few pages on the Goddess and Wicca. Includes a name index.

1180. Hensley, Charlotta. "'Womanspirit' and other Issues of Feminist Spirituality," *Serials Review*, Spring 1987, 13(1):5-18.

A listing of current and defunct feminist spirituality periodicals, with a good description of the movement.

1181. *Ladyslipper Catalog: resource guide; recordings by women.* Ladyslipper, Inc., Box 3124, Durham, NC 27715.

An astonishingly comprehensive mail-order catalogue of all kinds of recordings by women: music of every stripe, including hundreds of tapes and records of spiritual/New Age music; guided meditations; spoken recordings; videos; children's recordings and videos; calendars, posters, and other merchandise. Most of the audiocassettes and many of the videos listed in this bibliography are available from Ladyslipper.

1182. Mitchell, Carol. "The 20th Century Witch in England and the United States: an annotated bibliography," *Bulletin of Bibliography,* 1982, 39(2):69-83.

Includes articles on American and British covens in the 1960's from the popular press, and many books and articles on Afro-Americans and American folk traditions.

1183. O'Connor, June. "Rereading, Reconceiving and Reconstructing Traditions: feminist research in religion," *Women's Studies,* 1989, v. 17, p. 101-123.

A bibliographic essay on the literature of feminism and religion in the major world religions; African, Afro-American, and Native American religion; and feminist religious ethics. Also lists pertinent periodicals.

1184. Popenoe, Cris. *Inner Development*. Washington: Yes! Inc.; dist. by Random House, 1979. 654 p.

An annotated bibliography of all sorts of New Age, metaphysical, and spiritual subjects, from "African Philosophers" to "Women and Men," with lengthy introductions for each topic, many of them excerpted from well-known books in the field.

1185. Potter, Clare. *The Lesbian Periodicals Index*. Tallahassee: The Naiad Press, 1986. 413 p.

An exhaustive index of articles, poetry, artwork, and announcements from about two dozen lesbian periodicals chiefly from the seventies and early eighties. Includes many articles by authors such as Z Budapest and Cheri Lesh (Cerridwen Fallingstar) on the budding spirituality and feminist witchcraft movements.

1186. Ruud, Inger Marie. *Women and Judaism: a select annotated bibliography*. New York: Garland, 1987. 232 p.

Books, articles, dissertations, and essays on the religious and secular status of Jewish women, arranged by subject with indexes.

1187. Searing, Susan E. *Goddesses and Goddess Worship: a selected reading list*. Madison, WI: University of Wisconsin System, 1987. 4 p.

1188. Searing, Susan E. *Introduction to Library Research in Women's Studies*. Boulder, CO: Westview Press, 1985. 257 p.

Presents the basics of using a library and the kinds of research tools available. Lists guides, indexes, bibliographies in many areas of research (e.g. anthropology, lesbian studies, psychology, religion), with annotations. Useful for researchers at all levels.

1189. Taylor, Lillian McCulloch. *Readings For, By, or About Women of Faith: an annotated bibliography*. Louisville: Women's Ministry Unit, 1988. 30 p.

1190. Wynne, Patrice. *The Womanspirit Sourcebook: a catalog of books, periodicals, music, calendars & tarot cards, organiza-*

tions, video & audio tapes, bookstores, interviews, meditations, art. San Francisco: Harper and Row, 1988. 277 p.

As the subtitle explains, this essential resource is more than a bibliography of books and tapes, it is a kaleidoscope of the range of feminist spirituality, including material from the Christian, Jewish, and Buddhist traditions in addition to Goddess and Pagan. Besides compiling annotated entries, Wynne and other women interview many of the leaders of the feminist spirituality movement. The book also constitutes a catalogue of Gaia, Wynne's bookstore and mail-order business.

Subject Index

Numbers refer to entries

445, 450, 458, 496, 525, 543, 609, 654, 912

Great Mother, 387, 503

Greece, Ancient, 452, 894, 915, 1053

Green Man, 359, 496

Green Party, 137, 290

Guatemala, 9

Gurus, 333, 1080

Hagar, 844

Halloween, 646

Harappan civilization, 363

Healers, 1, 91, 174, 349, 651, 705, 872, 913, 1058

Healing, 23, 24, 66, 90, 110, 152, 160, 161, 165, 202, 215, 242, 259, 260, 297, 301, 320, 324, 326, 335, 337, 349, 583, 630, 637, 705, 897, 944, 1029, 1133

Healing, Psycho-spiritual, 77, 119, 220, 557, 1003

Healing—manuals, 301, 335, 337

Hebrews, 513, 856

Hecate, 378, 447, 481

Heidegger, Martin, 609

Hera, 94, 553, 1037

Herbal medicine, 21, 24, 202, 335, 337, 741, 960, 1099

Herbalists, 1, 22, 336

Herbals, 242

Herbs, 22, 1082

Heroines, 982, 1172

Herstory, 29, 71, 108, 192, 193, 218, 234, 298, 311, 478, 484, 580, 612, 738, 1014, 1042, 1061

Hestia, 76, 454, 548

Hinduism, 400, 429, 453; *see also under* Goddesses,

Hindu

Hispanic culture, 132

Hispanic women, 91, 651, 691

Hittites, 369, 471, 509

Holle, 566

Holy Spirit, 781, 824, 1147, 1150

Homophobia, 228

Horned God, 262

Horses, 540

Humor, 69, 397, 459, 626, 1012

Hygeia, 583

I Ching, 184, 303, 329, 1032

Iduna, 976

Imperialism, 424

Inanna, 383, 384, 524, 535, 600, 617, 899, 914, 1049

Incest, 652

Inclusive language, 321, 780, 788, 799, 807, 808, 852

India, 363, 371, 429, 477, 1119

Initiation, 26, 409, 421

Inuit, 37, 412, 599, 621, 979, 990

Ireland, 111, 393, 422, 581, 606

Ishtar, 600

Isis, 476, 620

Islam, 3, 47, 1080

Italy, 502, 710, 953, 954, 986, 1059

Jainism, 374

Jesus, 821, 832, 835, 920

Jewish women, 160, 498, 800, 822, 846, 1114

Journal writing, 140

Judaism, 3, 299, 497, 504, 550, 551, 687, 722, 742, 744, 745, 748, 762, 767, 776, 779, 783, 790, 800, 821, 822, 838, 839, 844-846,